MEAT SMOKING
AND
SMOKEHOUSE DESIGN

STANLEY MARIANSKI
ADAM MARIANSKI
ROBERT MARIANSKI

Bookmagic, LLC.
Seminole, Florida.

Meat Smoking And Smokehouse Design
Stanley Marianski, Adam Marianski, Robert Marianski.

ISBN: 978-0-9824267-0-8
Library of Congress Control Number: 2009903061
First edition 2006. Second edition 2009.

Bookmagic, LLC.
http://www.book-magic.com

Printed in the United States of America.

Contents

Introduction

Smoking is a topic that creates most of the questions on meat forums – wood chips or sawdust, dry wood or wet, hickory or oak, cold smoke or hot – the list has no end. There are little smokers and larger ones, there are small grills and there are big sophisticated units that cost thousands of dollars. There are drum smokers, box smokers, water smokers, and combination grill – smoker units. These definitions can make a newcomer confused and uncertain about making a choice. Very few books cover the subject of smoking in any meaningful manner. Most of them include a drawing or two, a few pages on generating smoke, and the rest of the pages are filled with hundreds of recipes. While various recipes usually get the spotlight, the technical know-how behind preparing meats and sausages is far more important. We feel it is more important to explain the ins and outs of meat smoking and not waste paper space with pictures of different knives that people use in the kitchen. There is a section with some basic recipes but our aim is to convince you that you can create your own recipes on the fly without much effort.

How our book differs from others

1. When we write about cold or hot smoke we don't end on just giving you the temperature range for a particular method. We also explain in great detail why one way is better for making certain products than the other. The same applies to smoking temperatures and curing. Behind every bit of information we try to provide an explanation as to why it is done in that particular way. This we hope will lay the foundation that will allow the reader to produce quality products and be in total control of the process.

2. The next way our book differs from others is in our second half, "The design of smokers and smokehouses". This section contains all that is known about smoker design and is supported with over 200 drawings and photographs. Many of them are detailed technical drawings with all dimensions and lists of needed materials for building fully functional units. After reading this book you will fully comprehend what can be expected of any particular smoker and how to build one that will conform to your individual needs.

Stanley Marianski

Chapter 1

Principles of Smoking

1.1 History of Smoking

The struggle for survival was an early man's main concern. He did not know how to cultivate foods or domesticate animals. Living in a cave his diet was simple - he ate anything that did not eat him. Having primitive weapons, our ancestors hunted in groups as this was the only way to kill larger animals. Those who survived had an ample supply of meat which would spoil soon. It had to be an awful feeling to leave a large amount of meat to rot away after such an exhausting and dangerous hunt. Then we discovered fire which provided warmth and became the center of social activities. One day a piece of meat was dropped into the fire and to everybody's amazement it tasted wonderful. It tasted good the next day, the following day and the day after. It eventually spoiled as well but it was already a huge improvement.

Then came another surprise as our ancestors discovered that smoke improved meat's flavor and further postponed its useful life. From that time on, meats were smoked and such was the beginning of the food preservation. Being a very curious by nature creature, man started to apply his newly acquired skills to other meat such as birds and fish. That only reinforced his beliefs in the mysterious power of smoke and fire.

The man was a practical creature and he ate everything that moved and did not manage to run away. After a while he developed a liking for some meats more than the others. He used the same powerful testing tool that we still use today and none of the supercomputers can compete even remotely. The tool is our tongue that we have been using for millions of years. Man discovered that a smoked wild boar, the hog's ancestor, tasted better than any other meat. The wild boar felt safe around humans as he was occasionally being fed leftovers. This led to wild boar acceptance by the humans and the boar became a pig. Unlike pragmatic animals like cows and horses, pigs were not of much practical benefit besides the fact that they were the first sanitation system. In ancient Rome they roamed the streets at nightfall and ate any leftover garbage.

In early Europe, there was a strong sentiment towards cows. They produced milk, which was processed into butter, cheese and cream. They were also used for labor, pulling ploughs and performing other chores. Upon death, they were buried, not eaten. On the other hand, pigs were not of much practical use, but they tasted good and were prepared in hundreds of different ways. Plus, they were the best meat for smoking.

In the USA native Indians were mainly drying meats in the sun. This technique was adopted by the first settlers and beef jerky became a standard item for people on the move. In 1539, Hernando de Soto came to the Tampa Bay area of West Florida bringing 13 pigs with him becoming the father of the pork industry in the USA. Contrary to other animals, a domesticated pig has no difficulty in adapting herself to living in the forest where it will become a wild boar in a few years. As they are great problem solvers they can find food in almost any surroundings and don't limit themselves to one particular diet. The hogs found perfect conditions in densely wooded lands and areas rich in water in the Eastern USA where they kept multiplying in large numbers. They became the meat of choice of slaves and the poor, and soon there was a makeshift smokehouse on every farm or dwelling. Smokehouses proliferated in the states such as Georgia, Carolinas, Virginia, Tennessee, Missouri and Kentucky and only the introduction of refrigeration in the 1900's has stopped smoking meats as a method of meat preservation. In those states pork popularity has not diminished at all and even today the word barbecue is synonymous with pork.

In the West cows had access to vast grassy areas to graze on and beef became the most popular meat. The cowboys looked down on any animal which did not resemble a cow and there were many armed conflicts between cow and sheep ranchers. If sheep or goat were not welcome it is not hard to imagine what a macho cowboy would think when seeing a pig. In the West, the art of barbecue developed to a very high degree, but the most popular meat was of course beef. Today there are all types of meats in a supermarket and one can smoke, grill or barbecue beef, pork, sheep, chicken, fish or a snake without danger of a fight with his neighbor.

1.2 Smoking - Reasons

Man discovered that in addition to salting and curing with nitrates, smoking was a very effective tool in preserving meats. Besides enhancing the taste and look, it also increases its longevity, and helps preserve the meat by slowing down the spoilage of fat and growth of bacteria. Smoking meat leads to more water loss, and results in a saltier and drier product, which naturally increases its shelf life. The advantages of smoking meat are numerous:

- Slows down the growth of bacteria.
- Prevents fats from developing a rancid taste.
- Extends the shelf life of the product.
- Develops a new taste and flavor.
- Changes the color; smoked products shine and look better.

Smoked fish develops a beautiful golden color. The meat on the outside becomes a light brown, red, or almost black depending on the type of wood used, heating temperatures, and total time smoking. The smell in an ethnic meat store specializing in smoked products can be overwhelming. This experience is not shared with our supermarkets since their products are rarely naturally smoked and they are vacuum-sealed to prolong shelf life. This unfortunately locks the aroma in. Certain classical sausages are smoked for up to three days and in today's era it is hard to imagine a manufacturer that will do that.

To survive the frantic pace of today's market, water is pumped into the meat, chemicals are added for aesthetic and preservation reasons, and smoking is virtually eliminated by adding liquid smoke. As long as the ingredients are not on the list of chemicals that present danger, the Food and Drug Administration does not care what goes into the meat. Taste plays a secondary role and if the price is low, people will buy the product and supermarkets will keep renewing orders.

The main reason to smoke meat at home today is to produce a product that can not be obtained in a typical store. One can order traditionally made products on the Internet but they will be very expensive. It is estimated that in the USA smoked meats account for about 30% of meats sold. And hot dogs and frankfurters constitute the largest portion of this number, though few people ever think of them as a smoked product.

1.3 Why Smoked Meats Are More Popular in Europe

In Europe smoking meats was practiced for thousands of years before the discovery of America and it was a necessary survival skill. The early immigrants brought this skill to America and for a few centuries meat smoking and sausage making became a part of everyday living on the farm. There was no need for food preservation on a national scale. With the exception of the short Civil War that had taken place in the Eastern part of the country, the American soil never felt the presence of World Wars the way Europe did. Our losses did not compare to the 25 million that died in Russia, 6 millions in Germany or 6 million in Poland during the II World War. Curing and smoking meats were survival skills which were not so important in the USA, but they were an absolute necessity in post-war Europe. Especially in East European countries which were severely damaged, but did not receive financial assistance from the West. Some Polish and German cities were completely destroyed and 20% of the population was gone. There was nothing in stores because there were no stores. Items like wine, sauerkraut, fruit preserves, meat and sausages, pickles, they all had to be prepared during the summer in such ways that they would last through the harsh winter. Everybody knew how to preserve food, make sausages and smoke meats because it was done in every house.

One had to buy carp from a street vendor a few days before Christmas as it was a traditional meal. As there were no refrigerators and the fish had to be kept fresh, the established routine was to let them swim in a bathtub. Kids loved it for two reasons: they liked watching the fish and they did not have to take a bath for a few days. Then on Christmas day, the fish was killed and cooked, everybody took in turn a bath and there was food on the table.

As time went by things improved, the hated system collapsed and big supermarkets with packaged foods appeared about 40 years later. Nevertheless, living in such conditions helped to develop and appreciate preserving skills that were passed down from generation to generation. When electricity and refrigeration became available, the need for meat curing and smoking as the means of preserving it had suddenly diminished. As the countries have entered into the new era of prosperity, grills and barbecue units become very popular and it's up to books like this one to keep up with the tradition.

1.4 What is Smoking ?

Smoke is a mixture of an air and gases created during wood combustion. What we see is a stream of gases such as nitrogen, carbon dioxide, carbon monoxide, water vapor, and sulphur dioxide that carry unburned particles such as tar, resins, soot and air borne ash. The actual composition of the smoke depends on the type of wood, its moisture content, combustion temperature, and the amount of available air. It is estimated that smoke consists of about 10,000 individual components and a few hundred of these are responsible for the development of a smoky flavor. The air draft, which might be considered the smokehouse sucking power, sucks in the outside air and combustion gases that in turn attract solid unburned particles such as soot, ash and others. This stream rushes inside of the smoking chamber where it collides with hanging meats and with the walls of the chamber. A stronger air draft and higher temperature increase the energy of the smoke which results in more intense smoking. This explains why the cold smoking process is much slower than the hot smoking method. The amount of moisture on the surface of a product plays a role in color formation and the color develops faster when the surface is wetter. This also results in a much darker color as particles such as tar and soot stick to the surface easier. That creates a barrier to smoke penetration and as a rule the surface of the product receiving smoke should be dry or at least feel tacky to the touch.

Smoking may or may not be followed by cooking. Some products are only smoked at low temperatures and never cooked, yet are safe to eat. The dry sausage has an almost indefinite shelf life and yet this sausage is not cooked. Generally we may say that smoking meats in most cases consists of two steps:

- Smoking
- Cooking

After smoking is done we increase the temperature to about 170° F (76° C) to start cooking. The smoked meats must be cooked to 154° F (68° C) internal temperature and here the quality and insulation of the smoker plays an important role. Nevertheless, the main smoking process is performed below 160° F (71° C). Smoked meats are usually eaten cold at a later date. Many great recipes require that smoked products hang for a designated time to lose more weight to become drier. It is only then that they are ready for consumption.

1.5 Cold Smoking

Continuous smoking at 52-71° F (12-22° C), from 1-14 days, applying *thin smoke* with occasional breaks in between, is one of the oldest preservation methods. We cannot produce cold smoke if the outside temperature is 90° F (32° C), unless we can cool it down, which is what some industrial smokers do. Cold smoking is a drying process whose purpose is to remove moisture thus preserving a product. You will find that different sources provide different temperatures for cold smoking. In European countries where most of the cold smoking is done, the upper temperature is accepted as 86° F (30° C). The majority of Russian and Polish meat technology books call for 71° F (22° C), some books ask for 77° F (25° C). The fish starts to cook at 85° F (29.4° C) and if you want to make delicious cold smoked salmon that is smoked for a long time, obviously you can not exceed 86° F (30° C). Anything higher and you are not cold smoking. Cold smoking assures us of total smoke penetration inside of the meat. The loss of moisture is uniform in all areas and the total weight loss falls within 5-20% depending largely on the smoking time. Cold smoking is not a continuous process, it is stopped a few times to allow fresh air into the smoker. In XVIII century brick built smokehouses a fire was started every morning. It smoldered as long as it could and nobody cared if it stopped altogether; it would be restarted again the following morning.

Cold smoked meats prevent or slow down the spoilage of fats, which increases their shelf life. The product is drier and saltier with a more pronounced smoky flavor and very long shelf life. The color varies from yellow to dark brown on the surface and dark red inside.

Cold smoked products are not submitted to the cooking process. If you want to cold smoke your meats, bear in mind that with the exception of people living in areas with a cold climate like Alaska, it will have to be done in the winter months just as it was done in the past. Ideally, the meat should be smoked at 80% relative humidity. If the humidity were increased, the intense smoke penetration would bring extra moisture inside. Extra moisture in the meat causes bacterial growth, which is exactly what we are trying to avoid.

Extremely low humidity such as in Arizona and New Mexico, will cause excessive drying of the sausage casing or the surface of the ham. This will prevent internal moisture from escaping the meat. Humidity control plays an important role when making products that cure very slowly in open air. In the pictures on the facing page, at the Catskill Mountains of New York, Waldemar Kozik is making meat products of the highest quality. There is no room for chemicals, binders or colorants here, just quality meats, Mother Nature and the art of smoking of Mr. Waldemar. The same way it has been done for centuries, the right way.

Not having enough humidity will produce meat that is still moist and raw on the inside and dry outside. Once the meat is cut, there will be two different noticeable shades. Using dry wood is of utmost importance when cold smoking. It is recommended to keep wood chips in a well defined single pile as they will have less contact with air, thus will smoke better without creating unnecessary flames and heat. By following these rules we achieve 75-85% humidity, creating the best conditions for moisture removal. Once the moisture content drops low enough, the salt present in the meat will further inhibit the development of bacteria and the products

Photo 1.1 Cold smoking at its best.

Photos courtesy Waldemar Kozik.

Photo 1.2 Smoking continues through the night.

can hang in the air for months losing more moisture as time goes by. Lox (smoked salmon) is smoked with cold smoke for an extended period of time. Applying hotter smoke (over 84° F, 28° C) will just cook the fish, the flavor will change and we will not be able to slice it so thin anymore. Cold smoking is a slow process and the hams, which lend themselves perfectly to this type of smoking, can be smoked from 2 to even 6 weeks. During smoking they will slowly be acquiring a golden color along with a smoky flavor.

1.6 Warm Smoking

Continuous smoking at 73-104° F (23-40° C), from 4-48 hours depending on the diameter of the meat, humidity 80%, and *medium smoke*. The weight loss varies between 2-10%, with the difference being largely dependent on the time spent smoking. The surface of the product becomes quite dry but the inside remains raw. Because of the warm smoke, the product receives more smoke in its outside layers. This dry second skin helps increase shelf life, as well as prevent the loss of its natural juices. The color ranges from yellow to brown and has a little shine due to some fat moving outwards. Warm smoke temperatures lie within the The Danger Zone (40-140° F, 5-60° C), which is the range of temperatures where all bacteria grow very fast. We may say that most bacteria love temperatures close to our body temperature, which is 36.6° C (98.6° F).

Optimum growing conditions for infamous *Clostridium botulinum* are 18-25° C (64-77° F) but it will still grow at 45° C (113° F). At those temperatures the only protection we have is the sodium nitrite (Cure #1 or 2) which should be added to smoked meats. As explained later in the book, the reason for using cures (nitrite) is not only to eliminate the risk of food poisoning (*Clostridium botulinum*) but to obtain the desired color, achieve better flavor and prevent the rancidity of fats.

1.7 Hot Smoking

Continuous smoking at 105-140° F (41-60° C), 0.5-2 hours, 5-12% weight loss, *heavy smoke*. This is not recommended for large pieces of meat. Although it is the fastest method, there is not enough time for adequate smoke penetration. This results in higher moisture content, reducing the product's shelf life. This type of smoking can be divided into three separate phases:

1. Drying out the surface of the meat for 10-40 min at 112-130° F (45-55° C), some very light smoke is acceptable, although not necessary. Besides drying out the surface of the meat, the temperature speeds up nitrite curing. Keep in mind that the draft controls must be fully opened to eliminate any moisture residing inside of the smoker. Initially smoking at temperatures higher than 130-140° F (54-60° C) will prematurely dry out the casings on the surface of the meat and will create a barrier to smoke penetration.

2. This is the proper smoking stage at 112-140° F (45-60° C) for 30-90 min, using medium to heavy smoke. The color becomes a light yellow to dark brown with a shade of red. In this state, the natural casings become strong and fit snugly on the sausages.

3. Baking the sausage at 140-176° F (60-80° C) for about 10-20 min. Temperatures as high as 194° F (90° C) are permitted for a short period of time. Proteins are denatured in the outside layers of the product, but the inside remains raw with temperatures reaching only 104° F (40° C). Natural casings fit very snugly, become shiny, and develop a few wrinkles. This is a welcomed scenario; lots of smoked products are subsequently poached. Acting like a barrier, the drier and stronger casings prevent the loss of juices. This type of cooking (poaching) is more economical to baking (less weight loss). If a smoker is used, the temperature in the last stages of the hot smoking process is increased to 167-194° F (75-90° C) until the inside of the meat reaches 154° F (68° C). This is the fastest and most common method of smoking. Because of a relatively short smoking time, hot smoked products should be kept in a refrigerator and consumed relatively quickly.

1.8 Wet Smoking

Smoked meats lose around 10% moisture during the smoking process. This of course depends on temperature, the length of smoking and humidity in the smokehouse. Eliminating moisture was a welcome scenario when the products were cold smoked for preservation purposes. Nowadays, the importance of preserving meats by dehydration plays the secondary role as losing moisture means decreasing weight that in turn leads to decreased profits. To prevent this loss, commercial manufacturers pump meats with water and recirculate moist air throughout the smokehouse.

Ready made charcoal briquettes or electric heating elements produce no moisture and placing a water filled pan inside of the smoker is of some help. This method is very common when barbecuing or smoking meats in commercially produced little barrel smokers. These are enclosed units that don't receive a steady supply of air. Fresh air contains moisture which cools sausage casings and prevents them from drying too fast. When smoking with an open fire, lots of fresh air enters the smoker and keeps the meat from drying out. No matter how cute a small factory unit may be, it will not be able to perform the same duty without a little help from a water pan. As water boils at the constant temperature of 212° F (100° C), placing a water filled pan inside of a small smoker will also help regulate temperature inside. Bear in mind that this is too high a temperature for smoking quality meats and sausages.

In short, *wet smoking is the type of smoking that employs a water dish placed inside of the smoker to increase humidity levels.* Dampening wood chips into water one hour before smoking will produce a similar effect using any kind of smoker. Wood always contains at least 20% moisture, even when perfectly dried on the outside. During the first stage of combustion this wood dries out and any remaining moisture evaporates with the smoke into the chamber. Once the wood has burned out, the remaining charcoal has no water left, and the only moisture the smokehouse gets is brought by the outside air. In dry climates known for little humidity the smoked product will benefit from extra moisture. Bear in mind that the surface of smoked meats or sausages must not be wet during the smoking process.

1.9 Smoking Without Nitrates

For those who smoke meats without cures, it will be advisable to smoke them at temperatures well above the danger zone (>160° F, 72° C). Such a product will not be pinked but will exhibit a typical grayish color of cooked meat. Adding cure to meats that will be smoked brings many benefits (explained later), one of them is preventing the danger of contracting food poisoning, known as botulism. Barbecued meats are smoked at much higher temperatures which eliminates the danger of *Clostridium botulinum* producing toxins. For those who insist on smoking meats without nitrates, the only solution is to smoke them at temperatures higher than 160° F (72° C) which in our opinion becomes *cooking with smoke.*

1.10 Why Did We Smoke Meats With Cold Smoke?

The main reason meats spoil is the moisture inside becomes a playground for food spoiling bacteria. With enough moisture eliminated a point is reached when meats will last almost indefinitely when kept in a cool and dry place. Climatic differences were a significant factor in the development of different methods of smoking, drying, and preserving meat products. It was relatively easy to dry out meats in countries with steady prevailing winds and moderate temperatures, such as Spain and Italy. The South had a drier climate with steady winds and the best air dried hams originated there (Spanish Serrano, Italian Parma). Those countries have been producing wonderful hams and sausages until today by air drying meats for months at the time. Given sufficient time a point was reached when meats were ready to eat although never submitted to any cooking. They would also last for long time.

In Northern Europe the climate was harsh, cold, humid, unpredictable and ill suited for air drying meat products. It was not possible to dry out meat in the winter time when temperatures were below the freezing point. But it was possible to hang them in a storage shack and either bring the smoke using a delivery pipe or start the smouldering fire right inside of the chamber. This slowly burning fire supplied enough heat to dry meat products, yet was not strong enough to burst into flames and burn down the chamber. There was no fire hazard present when the fire pit was placed outside. When fire was burned inside, the meats hung about five feet higher as this distance prevented flames from reaching the product. As the outside temperatures were cold so was the smoke.

Through trial and error it was soon established that the best results were obtained when the temperature of the smoke stayed below 22° C (72° F) and this limit is still used today by most producers in Europe. Thus we can say that the cold smoking method originated in Northern Europe. Higher temperatures would harden the surface area of a product and would inhibit the drying process. As a result moisture could have been trapped inside of the sausage and the product would have spoiled. Keep in mind that these product were smoked weeks at the time, and then were stored in the same chamber by moving them to an area which received less smoke. It was not unusual for some products to be stored inside for up to two years. Some of the best smoked products originated in Germany, Poland and Russia. Those regions became famous for the smoking art they developed and even today 60% of all meats sold in those countries are smoked.

1.11 Why Cold Smoke is Better for Preserving Meats

In processes such as curing, smoking or cooking, the action always starts from the outside towards the center. The skin, the fat or any hard surface will create a formidable obstacle to any process. On the contrary, in the drying process the moisture removed from the surface is replaced by the moisture coming from the inside of the sausage. Sausages are drying from inside out and the moisture removal from the surface is replaced by the moisture coming from the inside of the sausage. There must be a balance between moisture diffusion towards the surface and moisture evaporation from the surface. *When the diffusion rate equals the evaporation rate we are in the equilibrium state and drying is perfect.* Hot smoke will dry the meat too fast and the outside surface of the product will start to harden. This will be even more pronounced if humidity in a smokehouse is low or air movement is fast. If too high smoke temperature is applied the meat will start to cook as well.

This hardened surface acts as a barrier to successful smoke penetration and the meat will be only flavored with smoke in its outside areas. The anti-bacterial properties of the smoke will not act on spoilage bacteria active inside, and given sufficient time they will start to multiply. The meat will be protected in its outside layers only and will start to spoil in moist areas inside. To prevent this danger, smoking is followed by cooking which kills all bacteria. *Cold smoking is basically drying meat with smoke.*

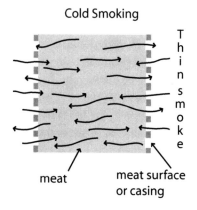

Fig. 1.1 Smoke behavior during cold smoking.

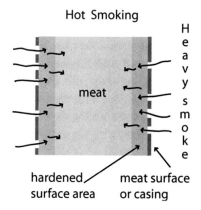

Fig. 1.2 Smoke behavior during hot smoking.

After prolonged cold smoking meat is hung in a cool dry area where it will continue to lose moisture reaching the point when it is preserved and will not spoil anymore. Such a product is perfectly safe to eat though never submitted to cooking. As smoke contributes to the microbiological safety of the products, in hot smoked products its positive action is limited to the surface area only. On the other hand cold smoke can diffuse into all areas of the product as the outside surface areas never get hardened. As a result its bacteria inhibiting properties are distributed in every part of the product. Cold smoking is seldom performed today as it is labor intensive and meats are preserved by keeping them in a refrigerator or a freezer. Some products, notably lox are still cold smoked as cold smoked meats offer better texture and have a more pronounced smoky flavor. They can be sliced paper thin and will still remain in one piece.

Traditionally made slow fermented dry products such as salami, chorizo, cervelat and others can be smoked only with cold smoke. Due to stricter government safety regulations many processors hot smoke and cook these products nowadays. Otherwise there is very little need for cold smoking today.

Hot smoking is the commonly used method and the process is accomplished in a matter of hours. Bear in mind that if you live in a hot climate the only time you can produce cold smoke using a home made smoker is December, January and February, and at night time. Commercial smokehouses can generate hot or cold smoke at will and the temperature and humidity are easily controlled.

1.12 Cold Smoke And Fermented Sausages

When smoking fermented products such as dry salami or German spread-able sausages it is of utmost importance to keep smoke temperature down. German meat technology books recommend applying cold smoke below 18° C (64° F) for about 3-4 days. Slow fermented dry sausages and fermented spreadable sausages can be cold smoked only. The reason being that these sausages are never cooked and applying smoke at higher temperatures will create favorable conditions for the growth of undesirable bacteria. The product will spoil and might become dangerous to consume.

Spreadable sausages are neither dried nor cooked and after cold smoking must be kept in a refrigerator. The initial drying temperature for fermented sausages falls into 15-18° C (59-64° F) range and cold smoke (< 22° C, 72° F) fits nicely into this range. Then drying continues at temperatures below 59° F, 15° C. To sum it up, the length of cold smoking is loosely defined, but the upper temperature should remain below 22° C (72° F). Unfortunately, this rule puts some restraints on making slow-fermented sausages in hot climates for most of the year, when using an outside smokehouse. You can't produce cooler smoke than the ambient temperature around the smokehouse, unless some cooling methods are devised. Semi-dry sausages, which are of fast-fermented type, are fermented at higher temperatures.

These sausages can be smoked with warmer smoke as they are subsequently cooked. The quote from *"The Art of Making Fermented Sausages"* follows below:

"Think of cold smoke as a part of the drying/fermentation cycle and not as the flavoring step. If the temperature of the smoke is close to the fermentation temperature, there is very little difference between the two. The sausage will still ferment and the drying will continue and the extra benefit is the prevention of mold that would normally accumulate on the surface. Cold smoking is performed with a dry, thin smoke. If we applied heavy smoke for a long time, that would definitely inhibit the growth of color and flavor forming bacteria which are so important for the development of flavor in slow-fermented sausages. As drying continues for a long time and cold smoking is a part of it, it makes little difference whether cold smoke is interrupted and then re-applied again".

1.13 Bacteriological Benefits of Smoke

Smoking provides some bacteriological safety but must be considered an additional safety hurdle and not the main one. Yes, it provides more microbiological protection in cold smoked products which are saturated with smoke in all areas, but we can not relay on this method alone. *Drying* is what makes cold smoked products safe and some dry salamis are smoked and others, notably Italian, are only dried without any smoking. In hot smoked products cooking provides safety to the product and smoking is just a *flavoring step*. Any bacteriological effects of smoke will be limited to the surface area only and not the inside. Dipping a sausage into a solution of salt and vinegar will provide extra safety to the outside of the sausage as well. Although we dislike the idea of liquid smoke, it can be used to impart a smoky flavor if a smokehouse is not available. Check the directions on the bottle but about a half teaspoon of liquid smoke to one pound of sausage is a typical dosage.

1.14 Smoke Generation

Smoke can be generated by:

- Burning firewood. Due to the danger of flames this method is limited to smokers with a separate fire pit.
- Heating wood chips or sawdust with an electrical wire (barbecue starter). Once started they will keep on smoldering and the wire starter is not needed anymore.

- Heating wood chips or sawdust over a gas flame or placing wood chips over hot coals. This method is commonly used when barbecuing meats.

The preferred method to handle wood chips or sawdust is to place them in a stainless steel pan, about 10-12" in diameter, not higher than 4", otherwise smoke may be too hot. To sustain smoke production more wood chips must be added. The wood chips should be kept together in a conical pile so that they will smolder and not burn. The moment they spread, they make contact with more air and are more inclined to burn. The same applies when adding wood chips directly on hot coals or ashes, keep them in a pile and if the flames start to grow bigger, add more wood chips to cut off the supply of fresh air. After a while a natural rhythm of adding sawdust will be established and the whole process will go on smoothly.

Photo 1.3 Hot plate.

Photo 1.4 Barbecue starter.   **Photo 1.5** Gas burner.

If smoking stops, the barbecue starter or hot plate is reconnected again. If the sawdust bursts into flames, any common spray bottle can bring it under control. All small and medium size factory made smokers use these methods to generate smoke. The bigger factory made models employ a free standing smoke generation unit that is connected with the smoker by a short pipe. Draft control plays no role here since an electrical blower blows the smoke into the smoker. Industrial smokehouses choose different methods of smoke generation but that does not necessarily mean that the quality is better. One method involves pressing blocks of pressed sawdust against rotating wheels. The resistance creates high temperatures and the block of wood starts to smoke. It's like cutting a piece of wood with a dull saw blade; it starts to smoke because of the heat generated.

1.15 Wood For Smoking

The wood used for smoking should be relatively new and kept in a well ventilated but covered area. A freshly cut tree contains 50% moisture, but when it is dried the moisture content drops to about 25%. That level of dryness requires about 6–9 months of drying. Wet wood can be recognized immediately because of the hissing sound it creates when burned. This is escaping vapor and billing particles of water. To achieve moisture contents of < 20%, the wood must be oven dried. This wood will burn quickly and cleanly, but will not be suitable for smoking products at higher humidity.

Any hardwood is fine, but evergreen trees like fir, spruce, pine, or others cause problems. They contain too much resin and the finished product has a turpentine flavor to it. It also develops a black color due to the extra soot from the smoke, which in turn makes the smoker dirtier, too. However, there is a region in Germany called Bavaria where they have been using evergreen for centuries. They have acquired this taste in childhood and they are very fond of it even though most people don't like it. And of course you cannot use any wood that was previously pressure treated, painted, or commercially manufactured. All wood must be natural. The type of wood used is responsible for the final color of the smoked product and it can also influence its taste.

The following woods are great for smoking:

Acacia – the same family as mesquite, though not as heavy. A very hot burning wood. Smoked color: yellow, lemon type.
Alder – light flavor that works well with fish and poultry. Contains a hint of sweetness, good with poultry and wild fowl. Traditionally used for smoking salmon in Pacific Northwest.
Almond – a nutty, sweet flavor.
Apple – mild, fruity flavor, slightly sweet. Good for poultry, pork.
Apricot – mild, sweet flavor. Good for fish, poultry, pork.
Birch – medium hard wood, flavor similar to maple. Good with poultry and pork.

Black Walnut – heavy flavor, can impart a bitter taste if not monitored carefully.

Cherry – mild, fruity. Good with poultry, pork, beef.

Citrus – lemon, grapefruit, orange, nectarine – light fruity flavor, good with fish, poultry, pork and beef.

Corncobs - dry corncobs make a perfectly acceptable smoking fuel.

Hickory – strong flavor, good with beef and lamb. Smoked products develop reddish color. Southern regions of U.S. Little known outside USA.

Maple – like fruit, sweet flavor. Northeast.

Mulberry – sweet, similar to apple.

Mesquite – very strong flavor, burns hot and fast. Good for grilling.

Oak – probably best all around wood for meat smoking. Popular in England. Strong but not overpowering, good for sausages, beef or lamb. Smoked products develop a light brown to brown color, depending on the length of smoking. Available worldwide.

Peach - mild, sweet flavor. Good on fish, poultry, pork.

Pear – light and sweet, products develop a dark red color. Excellent with poultry and pork.

Pecan – milder version of hickory. Burns cool. Southwest region.

Plum - mild, sweet flavor. Good on fish, poultry, pork.

Walnut – heavy smoke flavor. Can impart a bitter taste if not monitored. Good with red meats and game.

All fruit and citrus trees have a light to medium sweet flavor and are excellent with poultry and ham. Many say that cherry wood is the best. The Royal Couple of woods: King Hickory and Queen Oak can be used with poultry, pork, beef and lamb. Heavy smoke flavored woods (oak, hickory) lend themselves better for smoking red meats like beef and lamb. *Oak, available all over the world, is probably the most commonly used wood for smoking.* The famous Spanish hams "Iberrico" are produced from hogs that eat oak corns as the main staple in their diet. Wood types can be mixed to create custom flavors. For instance, walnut, which has a heavy smoke flavor, can be mixed with apple wood to create a milder version. For practical reasons a home sausage maker will probably use oak or hickory most of the time. Some sausages like German or Polish Hunter Sausages develop their characteristic flavors and aromas by adding juniper branches or berries to the fire. Juniper is the main ingredient for making gin, so we know it has to be a fine element.

Powdered bark of some trees have been used for medicinal purposes: (willow tree-aspirin, cinchona tree - source of quinine to fight malaria or to make tonic water) and they all taste bitter. Bark of the birch tree produces a lot of soot when it burns. Thus we can draw a conclusion that it will be much safer to remove the bark.

1.16 Dry or Wet Wood

Here is another question that never seems to go out of fashion: "what's better, wet or dry". Almost every book advocates using wet chips or sawdust, most likely because when wet they seem to produce more smoke. *This is simply not true; the extra amount of smoke is nothing else but water vapor (steam) mixed with smoke. This does make a difference when hot smoking at 105-140° F (40-60° C) and the smoke times are rather short. That extra moisture prevents the sausage casings from drying out during smoking.*

Besides, wet chips are not going to be wet for very long; the heat will dry them out anyhow. Wood chips produce good smoke when wet and they decrease temperature, but the moment they become dry, they burst into flames and the temperature shoots up. The grease from the sausage drops down on the little flames, the temperature goes up, and the once little flames are now big flames. In one minute we may have a raging fire inside of the smoker.

When a smoker has a separate standing fire pit, large pieces of wood can be burned as the resulting flames will never make it inside the smoker. As you already know, we don't use wet wood for cold smoking because we want to eliminate moisture, not bring it in. Cold smoke warms the surface of the meat up very finely, just enough to allow the moisture to evaporate. Creating cold smoke for two days with wet wood will never dry out the meat. When hot smoking, the smoke along with the air is drying out the casings, which develops a harder surface. The surface of the meat will become drier, too. By using wet wood when hot smoking, we moisten the surface of the product, aiding the smoking.

1.17 Wood Pieces, Wood Chips or Sawdust

The type of wood used will largely depend on the smoker used, and the location of the fire pit. If the smoker is connected with a fire pit by a pipe or a trench, it makes absolutely no difference what type of wood is burned as this design can take a lot of abuse and still provides efficient and comfortable smoke generation. Most people that use these types of smokers don't even bother with chips or sawdust and burn solid wood logs instead.

Burning wood inside of small one-unit smokers creates the danger of a fire erupting. We have to use wood chips or sawdust with a safety baffle above to prevent flames from reaching upwards. This would also prevent fat from dripping down on the wood chips and starting a big fire. When preparing sawdust, do not throw it into water, but place it in a bucket and then moisten it using a spray bottle. Mix sawdust by hand until it feels moist. This sawdust will burn longer and at lower temperatures than other woods and will be the material of choice for smoke generation in small electrical smokers.

When smoking in a home made barrel smoker with a fire pit in the bottom part of the drum, it is much easier to control the smoking process by using dry chips. These smolder and burn in a more predictable manner. Wet chips are just soaked in water on the outside, even when placed in a bucket overnight. The only way to make them really wet is to cover them with boiling water and leave them in it. Hot water penetrates wood all the way through.

1.18 Smoking Temperatures

Smoking temperature is one of the most important factors in deciding quality. There is no steadfast rule that dictates exact temperature ranges for different types of smoking. A few degrees one way or the other should not create any problem as long as the hot smoking upper temperature limit is not crossed. Crossing this limit will significantly affect the look and the taste of the product. When smoking, the inside temperature of the smoker cannot exceed 170° F (78° C) for any extended time. At this temperature, fat starts to melt quickly. It acts like glue, holding the meat fragments together, giving them a proper consistency and taste. Once it melts, the sausage inside will be a mass of bread crumbs, greasy outside, will lose its shine, and will have an inferior taste. If your sausage:

- Is greasy on the outside.
- Contains spots of grease under the sausage.
- Is too shriveled and wrinkled.
- Has lost its shine and looks opaque.
- Is crumbly inside with little empty pockets.

It means that the internal temperature of the sausage was too high during smoking or cooking. Determining temperature is as easy as inserting a stem thermometer through the wall or the door of the smoker, but unfortunately many smoke meats without it. Estimating the temperature by touching the smoker or inserting a hand is lucky at best. The fats start to melt at very low temperatures and we don't want them to boil and leak through the casings. When faced with excessive temperatures, they begin to melt, and there is no way to undo the damage.

Melting temperatures of some fats	
Pork	82-104° F, (28-40° C)
Beef	104-122° F, (40-50° C)
Lamb	110-130° F, (44-55° C)
Chicken	75° F, (24° C)

1.19 Smoke Deposition

The amount of smoke deposited on a product is influenced by:

- Smoke density-the thicker the smoke, the faster the rate of smoke deposition.
- Smokehouse relative humidity-high humidity favors smoke deposition but inhibits color development.
- The surface condition of the product-moist surface favors smoke but limits color development.
- Smokehouse temperature-higher temperature favors smoke deposition rate.
- Air draft-sufficient air velocity is needed to bring smoke inside. Too fast air might reduce smoke density, not enough air speed and product may be over smoked. Usually a compromise which is quite easy to figure out.

1.20 Humidity Control

The meat weight loss (moisture) is directly linked to the temperature and humidity and it is of great importance that we learn how to manipulate those two factors. Regulating humidity in a home made smokehouse can be done indirectly, and is relatively simple and cost free. When smoking in a home made smokehouse the humidity can be controlled by:

- Choosing the time of smoking.
- Placing a water filled pan inside the smoker.
- Using moist wood chips or sawdust.

The amount of needed humidity is dictated by:

- Type of a product - hot smoked sausage, cold smoked sausage, smoked and air-dried ham, or just air-dried ham.

- The smoking method that will be employed.

Geographical location plays a crucial role here. There is more humidity in areas containing many lakes, rivers or being close to the sea shore. Arid areas such as deserts or mountains have less water and subsequently less humidity. If you live in the Eastern part of the USA or Gulf states, you have a lot of humidity. If you live in the West (Arizona, New Mexico, California) you get less of it. As you cannot change the physical location of the smokehouse, you have to learn how to go around it and how to choose the time of smoking to your maximum advantage. The most important rule to remember that when the temperature goes up, the humidity goes down. When the temperature goes down, the humidity goes up (night). When the clouds come in and it starts to drizzle, the humidity will go up immediately. In a home refrigerator the humidity remains at about 45% at 40° F (4° C) and in a freezer it is about 70% at 0° F (-18° C). In an air-conditioned room the humidity remains at 40-45%. Different smoking methods require different humidity levels:

- Cold smoking - 75-85%. It is important to employ high humidity levels when cold smoking in order to keep drying at low speed.
- Warm smoking - 50-70%. It is advisable to start smoking at high humidity levels.
- Hot smoking - 40-50%. In case of hot smoking which is a relatively short process (about 2 hours), humidity control is of secondary importance. Use wet chips.

In dry climates like New Mexico or Arizona the relative humidity stays low at 15-20% during day time and it will not be advisable to smoke meats at such conditions. The meat will prematurely dry out. The remedy will be to place a water pan inside of the smoker and to use moist wood chips. The best solution is to smoke at night time when the temperature will drop and the humidity will increase.

Photo 1.6 Simple humidity tester.

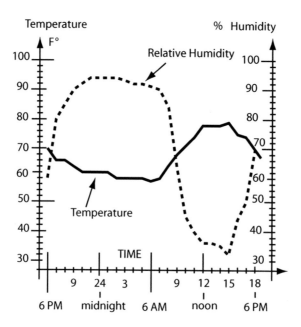

Fig. 1.3 Humidity and temperature in Florida on November 10/11, 2006. In the graph we can see the wild jumps in humidity levels: the relative humidity was over 94% at midnight and at 34% at 3 PM.

An often heard complaint when smoking in outside smokehouses is that the meat is wet on the surface and the final product tastes sour. In most cases it is a humidity problem. Outside smokers employ a free standing firebox that is connected to a smoker by an underground trench or pipe. After rain the ground is wet and the moisture will travel with smoke together. The remedy is to heat up the smokehouse well before smoking so that the moisture will evaporate away. Another problem that may occur is that when smoking in a popular metal drum at very low temperatures, the smokehouse temperature will be lower than the temperature of the entering smoke. Warmer smoke on contact with a cooler smoker surface will create moisture condensation on its walls.

Moisture from the outside or even moisture from the wood or the meat itself will condense on the walls of the drum. In other words water vapor present in the smoke will change into water droplets. Those droplets will combine with soot and other unburned particles and will start condensing on the meat or sausages. That of course will affect the color of the product and even worse, it will impart a sour flavor to the finished product. The solution is to insulate the drum on the outside with some material and heat up the drum before smoking. Ideally, the temperature in the smokehouse should be five degrees higher than the temperature outside but that requires a smoker with an inside located heat generating element. Controlling humidity levels is very important for commercial manufacturers who produce thousands of sausages a day. Proper humidity control during production and storage will decrease meat loss and will increase profits. It is of lesser importance for a home sausage maker unless he is making fermented sausages. Manufacturers of humidity sensors that could be inserted into a smokehouse can be located on the Internet although the prices are rather steep.

1.21 How Long to Smoke?

There isn't one universal time, use your own judgement and keep records. When cold smoking, the times are very long, days or even weeks as the purpose of cold smoking is to preserve the product for future use by removing moisture. There are not many people today that will have the time or patience to smoke products in this manner but those that will try it will be richly rewarded by creating products of different texture and flavor. When hot smoking, the times are short as we smoke and then cook the product trying to achieve the best flavor.

The diameter of the meat piece or sausage will be a deciding factor here but you can estimate smoking time by checking the color of the smoked piece as well. Sausages have a small diameter so the times are relatively short. For example, Kabanosy meat stick is stuffed into 24-26 mm sheep casings and 1 hour smoking time is plenty. Polish Smoked sausage stuffed in 36 mm hog casings will need about 1-2 hours. If the color of the sausage is yellow it is lightly smoked, if it is light brown the sausage is nicely smoked, if the color becomes dark brown the sausage is heavily smoked. If hickory is used, the color will have a more vivid red tint in it.

Keep in mind that sausages owe their characteristic flavors to the different spices they contain. Long smoking with heavy smoke can overpower these subtle spice aromas. A sausage will become nothing else but a piece of meat with a heavy smoky flavor. Smoking a thin ½" piece of meat like jerky for 3 hours with heavy smoke might make it bitter and non-palatable. When smoking, the rule "easy goes the long way" holds very much true. Large pieces of meat such as hams, bacon, and loins will require longer smoking times and should be smoked until the typical dark color is obtained.

1.22 Summary of Critical Issues

- All hot smoked products are cooked to a safe internal temperature and pose no health risk if the smoking times were very short.

- The pink color associated with smoked meats does not depend on smoking time or type of wood. It depends on the type of meat, nitrates and the inside cooking temperature it was submitted to. The outside color is influenced by the total time of smoking and to a smaller degree by the type of wood used.

- The gradual rising temperature in the smoker will prevent casings from hardening up.

- When smoking in dry desert areas containing little relative humidity, use wet wood chips because the smoke will bring extra moisture into the smoker. This will prevent the sausage casings from drying on the outside, not only creating a barrier for smoke diffusion into the meat but also preventing the escape of moisture from the inside of the meat.

- To provide extra moisture during hot smoking or when smoking using electrical smokers, a pan filled with water can be kept inside of the smoker. The rate that smoke is added to meat is affected by the relative humidity and the temperature.

- A relative humidity of 40-45 % is best for most products.

- A flow of uninterrupted fresh air is needed during smoking to remove moisture and unburned particles that have a tendency to sit in the upper part of the smoker. That is why meats should hang at least 4" below the top cover of the smoker. Delivering smoke without fresh air into a completely enclosed smoker may impart a bitter taste to the meat.

- Meats or sausages going into the smoker must be dry on the outside otherwise they will not develop a proper color.

- The bigger wood chips we use, the more available air they get and the smoke that gets generated is hotter.

- Meat pieces or sausages inside of the smoker should not touch each other; this will prevent those areas from receiving smoke and they will be a different, pale color when done.

- Sawdust or small wood chips work best in small smokers.

- Dry wood has to be used when cold smoking.

- Wood logs can be used in smokers with a free standing fire pit.

Chapter 2

Curing and Nitrates

2.1 Brining - Marinating – Sweet Pickle - Salting - Curing –What's the difference?

All tenderizing methods such as salting, curing, pickling and marinating rely on breaking down meat protein (denaturing them) to make meat more juicy and tender. The ingredients that break down those proteins are: *salt, vinegar, wine, lemon juice* and most marinades include them in their formulas. Salt is the strongest curing agent. Some definitions overlap each other and for example when we add salt and nitrites to water, we normally say we are preparing a brine or a pickle although technically speaking it is a curing solution.

Salting is the simplest form of curing and its objective is meat preservation. Water inside the meat spells trouble, it spoils everything and eliminating it by salting and drying allows meat to be stored for longer periods of time. A classical example will be an all American favorite beef jerky.

Brining is immersing meat in brine (salt and water) to improve the juiciness and flavor. Brined meats taste better and all cooks know it. When we cook any type of meat, there is an unavoidable loss of moisture, up to 30%. But if we soak the same meat in a brine first, the loss can be limited to as little as 15% because the meat absorbed some of the brine and it was more juicy at the start of the cooking. Another benefit we get from brining is that a salt solution dissolves some of the proteins in the meat, turning them from solid to liquid what in turn increases the juiciness of the meat. Normally there are very few ingredients in a brine: salt, water, sugar and sometimes spices.

Pickle is another definition of the brine. When sugar is added to a brine solution it is often called sweet pickle. Most brines contain sugar anyhow and both terms describe the same method. If you place chicken in a brine overnight you will roast it most likely at high temperature the next day and no nitrites are necessary. If you place chicken in a curing solution (salt, water, sugar, sodium nitrite) it can be safely smoked for many hours at low temperatures. It will have a different color, texture, taste and flavor. Some sweet pickles contain vinegar.

Marinade plays an important part in the barbecuing and grilling processes but it does not belong in the real world of curing as it does not call for nitrates. The purpose of marinating is to soak the meat in marinade which will tenderize the meat and add a particular flavor. Meat becomes tender and is able to hold more water which makes it juicier. It is a shorter procedure and a typical marinade contains ingredients which are known to tenderize meat by swelling meat proteins.

There are no fixed rules for the length of the marinating time but about 2-3 hours for 1" meat diameter sounds about right. A larger 6" chunk of meat should be marinating in a refrigerator overnight. Like in any other method a longer processing time will impart a stronger flavor on the marinated item. The composition of a marinade is much richer than that of a curing solution. There is a lot of room for improvisation for a creative cook.

2.2 What is Curing?

In its simplest form the word 'curing' means 'saving' or 'preserving' and the definition covers preservation processes such as: drying, salting and smoking. When applied to home made meat products, the term 'curing' usually means 'preserved with salt and nitrite.' When this term is applied to products made commercially it will mean that meats are prepared with salt, nitrite, ascorbates, erythorbates and dozens more chemicals that are pumped into the meat. Meat cured only with salt, will have a better flavor but will also develop an objectionable dark color. Factors that influence curing of meat:

- The size of the meat – the larger diameter the longer curing time.
- Temperature-higher temperature, faster curing.
- Moisture content of the meat.
- Salt concentration of dry mixture or wet curing solution-higher salt concentration, faster curing.
- Amount of fat-more fat in meat, slower curing.
- pH - a measure of the acid or alkaline level of the meat. (Lower pH-faster curing).
- The amount of nitrate and reducing bacteria present in the meat.

2.3 Curing Temperatures

The curing temperature should be between 36-40° F (4-10° C) which falls within the range of a common refrigerator. Lower than 36° F (4° C) temperature may slow down the curing process or even halt it. Commercial producers can cure at lower temperatures because they add chemicals for that purpose.

There is a temperature that can not be crossed when curing and this is when meat freezes at about 28° F (- 4° C). Higher than normal temperatures speed up the curing process but increase the possibility of spoilage. This is a balancing act where we walk a line between the cure and the bacteria that want to spoil meat. The temperature of 50° F (10° C) is the point that separates two forces: below that temperature we perform curing keeping bacteria in check, above 50° F (10° C) bacteria forces win and start spoiling the meat. Meats were traditionally cured with nitrates. Before nitrate can release nitrite (the real curing agent) it has to react with bacteria that have to be present in the solution. Putting nitrate into a refrigerator kept solution (below 40° F) will inhibit the development of bacteria and they may not be able to react with nitrate. On the other hand sodium nitrite works well at refrigerator temperatures. When used with nitrates/nitrites, salt is an incredibly effective preserving combination and there is not even one documented incident of food poisoning of a meat cured with salt and nitrates.

People in the Far East, Africa, South America and even Europe are still curing meats at higher than normal temperatures without getting sick. That does not mean than we recommend it, but if someone in Canada shoots a 1600 lbs (726 kg) Moose or a 1700 lbs (780 kg) Kodiak Bear he has to do something with all this meat. He is not going to spend 5,000 dollars on a walk-in cooler, is he? These are exceptional cases when curing can be performed at higher temperatures. After the Second World War ended most people in Europe neither had refrigerators nor meat thermometers but were curing meats and making hams and sausages all the same. Because of primitive conditions the curing temperatures were often higher than those recommended today but any growth of *C. botulinum* bacteria was prevented by the use of salt and nitrates.

They also predominantly used potassium nitrate which works best at temperatures of 46-50° F (8-10° C) and those were the temperatures of basement cellars. There was not much concern about longer shelf life as the product was consumed as fast as it was made. Salt and nitrite will stop *C. botulinum* spores from developing into toxins, even at those higher curing temperatures. The lower the temperatures when handling meats, the slower the growth of bacteria and the longer life of the product. Extending shelf life of the product is crucial for commercial meat plants as the product can stay on the shelf longer and has better chances of being sold.

Curing is a more complicated process than salting. In addition to physical reactions like diffusion and water binding, we have additional complex chemical and biochemical reactions that influence flavor and color of the meat. A thousand years ago there was no refrigeration but the merchants were moving barrel-packed salted fish from place to place. To preserve fish that way it had to be heavily salted. Before consumption fish were soaked in water to remove the excess salt and then were ready to be cooked. In highly developed countries refrigeration is taken for granted, but in many areas of the world even today the meat or fish has to be salted for preservation.

2.4 Methods of Curing

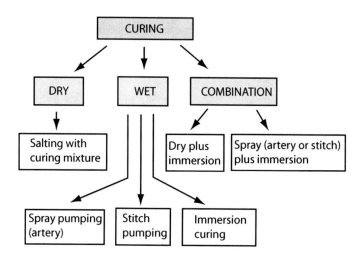

Fig. 2.1 Curing methods.

2.5 Salt Curing

Meat and salt are like two hands of the same body, they always work together and we cannot even imagine processing or eating meat without salt. When added to meat it provides us with the following benefits:

- Adds flavor (feels pleasant when applied between 2-3%).
- Prevents microbial growth.
- Increases water retention, and meat and fat binding.

Salt does not kill bacteria, it simply prevents or slows down their development. To be effective the salt concentration has to be 10% or higher. Salt concentration of 6% prevents *Clostridium botulinum* spores from becoming toxins though they may become active when smoking at low temperatures. Adding sodium nitrite (Cure #1) eliminates that danger. The two physical reactions that take place during salting are diffusion and water binding, and no chemical reactions are present. Salting is the fastest method of curing as it rapidly removes water from inside of the meat. The salt migrates inside of the meat and the water travels to the outside surface of the meat and simply leaks out. This gives us a double benefit:

- Less water in meat.
- More salt in meat.

Both factors create less favorable conditions for the development of bacteria. Today the products that will be only salted are pork back fat and some hams that will be air-dried for a long time.

2.6 Dry Curing

Dry curing has been performed the same way since the 13th century. Before smoking, the salt with nitrates had to be rubbed into hams or other meat cuts which was a tough job because it could only be done by hand. Then pork pieces were tightly packed in tubs, covered with more salt, and left there up to 6 weeks. The salt was dehydrating the meat and drawing the moisture out of it. The dry cure method can be used under wider temperature variations than other curing methods.

The dry curing method is best used for all types of sausages, bacon, and hams that will be air-dried. In most cases after curing, meats go for smoking, then for air drying and there is no cooking involved. In addition to salt and nitrates, the ingredients such as sugar, coriander, thyme, and juniper are often added to the dry mix.

Basic rules for applying dry cure:

When curing times are short, up to 14 days, use Cure #1 according to the standard limit of: 1 oz cure for 25 lbs of meat. For longer times use Cure #2 that contains nitrate which will keep on releasing nitrite for a long time. The amount of Cure #2 needed to cure 25 lbs of meat by the dry cure method when making dry products:

> 2 oz Cure #2
> 12 oz canning salt
> 6 oz dextrose or brown sugar
> seasonings

2.7 Dry Curing Times

The length of curing depends very much on the size of the meat and its composition. Fatty tissues and skin create a significant barrier to a curing solution. When curing a large meat piece, for example a ham, a curing solution will start penetrating on the lean side of the meat and then will progress deeper forward towards the bone and the skin side. There will be very little penetration on the fatty skin side.

The fat acts as a barrier not only to curing but to smoking and removal of moisture as well. It seems logical that removing the fat layer of the skin will speed up curing. It definitely will, but it is not such a good idea. After smoking the ham might be baked or poached in hot water. Here the fat acting as a barrier will prevent a loss of dissolved protein and meat juices that will try to migrate into the water. For more uniform curing, meats should be overhauled (re-arranged) on the third and tenth days of the cure. The curing time will depend on the size of the meat piece and your own preference for a strong or lightly salted product.

A basic rule is 2 days per pound for the small cuts and 3 days per pound for hams and shoulders. For example, a six pound bacon would require about 12 days in cure, while a 12 pound ham would need 36 days. Another formula calls for 7 days of curing per inch of thickness. A ham weighing 12-14 lbs and 5 inches thick through the thickest part will be cured 5 x 7=35 days. Smaller pieces should end up on top so they can be taken out first allowing larger pieces to continue curing. Otherwise they may taste too salty. Smaller meat cuts like bacon, butt, and loins can be cured with a dry mixture based on the following formula for 100 lbs of meat: 4 lbs salt, 1.5 lbs sugar, 2 oz. Saltpeter (1 lb Cure #2). Divide the mixture into three equal parts. Apply the first one-third and leave the meat to cure.

After three days overhaul and rub in the second part. After three more days apply the last third of the mixture and allow to cure for about 12 days. Generally, the addition of spices occurs after the last re-salting has been completed.

2.8 Wet Curing

The wet curing method, sometimes called brine (salt and water), sweet pickle (sugar added), or immersion curing has been traditionally used for larger cuts of meat like butts or hams that were smoked. It is accomplished by placing meats in a wet curing solution (water, salt, nitrites, sometimes sugar). Sugar is added only when curing at refrigerator temperatures, otherwise it will begin fermentation and start to spoil the meat. The wet curing is a traditional, time consuming method, going out of fashion as the large hams had to be submerged for up to 6 weeks and turned over on a regular basis.

With such a long curing time there is a danger of meat spoiling from within the center where the bone is located. During that time we have to scoop up the foam and any slime that might gather on the surface, as that might be a source of contamination. Most meat cuts require about 3-14 days of curing time even at 40° F (4° C). It is still a fine curing method for smaller cuts of meat that will have a shorter curing time.

The meats have to be turned over on a daily basis and prevented from swimming up to the surface. After curing the meats are washed in warm water and left to dry before going into the smoker. Cure meats at a refrigerator temperature of 38-40° F (3-4° C). We do achieve certain weight gain when curing meats, even without chemicals, but this is not the reason why a home sausage maker cures meats. Meats are cured to produce a top quality product. The weight gain is as follows:

- Canadian bacon   3%
- Bacon   3%
- Ham, butt   4%

Wet cure-spray pumping method

There are two methods of spray pumping:

1. The artery pumping - a wet cure method where a long needle, connected with a hose to a pump, will inject a brine solution into the ham's artery. It is a very efficient way of distributing the curing solution quickly and uniformly through the meat. The arterial blood system of the animal becomes a pipeline for the brine distribution throughout the ham. A leg will have to be carefully and professionally butchered so the artery will remain intact. There is of course no possibility of a bone removal prior to pumping. This method requires some anatomy knowledge on the part of the operator but is still too slow for commercial applications and is going out of fashion.

The stitch pumping is a wet cure method where the curing solution is applied under pressure to the surface of a ham, bacon, or butt with a bank of needles connected to a pump. A home sausage maker can use a manual meat syringe to perform the same function though on a somewhat limited scale. The syringe holds 4 oz of brine and has a 5 3/8" long needle with 12 tiny holes around its surface. Smaller syringes for kitchen use can be found in every major appliances store. They are used for pumping meats with marinade for barbecuing.

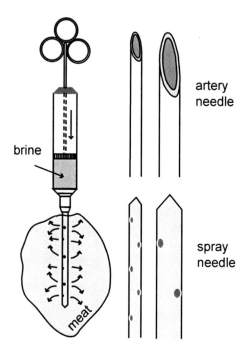

Fig. 2.2 Meat pump and needles.

2.9 Combination Curing

Combining the *dry cure* method with the *spray pumping*. A ham is spray pumped with a curing solution and the outside is rubbed with dry mix (salt and nitrite). That will allow the inside curing solution to penetrate the meat more evenly while the outside dry mix solution will be moving towards the inside. Combining the *wet cure* method with *spray pumping* (artery or stitch) shortens curing time.

A meat cut is spray pumped with a curing solution and then immersed in a container. The meat pieces should be completely covered and weighed down to prevent pieces from rising to the surface. They must also be turned over at least once every day for the duration of curing. The higher salt percentage in a curing solution the faster the curing process. When 26% of salt is added to water, the solution becomes saturated and extra salt will settle down on the bottom of the container. When forcefully rubbing salt into meat by hand we are introducing 100% of salt. This means that the dry curing method is much faster. Another benefit is that no moisture is added into the meat, on contrary, salt will draw water out of meat creating less favorable conditions for bacteria to grow. For these reasons traditional methods of ham preservation (countryside ham) relied on the dry cure method.

2.10 Making Brine - Be Professional And Use Tables And Brine Testers

There isn't a universal brine and every book and recipe provides customized instructions. Salt of different density and weight (table salt, Morton® Kosher, Diamond® Kosher) is measured with different instruments such as spoons, cups, ounces, pounds, kilograms - water measured by cups, quarts, gallons, liters... a total mess and chaos. We aim to explain the process in simpler terms using some common sense and logic. The main advantage of making your own brine is that you have total control over it and there is no guessing involved.

Firstly, it makes no sense at all to talk about curing time if we don't specify the strength of a brine. We can mix ½ cup salt with one quart of water or we can add 5 cups of salt into one gallon of water and it is obvious that *curing times will be different though both brines will do the job*. To prepare your own brine in a professional way and not to depend blindly on thousands of recipes you need two things:

1. Buy a brine tester. They are so cheap that there is no excuse for not having one. The salinometer consists of a float with a stem attached, marked in degrees. The instrument will float at its highest level in a saturated brine, and will read 100° (26.4 % salt solution). This is known as a fully saturated brine measured at 60° F. In weaker brines the stem will float at lower levels and the reading will be lower. With no salt present the reading will be 0°. To make brine put some water into a suitable container, add some salt, insert a brine tester and read the scale. Want a stronger solution: add more salt. Need weaker brine: add more water, it is that simple.

Photo 2.1 Brine tester also known as salinometer.

2. Learn how to use tables. The advantages of using tables are many: you can calculate the strength of any recipe you come across, you can find out how much salt to add to 1 gallon of water to create a particular brine strength, and you don't have to worry whether you use table salt, Morton® kosher salt or Diamond® kosher salt. Tables are especially useful when making a large volume of brine.

The Brine Tables and how to use them are in the Appendix A.

2.11 How Much Brine

You have to cover the meats and a lot of brine will be wasted if you cure only 1 chicken in a 55 gallon drum. A basic rule of thumb dictates that the amount of brine should come to 50% in relation to the weight of the meat. For 2 lbs of meat use 1 lb of brine. Try to use a container whose size and shape will accommodate the meat piece to use as little brine as possible. Many professionals use the following weight ratio: from 30% to 40% of water to 100% of meat. That means that for 1 kg (2.2 lbs) of meat we add 0.4 liters (400 mg) of water. Keep in mind that 1 liter of fresh water weighs exactly 1 kg. Then you choose the strength of the brine and keep on adding salt checking the reading with a salometer.

2.12 Strength of the Brine And Curing Times

There is no universal brine and its strength will be up to you. A brine tester is a must and a notebook for future reference will be of invaluable help. You can use a stronger brine and your curing time will be shorter or you can use a milder brine and the curing time can be longer. If you add sugar into your brine it will be heavier. For example, if we add 8 lbs of salt to 5 gallons of water we obtain 61° brine but if we add 8 lbs of salt plus 3 lbs of sugar to 5 gallons of water, we get 75° brine. *All our calculations are based on salt and water only.* Curing method used, curing times and brine strength all depend on each other:

- The strength of the brine – the stronger the brine the faster curing action.
- The size of the cured meat – a whole turkey requires more brining time than a shrimp.
- The method used – pumping and brining or just brining. Pumping meat shortens curing time.

Curing times estimates for the traditional wet cure method (brine strength 50–65 degrees) are as follows:

- 11 days per inch of thickness of the meat.
- About 3 ½ to 4 days per pound for 20 lbs. hams and picnics.
- 3 days per pound for smaller cuts.

Make sure you don't brine meats that have already been brined before you buy them, such as supermarket stocked pork, which has been treated with sodium phosphate and water to make it juicier. The following brine strengths are for orientation purpose only and feel free to improvise your own brines.

Meat	Brine Strength in Degrees	Time of Curing
Poultry	21	overnight
Bacon	50 - 65	1 1/2 - 2 days per pound
Spareribs	50 - 55	1 week
Loins	55 - 65	3 weeks
Ham, shoulders	65 - 75	4 days per pound
Fish	80	2 hours

Notice that sugar, though often added to brine after it is made, does not participate in calculation for making brine of a particular strength. That is due to the following reasons:

- A lot of brines do not call for sugar at all.
- A lot of brines call for different amounts of sugar (more sugar for a bacon, less sugar for a ham).
- People use different sugars, dextrose, maple syrup or honey.

Most meats like 70-75° brine, poultry likes a weaker solution of 21° and most fish are cured at 80° brine. Of course there are small diameter meat cuts and large ones (loins, butts, hams), chicken breasts, whole chickens and turkeys, fish fillets, small fish and big fish and all these different meats and cuts will have different curing times. Products like loins, hams, poultry, and spareribs taste good when more sugar is applied. *Sugar is not a curing agent and it has very little effect on the curing process.* Think of sugar in terms of flavoring.

To calculate the strength of the brine using the floating egg method makes very little sense as the readings are not reliable. There are books that advocate this method and each of them give different readings. The egg sinks in clean water and as the salt is added it should start lifting to the surface. Well, they do but in a very unpredictable manner. We have checked the floating egg method using five different size fresh eggs and the results were inconclusive. At 45° all eggs were breaking surface.

2.13 Brine Preparation

A brine solution (water, nitrite, salt) should be prepared 24 hours before use, then the surface foam and bottom sediment should be removed and the solution should be filtered using a fine cloth or paper towel. Before the use we should test the brine density using a brine tester to have a valuable reference for the future. Some people heat the brine with all ingredients to a boil to better dissolve salt in it, and then it is cooled and filtered. Reusing brine is a bad idea as the old brine may contain bacteria in it from the previous operation. Salt and cure mixes are so inexpensive that it makes no sense to take a risk of meat contamination. At the first suspicion of brine spoilage it should be replaced with a fresh one, in most cases there is nothing wrong with the meat itself. The accumulating foam on top of the brine should be periodically removed. In case the foam starts to give a foul odor, turn blue in color, or becomes a much thicker slime we will have to remove the ham, wash it in cool water, and place it again in a freshly made brine.

2.14 Curing With Nitrates/Nitrites

Meat cured only with salt, will have a better flavor but will also develop an objectionable dark color. Adding nitrites to meat will improve flavor, prevent food poisoning, tenderize the meat, and develop the pink color widely known and associated with smoked meats.

2.15 Curing And Meat Color

Meat color is determined largely by the amount of myoglobin (protein) a particular animal carries. The more myoglobin the darker the meat, it is that simple. Going from top to bottom, meats that contain more myoglobin are: horse, beef, lamb, veal, pork, dark poultry and light poultry. The amount of myoglobin present in meat also increases with the age of the animal. Different parts of the same animal, take the turkey for example, will have a different color as well.

This color is pretty much fixed and there is not much we can do about it unless we mix different meats together. Cured meats develop a particular pink-reddish color due to the reaction that takes place between meat myoglobin and nitrite. If an insufficient amount of nitrate/nitrite is added to the meat the cured color will suffer. This may be less noticeable in sausages where the meat is ground and stuffed but if we slice a larger piece like a ham, the poorly developed color will be easily noticeable. Some sections may be gray, some may be pink and the meat will not look appetizing.

At least 50 ppm (parts per million) of nitrite are needed to cure meat. Some of it will react with myoglobin and will fix the color, some of it will go into other complex biochemical reactions with meat that develop a characteristic cured meat flavor. If we stay within Food and Drug Administration guidelines (1 oz. Cure #1 per 25 lbs of meat-about 1 level teaspoon of Cure #1 for 5 lbs of meat) we are applying 156 ppm of nitrite which is enough and safe at the same time. Cured meat will develop its true cured color only after submitted to cooking (boiling, steaming, baking) at 140-160° F (60-71° C). The best color is attained at 161° F (72° C).

2.16 More About Nitrates

Nitrates have been used to cure meat since we can remember and how they were originally discovered is a matter of speculation. Rock salts were mined in different areas of the world and exhibited different properties which depended mainly on impurities contained within. Someone probably used salt to preserve meat that had more potassium nitrate in it and discovered that the meat had a different taste and color. Potassium nitrate was the main ingredient for making gun powder and it's commercial name was saltpeter, still used today. Potassium nitrate (KNO_3-Bengal saltpetre) or sodium nitrate ($NaNO_3$-Chile saltpetre) were even added to water causing the temperature to drop and that method was used to cool wine in the XVI century. *Nitrates and nitrites are powerful poisons* and that is why the Food and Drug Administration established limits for their use. So why do we use them?

The simple answer is that after testing and experiments, our modern science has not come up with a better solution to cure meats and prevent food poisoning. And now let's make something clear as almost all books written about sausages repeat one after another the same story: nitrates are used to prevent food poisoning known as botulism. Partly so… Nitrates were successfully added to meat for thousands of years and only in the XIX century a German fellow Justinus Kemer linked food poisoning to contaminated sausages. It took another 80 years to discover botulinum bacteria by Emile Pierre van Ermengem, Professor of bacteriology at the University of Ghent in 1895. The first scientific papers that explained the behavior of nitrates were published only in the XX century so why had we been using nitrates so much? Not to cure botulism of which we had never even heard of before.

We had been and still are using nitrates because:

- Nitrates can preserve meat's natural color. The same piece of ham when roasted will have a light brown color and is known as roasted leg of pork. Add some nitrates to it, apply smoke or boil it and it becomes ham with its characteristic flavor and pink color.

- Nitrates impart a characteristic cured flavor to meat.

- Nitrates prevent the transformation of botulinum spores into toxins thus eliminating the possibility of food poisoning.

2.17 What's Better, Nitrate or Nitrite?

Both nitrates and nitrites are permitted to be used in curing meat and poultry with the exception of bacon, where nitrate use is prohibited. *The use of nitrate is going out of fashion because it is difficult to control the curing process. Sodium Nitrate (NaNO₃) does not cure meat directly* and initially not much happens when it is added to meat. After a while micrococci and lactobacilli bacteria which are present in meat, start to react with nitrate and create *sodium nitrite (NaNO₂) that will start the curing process.* If those bacteria are not present in sufficient numbers the curing process may be inhibited. By adding sodium nitrite directly to meat we eliminate the risk of an insufficient number of bacteria and we can cure meats faster and at lower temperatures. Sodium nitrite is commonly used in the USA (Cure #1) and everywhere else in the world. To add to the confusion our commonly available cures contain both nitrite and nitrate.

Cure Agent	Nitrate	Nitrite
Cure #1	No	Yes
Cure #2	Yes	Yes
Morton ® Tender Quick	Yes	Yes
Morton ® Sugar Cure	Yes	Yes
Morton ® Smoke Flavored Sugar Cure	Yes	No

Many commercial meat plants prepare their own cures where both nitrite and nitrate are used. All original European sausage recipes include nitrate and now have to be converted to nitrite. So what is the big difference? Almost no difference at all. Whether we use nitrate or nitrite, the final result is basically the same. The difference between nitrate is as big as the difference between wheat flour and the bread that was baked from it. The nitrate is the Mama that gives birth to the Baby (nitrite).

Pure sodium nitrite is an even more powerful poison than nitrate as you need only about 1/3 of a tea-spoon to put your life in danger, where in a case of nitrate you may need 1 tea-spoon or more. So all these explanations that nitrite is safer for you make absolutely no sense at all. The main reason is that adding nitrite to meat does not leave much room for a question like: do I have enough nitrate or no? In other words, it is more predictable and it is easier to control the dosage. Another good reason for using nitrite is that *it is effective at low temperatures* 36-40° F, (2-4° C), where nitrate likes temperatures a bit higher 46-50° F, (8-10° C). By curing meats at lower temperatures we prevent the development of bacteria and we extend the shelf life of a product. When nitrates were used alone, *salt penetration was usually ahead of color development*. As a result large pieces of meat were too salty when fully colored and had to be soaked in water. This problem has been eliminated when using nitrite. Nitrite works much faster and *the color is fixed well before salt can fully penetrate the meat*. Estimating the required amount of nitrate is harder as it is dependent on:

- Temperature (with higher temperature more nitrite is released from nitrate).

- Amount of bacteria present in meat that is needed for nitrate to produce nitrite and here we do not have any control. The more bacteria present, the more nitrite released. Adding sugar may be beneficial as it provides food for bacteria to grow faster.

In the 1920's, the government allowed the addition of 10 lbs. of nitrate to 100 gallons of water (7 lbs. allowed today). The problem was that only about one quarter of the meat plants adhered to those limits and many plants added much more, even between 70 and 90 pounds. There was no control and as a result a customer was eating a lot of nitrates.

2.18 Nitrate Safety Concerns

There has been much concern over the consumption of nitrates by the general public. Studies have shown that when nitrites combine with by-products of protein (amines in the stomach) that leads to the formation of nitrosamines which are carcinogenic (cancer causing) in laboratory animals. There was also a link that when nitrates were used to cure bacon and the latter one was fried until crispy, it helped to create nitrosamines. But the required temperatures had to be in the 600° F (315° C) range and meats are smoked and cooked well below 200° F (93° C) so even this fact has no bearing on the use of nitrates in meats.

Those findings started a lot of unnecessary panic in the 1970's about the harmful effects of nitrates on our health. Millions of dollars were spent, a lot of research was done, many researchers had spent long sleepless nights seeking fame and glory, but no evidence was found that when nitrates are used within the established limits they can pose any danger to our health. A review of all scientific literature on nitrite by the National Research Council of the National Academy of Sciences indicates that nitrite does not directly harm us in any way. All this hoopla about the danger of nitrite in our meats pales in comparison with the amounts of nitrates that are found in vegetables that we consume every day. The nitrates get to them from the fertilizers which are used in agriculture.

Don't blame sausages for the nitrates you consume, blame the farmer. It is more dangerous to one's health to eat vegetables on a regular basis than a sausage: "Hey, doc, what about the food pyramid? Vegetables contain more nitrites than meat, can I still have my carrot?"

2.19 Nitrates in Vegetables

The following information about nitrates in vegetables was published by MAFF, Department of Health and the Scottish Executive before April 1st 2000 when the Food Standards Agency was established. Number 158, September 1998. MAFF UK - NITRATE IN VEGETABLES:

Vegetables contain higher concentrations of nitrate than other foods and make a major contribution to dietary intake. A survey of vegetables for sale in supermarkets was carried out in 1997 and 1998 to provide up-to-date information on nitrate concentrations, to assess the health implications for UK consumers and also to inform negotiations on a review of the European Commission Regulation (EC) No. 194/97 (which sets maximum levels for nitrate in lettuce and spinach).

A study on the effects of cooking on nitrate concentrations in vegetables was also carried out to provide further refinements for estimating dietary exposure. The vegetables were tested and the mean nitrate concentrations found were as listed in the table on the right. For comparison the permissible amount of nitrate in comminuted meat products (sausages) is 1718 mg/kg. If one ate 1/4 lb smoked sausage, the ingoing nitrate would be 430 ppm. That would probably account for less nitrates than a dinner served with potatoes and spinach.

Vegetable	Nitrate mg/kg
spinach	1631
beetroot	1211
lettuces	1051
cabbages	338
potatoes	155
swedes	118
carrots	97
califlowers	86
brussel sprouts	59
onions	48
tomatoes	17

Cooking by boiling reduced nitrate concentrations in most of the vegetables tested by up to 75 percent. Frying and baking did not affect nitrate concentrations in potatoes but frying caused increases in levels in onions. Dietary intakes of mean and upper range (97.5 percentile) consumers of these vegetables are 104 mg/day and 151 mg/day, respectively. These are below the Acceptable Daily Intake (ADI) for nitrate of 219 mg/day for a 60 kg adult set by the European Commission's Scientific Committee for Food (SCF). There are therefore no health concerns for consumers.

2.20 How Much Nitrite is Dangerous

According to the report prepared in 1972 for the U.S. Food and Drug Administration (FDA) by Battele-Columbus Laboratories and Department of Commerce, Springfield, VA 22151 – the fatal dose of potassium nitrate for humans is in the range of 30 to 35 grams (about two tablespoons) consumed as a single dose; the fatal dose of sodium nitrite is in the range of 22 to 23 milligrams per kilogram of body weight. A 156 lbs adult (71 kg) would have to consume, 14.3 pounds (6.5 kg) of cured meat containing 200 ppm of sodium nitrite at one time. Taking under consideration that nitrite is rapidly converted to nitric oxide during the curing process, the 14.3 lbs amount will have to be doubled or even tripled. The equivalent amount of pure sodium nitrite consumed will be 1.3 g. As nitrite is mixed with large amounts of salt, it would be impossible to swallow it at least from a culinary point of view. As our most popular cures are in a pink color it would be very hard to mistake them for common salt. Even if Cure #1 was misplaced in such an unusual way, the amount of salt needed to consume as a single dose will even be larger as there are only 156 ppm of sodium nitrite in it. That corresponds to eating 18.26 lbs of meat at one sitting. The only way to consume a fatal dose will be to mistake pure nitrite (it is white) for salt but the general public has no access to it.

2.21 Nitrates And The Law

Maximum In going Nitrite and Nitrate Limits in PPM (parts per million) for Meat and Poultry Products as required by the Food Safety and Inspection Service are:

Curing Agent	Curing Method			
	Immersion Cured	Massaged or Pumped	Comminuted	Dry Cured
Sodium Nitrite	200	200	156	625
Potassium Nitrite	200	200	156	625
Sodium Nitrate	700	700	1718	2187
Potassium Nitrate	700	700	1718	2187

- 1g of pure sodium nitrite is generally accepted as the life threatening dose. 1 PPM (part per million) equals 1 mg/kg.

There are more stringent limits for curing agents in bacon to reduce the formation of nitrosamines. For this reason, nitrate is no longer permitted in any bacon (pumped and/or massaged, dry cured, or immersion cured). As a matter of policy, the Agency requires a minimum of 120 ppm of ingoing nitrite in all cured "Keep Refrigerated" products, unless the establishment can demonstrate that safety is assured by some other preservation process, such as thermal processing, pH or moisture control. This 120 ppm policy for in going nitrite is based on safety data reviewed when the bacon standard was developed.

There is no regulatory minimum ingoing nitrite level for cured products that have been processed to ensure their shelf stability (such as having undergone a complete thermal process, or having been subjected to adequate pH controls, and/or moisture controls in combination with appropriate packaging). However, 40 ppm nitrite is useful in that it has some preservative effect. This amount has also been shown to be sufficient for color-fixing purposes and to achieve the expected cured meat or poultry appearance. Some thermally processed shelf-stable (canned) products have a minimum ingoing nitrite level that must be monitored because it is specified as a critical factor in the product's process schedule. By the time meats are consumed, they contain less then 50 parts per million of nitrite. It is said that commercially prepared meats in the USA contain about 10 ppm of nitrite when bought in a supermarket. Nitrite and nitrate are not permitted in baby, junior or toddler foods.

Note: how to calculate nitrates is presented in Appendix A

2.22 Cure #1 (also known as Instacure #1, Prague Powder #1 or Pink Cure). For any aspiring sausage maker it is a necessity to understand and know how to apply Cure #1 and Cure #2, as those two cures are used worldwide though under different names and with different proportions of nitrates and salt. Cure #1 is a mixture of 1oz of Sodium Nitrite (6.25%) to 1 lb of salt. It must be used to cure all meats that will require smoking at low temperatures. It may be used to cure meats for fresh sausages (optional).

2.23 Cure #2 (also known as Instacure #2, Prague Powder #2 or Pink Cure). Cure #2 is a mixture of 1 oz of Sodium Nitrite (6.25%) along with .64 oz of Sodium Nitrate (4%) to 1 lb of salt. It can be compared to the time-releasing capsules used for treating colds. It must be used with any products that do not require cooking or refrigeration and is mainly used for products that will be air cured for a long time like country ham, salami, pepperoni, and other dry sausages. Both Cure #1 and Cure #2 contain a small amount of FDA approved red coloring agent that gives them a slight pink color thus eliminating any possible confusion with common salt and that is why they are sometimes called "pink" curing salts. Cure #1 is not interchangeable with Cure #2 and vice versa.

2.24 Morton™ Salt Cures

In addition to making common Table Salt the Morton® Salt Company also produces a number of cures such as Sugar Cure® mix, Smoke Flavored Sugar Cure® mix, Tender Quick® mix, and Sausage and Meat Loaf® seasoning mix. To use them properly one has to follow instructions that accompany every mix.

2.25 European Cures

There are different cures in European countries and for example, in Poland a commonly used cure goes by the name "Peklosól" and contains 0.6% of Sodium Nitrite to salt. No coloring agent is added and it is white in color. In European cures such a low nitrite percentage in salt is self-regulating and it is almost impossible to apply too much nitrite to meat, as the latter will taste too salty. Following a recipe you could replace salt with peklosól altogether and the established nitrite limits will be preserved. This isn't the case with American Cure #1 which contains much more nitrite (6.5%) and we have to color it pink to avoid the danger of mistakes and poisoning.

Country	Cure	% of nitrite in salt
USA	Cure #1	6.25
Poland	Peklosól	0.6
Germany	Pökelsalz	0.6
France	Sel nitrité	0.6
Sweden	Colorazo	0.6
England	Nitrited salt	various
Australia	Kuritkwik	various

2.26 How to Apply Cures

Well, there are two approaches:

- Like an amateur - collecting hundreds of recipes and relying blindly on each of them. You lose a recipe and you don't know what to do. And how do you know they contain the right amount of cure?

- Like a professional - taking matters in your own hands and applying cures according to the USA Government requirements.

In case you want to be the professional, we are enclosing some useful data which is based on the FSIS nitrate limits presented in the table on page 42.

Comminuted products - small meat pieces, meat for sausages, ground meat, poultry etc. Cure #1 was developed in such a way that if we add 4 ounces of cure # 1 to 100 pounds of meat, the quantity of nitrite added to meat will comfort to the legal limits (156 ppm) permitted by the Meat Division of the United States Department of Agriculture. That corresponds to 1 oz (28.35 g) of Cure #1 for each 25 lbs (11.33 kg) of meat or 0.2 oz (5.66 g) per 5 lbs (2.26 kg) of meat.

Comminuted Meat (Sausages)	Cure #1 in ounces	Cure #1 in grams	Cure #1 in teaspoons
25 lbs	1	28.35	5
5 lbs	0.2	5.66	1
1 lb	0.04	1.1	1/5
1 kg	0.08	2.5	1/2

Cured Dry Products - country ham, country style pork shoulder, proscuitto, etc. These products are prepared from a single piece of meat or poultry, that has had the curing ingredients directly applied to the surface, and has been dried for a specific period of time. For larger pieces of meat, the curing ingredients must be rubbed on the surface several times during the curing period. The rubbed meat or poultry cuts are placed on racks or in boxes and allowed to cure. Nitrite is applied to the surface of the meat or poultry as part of a cure mixture. If you look at the FSIS nitrite limits table on page 42 you will see that the maximum nitrite limit for Dry Cured Products (625 ppm) is four times higher than for Comminuted Products (156). All you have to do is look at the Comminuted Products table on a previous page and multiply the amount of Cure #1 four times. It uses the same formula for nitrite calculations as the comminuted products. For example, to cure meat for sausages (comminuted) and to stay within 156 ppm nitrite limit we have to apply no more than 1 oz of Cure #1 for each 25 lbs of meat. To dry cure 25 lbs of pork butts and to stay within 625 nitrite limits we need 4 times more of Cure #1, in our case 4 ounces. Keep in mind that when you add Cure #1 (there is 93.75% salt in it) you are adding extra salt to your meat and you may re-adjust your recipe.

Meat for Dry Curing	Cure #1 in ounces	Cure #1 in grams	Cure #1 in teaspoons
25 lbs	4	113.4	20
5 lbs	0.8	22.64	4
1 lb	0.16	4.4	3/4
1 kg	0.35	10.0	1.5

The reason that there are much higher allowable nitrite limits for dry cured products is that nitrite dissipates rapidly in time and the dry cured products are air dried for a long time. Those higher limits guarantee a steady supply of nitrite.

Immersed, Pumped and Massaged Products such as hams, poultry breasts, corned beef. Here, it is much harder to come up with a universal formula as there are so many variables that have to be determined first. The main factor is to determine % pump when injecting the meat with a syringe or % pick-up when immersing meat in a curing solution. We will calculate the formula for 1 gallon of water, Cure #1 and 10% pick-up gain. Then the formula can be multiplied or divided to accommodate different amounts of meat. 10% pump or 10% pick-up mean that the cured meat should absorb 10% of the brine in relation to its weight. For immersion, pumped or massaged products, the maximum ingoing nitrite limit is 200 ppm and that corresponds to adding 4.2 oz of Cure #1 to 1 gallon of water.

1 gallon (8.33 lbs) of water	Cure #1 in ounces	Cure #1 in grams	Cure #1 in teaspoons
	4.2	120	20 tsp (6 Tbs)

This is a very small amount of brine and if you want to cure a turkey you will need to increase the volume. Just multiply it by a factor of 4 and you will have 4 gallons of water and 1.08 lbs of Cure #1. The following is the safe formula for immersed products and very easy to measure: 5 gallons of water, 1 lb of Cure #1. In the above formula at 10% pick-up the nitrite limit is 150 ppm which is plenty. Keep in mind that adding 1 lb of Cure #1 to 5 gallons of water will give you 4.2% salt by weight and that corresponds to *only 16 degrees brine (slightly higher than sea water)*. If we add an additional 2 lbs of salt we will get:

5 gallons of water, 1 lb of Cure #1, 2 lbs of salt and that will give us a 25 degree solution which is great for poultry.

2.27 What Will Happen if Too Little or Too Much Cure is Added?

With not enough cure, the color might be weaker, some loss of cured flavor, too. FSIS regulations dictate the maximum allowed nitrite limits and there are no limits for the lower levels. It has been accepted that a minimum of 40-50 ppm of nitrite is needed for any meaningful curing. Too much cure will not be absorbed by the meat and will be eaten by a consumer. Adding an excessive amount may make you sick, read page 42.

2.28 What Will Happen if Curing Time is Shorter or Longer?

If the curing time is too short, some areas of meat (inside or under heavy layers of fat) will exhibit an uneven color which might be noticeable when slicing a large piece of meat. It will not show in sausages which are filled with ground meat, although the color may be weaker. If curing time is longer by a few days, nothing will happen providing the cured meat is held under refrigeration. You don't want to cure bone-in meats longer than 30-45 days as they may develop bone sour even when kept at low temperatures.

2.29 Commercial Curing Methods

Meat plants can not afford the luxury of the traditional wet curing as it requires storage space and extra time. The process they employed consists of pumping meats with needle injectors with specially formulated and often patented formulas, then massaging the meats in tumblers to distribute the curing solution more evenly. Needle injectors pump the meat under pressure with a prepared solution that contains everything that is allowed by law to make the process the shortest and most economical. Some methods allow pumping meat with a curing solution and microscopic parts of meat of any kind.

Meat plants don't use these machines to improve quality, they use them to work faster and save money. A pork butt left for 10 days in a brine solution will be perfectly cured in every area, something a needle injector and tumbler will not do. There is a limit to how many holes can be made in meat with needles as they damage the texture of the meat. These machines are only effective if used with chemicals that will help to cure meat faster. By injecting the curing solution directly into the meat we speed up the process. The tumbler machine helps to distribute the solution evenly inside but nitrite needs time to create a pink color. Salt also needs time to cure meat but there is no easy way to notice how well salt did its job. If curing time is too short, some areas of the large piece of meat will be grey, some lightly pink and some will be red-pink. That is why we use cure accelerators so they can cure and color meat at a much faster rate.

Photo 2.2 Needle injector.
Photo courtesy Koch Equipment, Kansas City, MO

Photo 2.3 The tumbler is a machine with a rotating drum. The meat pieces bounce around its moving walls providing better brine distribution inside of the meat.

Photo courtesy Koch Equipment, Kansas City, MO

Using high production stitch pumping machines and a tumbler, a ham can be ready for the smoker in 24 hours. A home processor can use a manual syringe to inject brine into the meat but I don't believe anybody wants to keep a tumbler machine in the kitchen. You could massage meat with your hands or pound it through a towel with a rubber mallet. Unfortunately, that will require a lot of time and at temperatures prevailing in an ordinary kitchen that will create more harm than good.

After losing moisture during smoking and cooking commercially produced hams still weigh the same as what the original weight was. This miracle is due to the water that is injected into the meat and held there by phosphates. The present day ham might be juicier (extra water) than those old European products but its flavor does not even come close. As a curiosity matter the Soviet hams were: salted, cured, soaked, air-cured for 10 days at 54-64° F (12-18° C) and the relative humidity not exceeding 80%. Then they were smoked for 3 days at 86-95° F (30-35° C) or for 15 days at 64-68° F (18-20° C) and dried for 10 days. The yield of the finished product was 70% of the original meat weight. As you can see from the above example, the same product can be successfully smoked at different times and temperatures.

Taste your meats after curing is done. You can always cure them longer in a heavier brine (to increase salt content) or soak them in cold water (to lower salt content).

2.30 Curing Accelerators And Water Retention Agents

The time required to develop a cured color may be shortened with the use of cure accelerators. Ascorbic acid (vitamin C), erythorbic acid, or their derivatives, sodium ascorbate and sodium erythorbate speed up the chemical conversion of nitrite to nitric oxide which in turn will react with meat myoglobin to create a pink color. They also deplete levels of meat oxygen which prevents the fading color of the cured meat in the presence of light and oxygen.

Phosphates are the most effective water holding agents. Salt and most water binding agents force meat protein to swell which helps them trap and hold more water. Phosphates are able to open the structure of the protein which helps them to hold even more water. This increased water holding capacity of the protein is what prevents water losses when smoking and cooking.

Soy protein concentrate being a *natural product* can bind water, prevent melting of fat and improve the texture of the sausage. The sausage will be juicier and plumper but the amount of added soy protein concentrate should not exceed 3% otherwise it may impart a "beany" flavor to the product.

Non fat dry milk powder can bind water and is often used in making sausages, including fermented types. Non fat dry milk is cheaper and available in a local supermarket. Dry milk powder contains sugar and is used in fermented sausages as a source of food for lactic acid producing bacteria. Dry milk powder greatly improves the taste of low fat sausages.

MSG (monosodium glutamate) is a very effective flavor enhancer which is produced by the fermentation of starch, sugar beets, sugar cane, or molasses. Although once stereotypically associated with foods in Chinese restaurants, it is now found in many common food items, particularly processed foods.

Name	Common amount	Max allowed by law
phosphate		0.5% (5g/1kg of meat)
ascorbic acid	around 500 mg	as needed
erythorbic acid		< 500 mg/kg
sodium erythorbate		< 500 mg
soy protein concentrate	1-3% (10-30 g/kg)	as needed
non fat dry milk	1-3% (10-30 g/kg)	as needed
monosodium glutamate	0.5-0.2% (0.5-2g/kg)	as needed

The chemicals listed above are not used to improve flavor of the product, but to increase its water holding capacity and shorten curing. This results in increased yield and higher profits.

Chapter 3

Cooking

3.1 Methods of Cooking

It really does not matter which method you will use to cook meats. You could smoke meat in the most primitive conditions outdoors, then bring it home and poach it in a pot and it will be a great product. We can use the following cooking methods:

- Cooking in a smoker.
- Baking in the oven.
- Poaching in water.

All we have to do is remember that the fat melts down at quite low temperatures and although it solidifies again, its looks are already gone. Fry a piece of solid fat on a frying pan and see what happens when it solidifies, it doesn't look the same. We can't avoid it altogether (unless we make cold smoked and air dried products), but there is no reason to intensify the problem by creating unnecessarily high temperatures.

3.2 Cooking in a Smoker

It makes a lot of sense to cook meat in the smoker as it is already there. Besides, it will have a slightly better taste than by using the poaching method and it will shine more. On a downside, it will lose more weight than by other methods. It is also the slowest and the most difficult method that largely depends on the technical possibilities of the smoker. Slowly increasing the temperature inside the smoker will achieve the best effects.

Two thermometers are needed-one to monitor the temperature of the smoker, cooking pot or oven (oven has its own temperature dial), and the other to monitor the inside temperature of the meat or sausage in its thickest part. It helps to have a thermometer with an alarm sounder in it, this way we get an audible warning when meat has achieved its pre-set temperature. While it takes 2-3 hours to smoke a sausage, it may take an additional 5 hours to cook it inside the smoker. It will largely depend on the inside temperature of the meat when smoking was stopped.

If it was 100° F (38° C) we have a long way to go, if it was 150° F (66° C) we are almost there. That shows a need for some intelligent planning and when cooking in a smoker it is advisable to slowly increase the smoking temperature to about 160° F. When smoking is done, the temperature should be increased to 170° F (77° C) and maintained at that level until the inside temperature of the smoked meat reaches 154° F (68° C).

This way the process will be relatively short. That sometimes might be difficult to achieve and we will have to increase the temperature of a smoker to about 185° F (85° C) to bring the internal temperature of the meat to the required level. A lot will depend on outside conditions and how well the smoker is insulated. The other easier method is to set the temperature of the smoker to 170° F (77° C) and wait until the meat's inside temperature reaches 154° F (68° C).

3.3 Poaching in Water

Poaching is a proper, acceptable and professional way of cooking sausages and there are dozens of well known sausages that are made this way. It is also easier and faster to apply than cooking in the smoker and the meat weight loss is smaller. When poaching sausages, water is brought to the temperature of 158-194° F (70-90° C) and the meats or sausages are immersed in it. For instance, home made hams are poached at 176° F (80° C) and this temperature is maintained until the meat's inside temperature reaches 154° F (68° C). Some recipes call for preheating the water before adding the sausages and some call for adding the sausages to cold water. Most people prefer the latter method. The poaching water should be heated rapidly to 175-185° F (80-85° C). A product taken out of the hot vessel might still increase its internal temperature by one or two degrees. A cooking pot remains uncovered during poaching.

The poaching method is the preferred choice for sausages that are smoked with hot smoke. The short hot smoking process creates a dry layer on the outside of the sausage, similar to a second skin, that prevents the migration of moisture and juices from inside of the sausage to the water in the pot. Exact times and temperatures of poaching are given with particular recipes. At 176° F (80° C) the sausages are poached from 10-120 minutes, depending on the type and size of the product. A rule of thumb calls for 10 minutes for each 1 cm of the width (diameter) of the sausage.

3.4 Baking in Oven

You can bake your meat or sausages in the oven as long as your unit can maintain temperatures of 190° F or lower (preferably 170° F) and home ovens are normally capable of delivering such low temperatures. If the oven's lowest temperature will be higher than 190° F (88° C) switch to the poaching method.

3.5 Cooking Pork

Sausages, hams and other pieces of meat are considered raw products and must be cooked after smoking. A sausage smoked at 100° F (38° C) for 6 hrs, will have a great smoky taste, flavor and color but it will still be a raw sausage like a fresh sausage that was only ground, mixed with spices, and stuffed into casings. Both of them must be cooked to safe temperatures before consumption. The U.S. Department of Agriculture recommends cooking fresh pork to an internal temperature of 160° F (71° C) and The National Pork Producers Council recommends an internal cooking temperature of 155° F (68° C) for maximum juiciness and flavor. Those extra 6° F (between 154° and 160° F) might kill a few more microbes and as a result the sausage might have a few hours longer shelf life, which is more important from a commercial point of view.

For a home sausage maker the inside temperature of the meat should fall between 154-160° F (68-72° C). We can stop cooking at 154° F (68° C) as most products will be of smoked variety and thus previously cured with salt and nitrite which gives us considerably more safety. Meats, which were not previously cured, will not be smoked, just cooked before consumption and the recommended temperature of 160° F should be observed. The lower cooking temperature, the juicier and tastier the product is and the weight loss is also smaller. Fats start to melt at 95-104° F (35-40° C) and going over 170° F (76° C) internal meat temperature will decrease the quality of the sausage. Staying within 154-160° F (68-72° C) will produce the highest quality product.

3.7 Cooking Beef and Poultry

There are some sausages made entirely of beef though in most cases beef is mixed with pork. As beef can develop *Salmonella*, the Food Safety and Inspection Service of the United States Department of Agriculture has issued the following guidelines in June, 1999:

"Cooked beef and roast beef including sectioned and formed roasts, chunked and formed roasts, and cooked corned beef can be prepared using one of the following time and temperature combinations to meet either a 6.5-log10 or 7-log10 reduction of Salmonella":

F°	C°	6.5-log10 lethality	7-log10 lethality
130	54.4	112 minutes	121 minutes
140	60.0	12 min	12 min
145	62.8	4 min	4 min
150	65.6	67 seconds	72 seconds
152	66.7	43 sec	46 sec
154	67.8	27 sec	29 sec
158	70.0	**0** sec	**0** sec

*"Cooked poultry rolls and other cooked poultry products should reach an internal temperature of at least 160° F (71° C) prior to being removed from the cooking medium, except that **cured and smoked** poultry rolls and other **cured and smoked** poultry should reach an internal temperature of at least 155° F (69° C) prior to being removed from the cooking medium". (FSIS, June, 1999).*

3.7 Cooking Fish

Fish is considered done when cooked to 145° F (63° C) internal temperature. A reliable test is to insert a fork or knife into the thickest part of the fish and twist. The flesh should "flake" (separate).

3.8 Summary

The thermometer should be inserted in the thickest part of the meat.

- The previously cured meat will develop the best color when heated to 160° F (72° C). Most sausage recipes contain smoking instructions on required temperatures and times.

- At higher cooking temperatures sausage shrivelling will be more pronounced.

- In many poorly insulated smokers the cooking temperature must be almost 25° F higher than the corresponding meat temperature to notice any practical progress (The meat temperature follows the smoker's temperature but is behind by about 25° F).

- The surface area of a cooked product exhibits a higher temperature than the inside and even after the heat source is switched off, the heat will continue to transfer towards the inside. The internal temperature of the meat will still advance by a few degrees.

Meats that were not cured and smoked should be cooked to the following temperatures:

- Fish should reach 145° F (63° C) as measured with a food thermometer.
- All cuts of pork to 160° F (72° C).
- Ground beef, veal and lamb to 160° F.
- All poultry should reach a safe minimum internal temperature of 165° F (74° C).
- Leftovers to 165° F.

Photo 3.1 Cooking in the wild.

Photo courtesy Waldemar Kozik

Dutch Oven

The Dutch oven is an extraordinary vessel for slow cooking. Although it does not have much in common with traditional meat smoking, nevertheless it a great way of cooking outdoors. A proper traditional oven is made of cast iron and is quite heavy, depending on its diameter. There are different sizes, starting from 8" diameter and up. A Dutch oven made of cast iron can handle heat up to 2,000° F (1093° C) and a fast burning open fire can sometimes reach 1,500° F (815° C). A good oven must have three strong legs, a hanging bail, rimmed lid and the cover handle. A good lid is concave shaped so it can be flipped over and used as a frying pan.

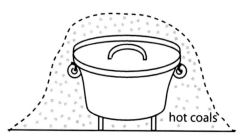

covered with hot coals

hot coals

Fig. 3.1 Dutch oven can stand on its legs or can hang on the hook.

Fig. 3.2 Dutch oven covered with hot coals. If kept clean and properly maintained, it is virtually indestructible.

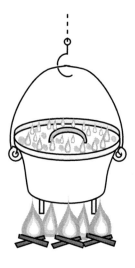

A good lid must fit tight and must be thick enough to handle hot coals which are placed on it. The lid has a raised lip to confine coals inside. Dutch ovens can handle all cooking needs such as bread, stew, pulled pork, pies, turkey and other dishes.
Fig. 3.3 - left. Oven hanging over camp fire.
Fig. 3.4-right. Ovens stacked up.

Chapter 4

Food Safety And Bacteria

4.1 All About Bacteria

Food safety is nothing else but the control of bacteria and to do it effectively first we have to learn how bacteria behave. Once one knows what bacteria like or dislike, it will be very simple to produce safe products with a long shelf life. Let's make something clear: it is impossible to eliminate bacteria altogether, life on the planet will come to a halt. The best we can do is coexist with them and try to manipulate them to our advantage.

All microorganisms can be divided into the following classes:

- Bacteria
- Yeasts
- Molds

They all share one thing in common: they want to live and given the proper conditions they will start multiplying. They don't grow bigger, they just divide and divide and divide until there is nothing for them to eat, or until conditions become so unfavorable that they stop multiplying and die.

All bacteria need moisture, nutrients, and warm temperatures to grow. Meat contains about 75% of water and this moisture is the main reason that it spoils. Bacteria love temperatures that revolve around the temperature of our body (36.6° C, 98.6° F). Holding products at higher temperatures (greater than 130° F, 54° C) restricts the growth of bacteria. Increasing temperatures over 60° C (140° F) will start killing them. Most bacteria need oxygen (aerobic), others thrive without it (anaerobic). All of them hate cold, and around 32° F, (0° C) they become lethargic and dormant when the temperature drops lower. *Keeping them at low temperatures does not kill them, but only stops them from multiplying.* Once when the conditions are favorable again, they will wake up and start growing again. Some bacteria tolerate the presence of salt better than others and we take advantage of this when curing meats. Other bacteria (e.g. *Clostridium botulinum*) are able to survive high temperatures because they form spores.

Spores are special cells that envelop themselves in a protective shell and become resistant to harsh environmental conditions. Once conditions become favorable, the cells return to their actively growing state. Given favorable conditions bacteria can double up in numbers every 20 minutes. In a refrigerator their number will also grow, albeit at a reduced pace, but they can double up in 12 hours. Short of deep freezing, it is impossible to stop bacteria from contaminating meat, but we can create conditions that will slow down their growing rate. At room temperatures bacteria will grow anywhere they have access to nutrients and water. Microorganisms which are of special interest when processing meats:

- Food spoilage bacteria.
- Dangerous (pathogenic) bacteria.
- Beneficial bacteria.
- Yeasts and molds.

4.2 Food Spoilage Bacteria

Spoilage bacteria break down meat proteins and fats causing food to deteriorate and develop unpleasant odors, tastes, and textures. Fruits and vegetables get mushy or slimy and meat develops a bad odor. Most people would not eat spoiled food. However, if they did, they probably would not get seriously sick. Bacteria such as *Pseudomonas spp.* or *Brochotrix thermosphacta* cause slime, discoloration and odors, but don't produce toxins. There are different spoilage bacteria and each reproduces at specific temperatures. Some can even grow at the low temperatures in the refrigerator or freezer.

4.3 Pathogenic Bacteria

It is commonly believed that the presence of bacteria creates an immense danger to us but this belief is far from the truth. The fact is that a very small percentage of bacteria can place us in any danger, and most of us with a healthy immune system are able to fight them off. *Pathogenic bacteria cause illness.* They grow rapidly in the "Danger Zone"-the temperatures between 40 and 140° F-and *do not generally affect the taste, smell, or appearance of food.* Food that is left too long at warm temperatures could be dangerous to eat, but smell and look just fine. *Clostridium botulinum, Bacillus cereus* or *Staphylococcus aureus* infect food with toxin which will bring harm to us in just a few hours. Still others, like *Salmonella* or *Escherichia coli* will find its way with infected meat into our intestines, and if present in sufficient numbers, will pose a serious danger. Pathogenic bacteria hate cold conditions and lie dormant at low temperatures waiting for an opportunity to jump into action when the conditions get warmer again. They all die when submitted to the cooking temperature of 160° F (72° C), but many fermented sausages are never cooked and different strategies must be implemented to keep them at bay. Fighting bacteria is a never ending battle, but at least we can do our best to turn the odds in our favor.

4.4 Beneficial Bacteria

Without beneficial bacteria it will not be possible to make fermented sausages. They are naturally occurring in meat but in most cases they are added into the meat in the form of starter cultures. There are two classes of beneficial (friendly) bacteria:

- Lactic acid producing bacteria - *Lactobacillus, Pediococcus.*
- Color and flavor forming bacteria - *Staphylococcus, Kocuria* (previously known as *Micrococcus*).

Although lactic acid producing bacteria are used mainly to produce fermented products, color and flavor forming bacteria are needed to brake nitrate into nitrite and are often added to develop a stronger red color of meats.

4.5 Yeasts And Molds

Yeast and molds grow much slower than bacteria and they develop later in the drying process. This means they are normally part of the traditionally made sausage process. Yeasts need little oxygen to survive, and live on the surface or near the surface inside of the sausage. Molds are aerobic (need oxygen) and will grow on the surface of the sausage only. On fermented European sausages, the development of mold is often seen as a desired feature as it contributes to the flavor of the sausage. Smoking sausages during or after fermentation, will prevent the growth of mold. If mold develops and is not desired, it can be easily wiped off with a cloth saturated in vinegar. Because molds can grow only on the outside of the sausage, there is nothing wrong with the meat itself.

4.6 Effects of Time And Temperature on Bacteria Growth

Under the correct conditions, spoilage bacteria reproduce rapidly and the populations can grow very large. Temperature and time are the factors that affect bacterial growth the most. Below 45° F bacteria grow slowly and at temperatures above 140° F they start to die. In the so called "danger zone" between 40-140° F (4-60° C) many bacteria grow very well. Most bacteria will grow exponentially at temperatures between 70° F and 120° F. When bacteria grow, they increase in numbers, not in size. After cooking, meats are free of bacteria, but leaving them warm for an extended time will invite new bacteria to settle in and start growing. For this reason smoked and subsequently cooked meats are submitted to cold showers to pass through the "danger zone" as fast as possible. Let's see how fast bacteria grow at ideal temperature:

Number of bacteria	Elapsed time
10	0
20	20 minutes
40	40 minutes
80	1 hour
160	1 hour 20 min
320	1 hour 40 min
640	2 hours
1280	2 hours 20 min
2560	2 hours 40 min
5120	3 hours
10,240	3 hours 20 min
20,480	3 hours 40 min
40,960	4 hours
81,920	4 hours 20 min
163.840	4 hours 40 min
327,680	5 hours
655,360	5 hours 20 min
1,310,720	5 hours 40 min
2,621,440	6 hours

Now it becomes evident what happens to a piece of meat left out on the kitchen table for many hours on a beautiful and hot summer day. The thermometer drawing that follows below has been compiled from the data we found at the College of Agriculture, Auburn University, Alabama. It shows the time that is required for 1 bacteria cell to become 2 at different storage temperatures. Looking at the drawing on the facing page we can see that once the temperature rises above 50° F (10° C), bacteria will double up every time we raise the temperature by about 5° F.

From the above examples we can draw a logical conclusion that if we want to process meats we should perform these tasks at temperatures not higher than 50° F (10° C). And those are the temperatures present in meat processing plants. You might say that lowering the temperature of the room will be better still. Of course it will be better, but people working in such conditions for 8 hours a day will find it very uncomfortable.

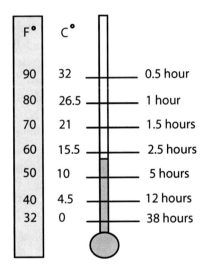

F°	C°	
90	32	0.5 hour
80	26.5	1 hour
70	21	1.5 hours
60	15.5	2.5 hours
50	10	5 hours
40	4.5	12 hours
32	0	38 hours

It can be seen that at 32° F (0° C) bacteria needs as much as 38 hours to divide in two. That also means that if our piece of meat had a certain amount of bacteria on its surface, after 38 hours of lying in a refrigerator the amount of bacteria in the same piece of meat will double. If we move this meat from the refrigerator to a room having a temperature of 80° F (26.5° C) the bacteria will double up every hour (12 times faster). At 90° F (32° C) they will be dividing every 30 minutes.

Fig. 6.1 Bacteria growth with temperature.

Effects of temperature, acidity (pH) and moisture (Aw) on bacteria behavior:

Name	Temperature in ° C			Min pH	Min Aw
	Minimum	Optimum	Maximum		
Salmonella	7	35 - 37	45	3.8	0.94
Cl.botulinum	3	18 - 25	45	5.0	0.97
Cl.perfringens	12	43 - 47	50	5.5	0.93
Staph.aureus	6	37	48	4.2	0.85
Campylobacter	30	42	45	4.9	0.98
Listeria	-1.5	37	45	4.4	0.92
E.coli	7	37	46	4.4	0.95
Shigella	7	35-37	47	4.0	0.91
Bacillus	4	30 - 37	55	4.3	0.91

Controlling pH and Aw is crucial when making fermented products, for the purpose of this book it is enough to know that bacteria hate high acidity (low pH) and low water levels (Aw).

4.7 Destruction of Bacteria

Most pathogenic bacteria, including *Salmonella, Escherichia coli 0157:H7, Listeria monocytogenes*, and *Campylobacter,* can be fairly easily destroyed using a mild cooking process. Maintaining a minimum temperature within the range of 130-165° F (54 -74° C) for a specific amount of time will kill them. However, cooking at low temperatures will not destroy these toxins once they have formed in food.

Spoilage bacteria (*Pseudomonas* spp.) need oxygen to survive and applying a vacuum (removing air) during mixing and stuffing is an effective way to inhibit their growth. At home, a precaution must be made so that the sausage mix is stuffed firmly and any air pockets which are visible in a stuffed casing are pricked with a needle. Oxygen also affects the development of proper curing color and promotes rancidity in fats.

4.8 Toxins

Toxins of most concern are produced by *Clostridium botulinum, Clostridium perfringens, Bacillus cereus*, and *Staphylococcus aureus.* All are the result of the growth of bacteria in foods that have been mishandled. These bacteria are common in the environment and are often found on carcasses. Proper cooking, fermentation, cooling, and storage of food can prevent the growth of these bacteria and more importantly, the production of their toxins. Thermal processing (canning) at temperatures of greater than 240° F (115° C) for a specific amount of time is necessary to destroy most spores and toxins.

4.9 What is Botulism?

Botulism, once known as a sausage disease, is a rare but serious food borne disease that can be fatal. The symptoms of botulism include difficulty swallowing, talking, breathing, and double vision. Without medical care, respiratory failure and death are likely. Botulism symptoms typically appear within 18 to 36 hours of eating the contaminated food, although it can be as soon as four hours and last up to eight days. Food borne botulism can be especially dangerous because many people can be poisoned at once. The optimal temperature range for the growth of botulinum bacteria is 78-95° F (26-35° C) and it significantly slows down at 118° F (48° C). When threatened, they envelop themselves in protective shells called "spores" which can only be killed by boiling at 212° F (100° C) for at least 10 minutes. At 140° F (60° C), botulinum spores do not develop into toxins, although they are heat resistant.

4.10 Where Does Botulism Come From?

C. botulinum is found in soil and aquatic sediments all over the world. Like plant seeds, they can lie dormant for years. They are not threatening until they encounter an adequate environment for growth. The spores that germinate produce the deadly botulinum toxin. To grow, these bacteria require a slightly acidic, oxygen free environment that is warm and moist. That is exactly what happens when smoking meats:

1. First of all, meats contain a lot of moisture. Water is then also added to sausages to facilitate stuffing. Hams and other meats are pumped up with water.

2. Lack of oxygen – when smoking we intentionally decrease the amount of available air. This allows our sawdust or wood chips to generate lots of smoke.

3. Temperatures between 40° and 140° F - most smoking is done at this temperature range. The most dangerous range is from 78-95° F (26-35° C), and that fits into the "warm smoking" method. Bacteria thrive at this temperature range. It looks like we have created ideal conditions for botulin toxin. Clearly, we have to come up with a solution.

4.11 How to Prevent Botulism

The answer lies in the use of *nitrates/nitrites*. When present, they prevent the transformation of *C. botulinum* spores to toxins. It is almost like applying a vaccine to eliminate a disease. By curing meats with nitrates, we protect ourselves from possibly contracting a deadly disease. Nitrates are cheap, commonly available, and completely safe in amounts recommended by the Food and Drug Administration. So why not use them? All commercial plants do. Nitrates are needed only when smoking meats or making fermented sausages. You don't need nitrates when barbecuing or grilling, as the temperatures are high enough to inhibit the development of botulinum spores into toxins. Sausages are the second biggest source of food contamination and food poisoning, second only to home-canned food products.

4.12 Trichinae

There are some cold smoked pork sausages and pork products that will not be submitted to the cooking process. Raw pork or wild game meat can be at risk of being infected with trichinae. Trichinae is an illness caused by the consumption of raw or under cooked meat infected with *"trichinella spiralis"*. It is a round worm that can migrate from the digestive tract and settle in the form of cysts in various muscles of the body. The disease is almost non-existent in American pigs due to their strictly controlled feed, but it can still be found in meats of free roaming animals. The illness is not contagious, but the first symptoms appear within 1-2 days of eating contaminated meat. They include nausea, diarrhea, vomiting, abdominal pain, itchy skin, and may be mistaken for the flu. Trichinae in pork is killed by raising its internal temperature to 137° F (58° C). The U.S. Code of Federal Regulations requires pork to be cooked for 1 minute at 140° F (60° C). Traditionally made fermented sausages, also called dry or slow-fermented sausages are normally never cooked and the heat treatment does not apply here. Fortunately, *storing pork at low temperatures also kills trichinae.* The U.S. Department of Agriculture's Code of Federal Regulations, Title 9, Volume 2, Cite: 9 CFR318.10 requires that pork intended for use in processed products be frozen at:

Group 1 - comprises product in separate pieces not exceeding 6" (15 cm) in thickness, or arranged on separate racks with layers not exceeding 6" (15 cm) in depth, or stored in crates or boxes not exceeding 6" (15 cm) in depth, or stored as solidly frozen blocks not exceeding 6" (15 cm) in thickness.

Group 2 - comprises product in pieces, layers, or within containers, the thickness of which exceeds 6" (15 cm) but not 27" (68 cm) and product in containers including tierces, barrels, kegs, and cartons having a thickness not exceeding 27" (68 cm).

Table 1. Required Period of Freezing Indicated			
Temperature		Days	
° F	° C	Group 1	Group 2
5	-15	20	30
- 10	-23.3	10	20
- 20	-28.9	6	12

The product undergoing such refrigeration or the containers thereof shall be so spaced while in the freezer as will insure a free circulation of air between the pieces of meat, layers, blocks, boxes, barrels, and tierces in order that the temperature of the meat throughout will be promptly reduced to not higher than 5° F (-15° C), -10° F (-23.3° C), or -20° F (-28.9° C), as the case may be. In lieu of the methods prescribed in Table 1, the treatment may consist of commercial freeze drying or controlled freezing, *at the center of the meat pieces*, in accordance with the times and temperatures specified in Table 2.

| Table 2. Alternate Periods of Freezing at Temperatures Indicated | |
| *Maximum Internal Temperature* | |
Temperature	Minimum Time
0° F (- 18° C)	106 hours
- 5° F (-21° C)	82 hours
-10° F (-23° C)	63 hours
-15° F (-26° C)	48 hours
-20° F (-28° C)	35 hours
-25° F (-32° C)	22 hours
-30° F (-34° C)	8 hours
-35° F (-37° C)	0.5 hours

Microwaving, curing, drying or smoking is not effective in preventing Trichinae. It should be noted that *freezing will not kill larval cysts in bears and other wild game that live in Northwestern U.S. and Alaska.* That meat has to be cooked to 160° F internal temperature.

4.13 Good Manufacturing Practices that Can be Applied in the Everyday Kitchen

Meat of a healthy animal is clean and contains very few bacteria. Any invading bacteria will be destroyed by the animal's immune system. Most bacteria are present on the skin and in the intestines. The slaughtering process starts introducing bacteria into the exposed surfaces. In a large piece of meat the outside surface serves as a natural barrier preventing access to bacteria. *Every time we create a new surface cut with a knife we create an opening for bacteria to enter the meat from the outside and start spoiling it.*

The more cuts, the more spoils of meat and that is the reason why ground meat has the shortest shelf life. In a stressed animal bacteria are able to travel from the animal's gut right through the casing into the meat. Duties like cutting meat, grinding, mixing or stuffing all increase meat temperature and should be performed in the kitchen at the lowest possible temperatures as fast as possible. Otherwise we create conditions for the growth of bacteria and that will decrease the shelf life of the product.

To sum it up make sure that:

- *Meat is very fresh and always kept cold.*
- *Facilities and tools are very clean.*
- *Working temperatures are as low as possible.*
- *Take what you need rule always applies.*

4.14 Temperature Control

If you live in a tropical climate without air conditioning, try to process meat in the evening or early morning hours and work with a small portion of meat at one time. Other factors which influence your product quality and can eliminate the danger of any food poisoning are the 4 C's of Food Hygiene:

- Cleanliness-wash hands, prevent insects, use clean equipment.
- Cooking-cook meat, poultry and fish to proper internal temperature.
- Chilling and storage-keep food at refrigerator temperature.
- Cross-contamination-don't mix raw and cooked meats, use clean knives, keep separate chopping boards for cooked and raw meat.

4.15 Storing Meat

When making fresh or smoked meats or sausages, it should be treated as fresh meat. We can keep at hand an amount that will be consumed within a few days and the rest should be frozen. A ready to eat product should not be stored for more than 7 days if held at 41° F, or 4 days at 45° F. This practice will help control the growth of *Listeria monocytogenes*, a harmful bacteria. Meats should be stored at 32-40° F (0-4° C). We should bear in mind that there are differences between home and commercial refrigerators and freezers:

Home refrigerator	Butcher's cooler
36° - 40 F° (2° - 4° C)	32 F ° (0° C)
Home freezer	Butcher's freezer
0° F (-18° C)	-25° F (- 32° C)

4.16 Freezing Meat

Freezing prevents the spoilage of sausage, however, keeping it in a freezer for longer than 6 weeks will lower it's flavor, though it will still be nutricious and perfectly safe to eat. To understand the concept of freezing it is necessary to remember the fact that the meat (or our own body) consists of up to 75% of water.

When water is placed in a freezer it freezes but also increases in volume. The same applies to meat – it contains water everywhere, on the surface and inside. The water inside of the meat, like the water inside of a bottle, will become ice and because of its increased volume will expand and do damage to the meat protein, resulting in a loss of elasticity and its ability to hold water. It damages the meat's structure though we can't see it with a naked eye. This happens mainly when the freezing process is slow as it allows for the creation of large crystals of ice.

When freezing *at very low temperatures* the formed ice crystals are smaller as the freezing of water happens so rapidly that it does not allow time for ice crystals to grow, and there will be less damage to the internal meat structure. Meat freezes at 28° F (-2° C) but to freeze all water present inside of the meat we have to create temperatures of -8°-22° F (-22°-30° C), which is well beyond the range of a home refrigerator. Industrial freezers solve this problem by blasting fast moving cold air over the product that drops the temperature to - 40° F (- 40° C). In frozen meat, light accelerates discoloration. Meats kept in freezers, should therefore be covered, as a precaution against the normal lighting.

4.17 Thawing Meat

Thawing must be done slowly, preferably at refrigerator temperature, which will allow for the ice crystals to dissipate slowly without creating significant damage to the texture of the meat. Preferred methods of thawing are:

- In the refrigerator 36-40° F (2-4° C).
- In cold and fresh running water, you can leave it in a container with ice and water, but add more ice as needed.
- In the microwave.

Photo 5.1 Having a computer science degree from Georgia Tech does not prevent Robert Marianski from continuing a family tradition.

Chapter 5

Smoking Meats and Sausages

5.1 Smoking Meats

Traditionally smoked meats come almost always from cured parts of pork. The most popular large cuts used for smoking are ham, bacon, butt, loin, back fat and smaller parts such as hocks and jowls. Ribs are normally barbecued. Due to their large size those popular cuts require longer curing times although those times can be somewhat shortened when needle pumping precedes the common wet curing method. Hams can be dry or wet cured, butts and loins are normally wet cured and bacon and back fat are commonly dry cured. Trimmings end up for making sausages.

5.2 Making And Smoking Sausages

Sausages require some extra work as the meat has to be ground, mixed and stuffed into the casing. Making sausage is like making hamburger - the meat is ground, salt, pepper and the required spices are added, and then it is cooked until it is safe for consumption. If this prepared meat were stuffed into casings it would become a sausage. Most home made sausages are made of either pork or a combination of pork and beef.

While various recipes usually get the spotlight (there are thousands on the Internet), the technical know-how behind preparing sausages is far more important. These basic rules will dictate how to make your meal both delicious and safe. Basically, a sausage is meat, salt and pepper. Most sausages will include a dominant spice plus other spices and ingredients.

The proper amount of salt in meat (tastes pleasant) is between 1.5-2% and 3.5-5% will be the upper limit of acceptability; anything more and the product will be too salty. There is less room for compromise when making fermented sausages where salt is used as a safety hurdle to prevent the growth of bacteria in the first stage of processing. Dry sausages require about 3% of salt and semi-dry around 2.5%. Usually, most home sausage makers omit the curing step. This can be attributed to the lack of information available on curing meats for sausages as many recipes on the Internet are very amateurish at best. A commercial plant might avoid the traditional way of curing meats in order to save time and space but they make up for it by injecting larger cuts with curing solution or adding salt, nitrite, and curing accelerators during meat chopping and mixing. For example, a frankfurter which is a smoked sausage is cured, smoked, peeled and packed in about 30-45 minutes. The sausage making process:

- Meat selection.
- Curing.
- Grinding.
- Mixing.
- Stuffing.
- Drying.
- Smoking.   (covered in Chapter 1)
- Cooking.
- Cooling.
- Storing.   (covered in Chapter 4)

5.3 Meat Selection

Good cuts of meat make good sausages. Trim out all gristle, sinew, blood clots, and excess fat. Don't store the meat in the refrigerator for more than a couple of days, especially if it was ground, because it will start turning a dark grey color. Note that the meat is still fine, it just looks unpleasant. If you use a cut that is too lean, your sausage will definitely be healthier and cleaner, but you will miss out on the taste. Sausages need about 25-30% of fat in them and pork butts lend themselves as excellent choices.

The type of meat used to make sausage is not set in stone. Most sausages are made of either pure pork, or a combination with other meats, most often beef (about 20%). Emulsified sausages (finely comminuted) such as high quality frankfurters usually contain more beef (40-60%) due to its excellent water holding capacities. Cheaply produced commercial versions include machine deboned meat, different trimmings, and phosphates which have very strong water binding properties. People living in off beaten track areas, (i.e. Central Alaska) might use wild game meats such as moose, bear, elk, reindeer, or rabbit. However, it is still recommended to mix these lean meats with pork to achieve better texture and flavor. You can mix fresh and previously frozen meats together but there should be no more than 20-30% frozen meat. When fat is added, the best choice is pork hard fat as it is white and tastes best.

5.4 Curing Meat For Sausages

Curing imparts a certain peculiar flavor which is in demand by the consumer and if we cure hams, bacon, chops, butts, and fish because they taste better, so why not cure meat for sausages? The fact that we grind meat makes it only easier on our teeth to chew it – it does not improve the color, texture or the flavor of the sausage. Someone might say: but I've mixed nitrite and spices with ground meat before stuffing so that's OK. Well, it's not ok, the problem is that not enough time was allowed for proper curing to take place and the sausage is only partially cured. *The dry method of curing is used to cure meat for sausages.* Meat should be cut into smaller pieces, about 2 inches (5-6 cm) and not heavier than 0. 5 lb (250 g).The curing process depends directly on the length of time involved and we can decrease this time by making meat cuts even smaller by grinding them in a grinder. Meat should be thoroughly mixed with salt, Cure #1 (salt, nitrite), sugar (if used) and packed tightly in a container, not higher than 8 inches (20 cm). Then it should be covered with a clean cloth and stored in a refrigerator. There are chemical reactions taking place inside and the cloth allows the gases to evaporate through. It also prevents the surface of the meat from reacting with oxygen which sometimes creates gray color areas on the surface. This is normal, the meat is fine and there is nothing to worry about. With the use of ascorbates and erythorbates it is possible to cure meats at even lower temperatures, which is commonly practiced by commercial establishments. The curing times at 40° F (4° C) (refrigerator temperature) are as follows:

- Meat pieces size 2"–72 hours.
- Meat ground in grinder – 24-36 hours, depending on a plate size.

What will happen to smoked sausages if the meat is not cured? Basically nothing as long as you add salt and Cure #1 (sodium nitrite) to ground meat during mixing (you are still curing meat). Then let it hang for 1-2 hours at room temperature to gain some curing time and to dry out the casings. *Chemical reactions proceed much faster at higher temperatures and so does curing.* The final color might not be as good as the properly cured sausage but it will still be a great sausage.

5.5 Grinding

The lean meat should be separated from the fat. As a rule, lean meat is ground coarsely while fatty cuts are ground very finely. This way our sausage is lean-looking and the fat is less visible. It is much easier to grind cold meat taken directly out of the refrigerator. The knife must be sharp, otherwise the meat will smear. The locking ring on a grinder head should be tight. After a while, the meat will lubricate the grinder and the crank will begin to turn with ease. Bear in mind that the grinder, whether electric or manual, generates heat and if it were washed in hot water, it should be cooled off before use. Otherwise we would have meat smearing and the sausage will look greasy even when lean meat was used. Ideally, meat should always be chilled between 32-35° F (0-2° C) for a clean cut. The fat should be partially frozen or a smeared paste will be produced. When a recipe calls for a second grind, grind the chilled meat first, refreeze it, and then grind it a second time.

5.6 Mixing

If the meat was previously cured, then salt, nitrite, and sugar were already added to it. Now we have to add the remaining spices. The lean meat should be mixed with spices first, and the fat should be added at the last moment. Mixing meat by hand also raises its temperature and should be done as quickly as possible. It takes roughly about 5 minutes to thoroughly mix 10 lbs. of meat. The time is important because fat specks start to melt at 95-104° F (35-40° C). We want to prevent this smearing to keep the sausage texture looking great. The ingredients may be mixed with cold water in a blender, and then poured over the minced meat. The water helps to evenly distribute the ingredients and it also helps soften the mass during stuffing. We can easily add 1 cup of cold water to 5 lbs. of meat because it is going to evaporate during smoking anyway.

5.7 Stuffing

Remember to taste your sausage now, before you stuff it since you still have time to implement any changes. People make mistakes when reading recipes, they get confused with ounces and grams, they use different size spoons to measure ingredients, etc. Just make a very tiny hamburger, like a quarter, throw it on a frying pan and in two minutes you can taste your sausage. After the meat is ground and mixed it has to be stuffed into a casing preferably as soon as possible. Allowing the meat to sit overnight causes it to set up and absorb all this moisture that we have added during mixing and stuffing. The ample amount of salt inside will perform this trick and we'll be struggling with stuffing casings blaming the whole world for it. It is important to stuff sausages hard and without air as the resulting air pockets might fill with water or become little holes later. When stuffing fermented and dry products, such moisture pockets will become breeding grounds for bacteria. Pack the meat tightly in the grinder, horn, or piston stuffer to prevent the air from entering into the casing. The air also creates unnecessary resistance during stuffing. Better piston stuffers come equipped with an air valve that allows accumulating air to escape outside. After the sausage is stuffed, any accumulated air pockets visible to the naked eye are simply pricked with a needle. The casing should have about a third of a cup of water inside as it acts as a lubricant for the entering meat. By the same token pouring water over the stuffing tube is recommended to increase lubrication. Some people grease the tube lightly. Use the largest stuffing tube which fits the casing but make sure it goes on loosely otherwise the casing might break.

It is a known fact that a smoked sausage will be of higher quality when the meat is seasoned overnight which is basically a shorter, simplified version of a curing process that should have been performed earlier. If you want to cure a sausage that way (why not to cure it the proper way), grind, mix and stuff it first, then it can be stored overnight in a refrigerator. Note that when a cold sausage will be transferred from a cooler to a warm room, the condensation will likely appear on its surface. Sausages that have been kept in the refrigerator overnight should be permitted to hang at room temperature for at least one hour before being placed in the smokehouse.

It is impossible to match the quality of natural hog or sheep casings. They can be used for almost any product. The biggest advantage of using natural casings is that they shrink equally with the meat and thus are great for making dry or semi-dry salami or sausages. That leaves their use to smaller butchers or sausage makers and it is the preferred choice for a home producer. Another advantage is that they are edible and you don't even feel them when eating a well made smoked sausage.

The main reason that commercial manufacturers cannot use natural casings is the fact that they are not uniform and have a different diameter, texture and length. The meat plant even knowing the length of the sausage, cannot precisely estimate the weight of meat it contains and by the same token cannot arrive at the correct price. And you cannot run a business when no two samples are alike. Natural casings are usually packed and stored in salt and have to be rinsed on the outside and flushed out with water inside. Then they should be left for 30 minutes in a water filled container. That removes more salt from the casings and makes them softer and easier to work with when stuffing. After stuffing any remaining casings should be packed with canning salt and stored at refrigerator temperature (38-40° F) where they will last for a long time.

5.8 Drying

Stuffed sausages that are subject to smoking follow a drying procedure which lasts from 0.5-2 hrs at 68-86° F (20-30° C). This simple process dries out the surface of the casing so it can acquire smoke better and develop the proper smoking color. This is a short, hardly noticeable process and before the last casings are stuffed, the first ones are ready for smoking.

5.9 Cooling

Immediately after cooking the sausages should be showered with hot and cold water. Showering with hot water cleans the surface from any soot or grease accumulation. A hot spray is applied by commercial producers but very seldom by the hobbyist. At home conditions a cool spray is normally practiced. This prevents sausages from shriveling and helps cross the danger zone where dangerous bacteria thrive. Once the temperature drops below 68° F (20° C) it is safe to hang sausages for further cooling. The sausages will develop a darker color and better looks but may also become more shriveled, though some shriveling is normal. The solution is to poach them again for 30-60 seconds with hot water (194° F, 90° C) and then cool as before. During this cooling/drying process a smoked sausage will further improve its shine, color, and will develop a darker shade of brown. This shine is created by fat deposition on the surface of the sausage, just put some grease on your shoe and you will see that it becomes darker and shinier. Some books call it "blooming" but this is the air drying we are writing about. Sausages should be hung in a dark place and a newspaper is placed on the floor to catch any grease and moisture dripping down. After that, the sausage can be refrigerated. The official recommendation of the Food Safety and Inspection Service of the USDA (June 1999) issues the following guidelines:

"During cooling, the product's maximum internal temperature should not remain between 130° F (54° C) and 80° F (27° C) for more than 1.5 hours nor between 80° F (27° C) and 40° F (4° C) for more than 5 hours" (6.5 hours total time). "Products cured with a minimum of 100 ppm ingoing sodium nitrite may be cooled so that the maximum internal temperature is reduced from 130° F (55° C) to 80° F (27° C) in 5 hours and from 80° F (27° C) to 45° F (7 C) in 10 hours" (15 hours total time).

Chapter 6

Smoking Poultry

When overcooked, most meats will have an inferior taste, but poultry is particularly vulnerable because it is so lean. Fortunately, soaking birds in brine - a solution of salt and water will help to achieve a moister, juicier product. If a product will be smoked at low temperatures nitrite (Cure # 1) must be used.

6.1 Making Brine

Brine is a solution of water and salt. A sweetener such as brown or white sugar, molasses, honey, maple-flavored sugar, or corn sugar may be added to the solution for flavor. The salt has two effects on poultry, reports Dr. Alan Sams, a professor of poultry science at Texas A & M University. "It dissolves protein in muscle, and the salt and protein reduce moisture during cooking. This makes the meat juicier, more tender, and improves the flavor. The low levels of salt enhance the other natural flavors of poultry".

Curing and smoking imparts a unique, delicate flavor and pink color to poultry meat and increases its storage life. Mild cures with relatively low salt content are used in preparation for the smoking to maintain the poultry flavor. A light smoke will add to the delicate flavor of the poultry, a heavy smoke will add flavor similar to smoked red meat products. Poultry is cured by a wet method using mild cure. It is very easy to end up with a product that's too salty to use. One of the reasons is that the brine is prepared as if poultry were a piece of ham and no consideration is given to the fact that a large part of any bird consists of bones.

The bones are not going to absorb any salt and the curing times need to be shorter. It is safer to brine on the low end of the time range on the first attempt and keep notes for future reference. You can always brine longer the next time if required. To prepare a brine dissolve salt in cold water by mixing it thoroughly (salt dissolves much faster in hot water than in cold water). Cover and refrigerate before adding poultry.

The FSIS (Food Safety and Inspection Service) of the USDA (United States Department of Agriculture) recommends: *"To prepare a brine solution for poultry, add ¾ cup salt to 1 gallon of water, or 3 tablespoons of salt per quart of water. For best flavor use, use sodium chloride-table salt"*. Taking this as common table salt (non-iodized) this works out as ¾ of a cup equal to 219 g (0.49 lb). This in turn works out to be a brine concentration of 5.55 % or salinometer reading of **21.** A noted expert on sausage making and meat curing, Parson Snows, recommends 1 part table salt to 16 parts water.

1/1+16 = 1/17 = 0.0588 (5.88%)

Using the ratio of 1 lb of salt per 16 lbs of water (1.92 US gallons) or 0.52 lbs of salt per US gallon of water equals a brine concentration of 5.88 % or a salinometer reading of **22.5** degrees.

Rytek Kutas presents the following formula in his book:

    5 gal water
    2 lbs salt
    1 lb Cure # 1 (there is 0.93 lb salt in it)
    1 ½ lbs powdered dextrose

and that equals a brine concentration of 6.5% or a salinometer reading of **25** degrees (salt present in Cure #1 is included in calculations).

Dr. Estes Reynolds, a brining expert at the University of Georgia recommends using 9.6 ozs of salt for every US gallon of water for products that brine longer than several hours. This works out to be a brine concentration of 6.68% or a salinometer reading of **25** degrees. There are many sources that recommend using 1 lb of salt to 1 gallon of water. This works out a brine concentration of 10.71% or a salinometer reading of **40** degrees which is rather high if the bird will be brined for more than a few hours.

With salt everyone's tastes are different, but it can be concluded that any salinometer reading between 17 and 26 degrees will work out fine with the 21 – 22 degrees being in the middle of the safe range. It should be noted that the higher salinometer reading, the saltier the brine.

Products that are going to be smoked at low temperatures (below 200° F, 93° C) need Cure # 1 to be added to the brine. Cure #1 contains 93.75 % of salt which has to be taken under consideration. Using ½ cup of salt and 3 oz of Cure #1 for 1 gallon of water we obtain a brine concentration of 5.6 % which corresponds to a salomter reading of **21** degrees.

A typical brine solution (with Cure #1) at 21 degrees salometer reading:

  1 gal of cold water
  ½ cup (146 g) of salt
  3 oz (85 g) of Cure #1 – corresponds to 79 g of pure salt
  3 oz (85 g) sugar (brown or white).

A typical brine solution (no Cure #1 added) at 21 degrees salometer reading:

  1 gal of cold water
  ¾ cup of salt
  3 oz (85 g) sugar (brown or white)

Curing time depends on the size of the bird:

Cornish Game Hens	1 - 2 hours
Chicken Pieces	2 – 4 hours
Whole Chickens (2 lbs)	1 day
Whole Chickens (4 lbs)	1 - 2 days
Turkey Breast	4 – 8 hours
Whole Turkeys (up to 10 lbs)	1 - 2 days
Whole Turkey (over 10 lbs)	2 - 3 days
A Very Large Turkey	4 - 5 days

To shorten curing time, poultry may be pumped with a brine mixture in an amount equivalent to 10% of the bird's weight. A 10 lb turkey should receive 1 lb of brine. Birds weighing less than 3 lbs don't need to be pumped and can be immersed in a brine mixture.

The poultry should now be placed in a stainless steel, clay or food grade plastic container and covered fully with the remaining brine (use weight plate if needed). It should be placed in the refrigerator or in case the container is too large, ice should be added periodically to the brine if the temperature goes over 40° F (4° C). Added ice should be taken under consideration if we want to maintain the proper proportion of ingredients in the brine.

6.2 Draining And Drying

After curing, the poultry should be rinsed in cold tap water for 5 minutes to remove any crystalized salt from its surface, then it should be left to drain. Poultry holds its shape after hanging in a smoker for many hours and it will look like a bat with spread wings and legs. To retain its original shape it should be smoked in a stockinette bag.

6.3 Smoking

When the birds are dry or tacky to touch, they should be placed in a pre-heated smoker. Keep the damper wide open to allow moisture to escape. Once the birds feel dry, leave the damper in ¼ open position and smoke at 130° F (54° C) for about five hours. Then continue smoking slowly raising the temperature to 165-170° F (74-77° C) and hold until the inside temperature in the thickest part of the breast is 155-160° F (68-71° C). You could insert a thermometer close to the ball and socket joint of the thigh as this is also the last place the meat becomes fully cooked. If the thermometer is not available, you can check the turkey by twisting the leg slightly. If it moves easily, the cooking is done. Small birds like cornish game hens or small chicken will need shorter smoking and cooking times.

Sodium nitrite (Cure #1) in the brine will cause the poultry meat to become pink when it is smoked. If you smoke turkey without Cure #1 higher temperatures are needed to eliminate food poisoning (botulism) that Cure #1 prevents. The turkey should be placed in a smoker preheated to 180° F (82° C) for at least one hour. Then the temperature should be increased to 200-225° F (93-108° C) and smoke applied. The turkey breast should be smoked/cooked to an internal temperature of 165° F (74° C). We are now smoking/baking the turkey without worrying about food poisoning. *And be careful when making stuffing.* Let's follow a beautifully presented scenario on stuffing a turkey from the 1984 classic "The Great Sausage Recipes and Meat Curing" by Rytek Kutas.

"The well-intentioned cook decides to make the dressing for the turkey the night before. This gives her more time to do many other important things the next day. She stuffs the turkey the night before, and places it in the refrigerator to be cooked the next day. Unfortunately, she doesn't know she is creating ideal conditions for food poisoning. Obviously, the stuffing that she put into the turkey is somewhere between 40° and 140° F. Because the various parts of dressing have some liquid in them, the moisture is also there. Lastly, she sews up the turkey to create a lack of oxygen in its cavity".

It is that simple to create food poisoning. You can make turkey stuffing a day earlier, just make sure it is left in a refrigerator.

Duck and Goose

Duck and goose are more fatty than turkey and they taste very good when smoked. Follow procedures for smoking turkey.

Chapter 7

Smoking Fish

Fish has always played a very important part in our diet and was a precious commodity especially in areas without direct access to the oceans or even lakes or rivers. For those reasons the preservation played the main role and the taste was less important. Preservation was achieved by storing heavily salted fish in barrels where they were kept for months at the time. Caravans were able to move salted fish large distances and all the consumer had to do was to soak the fish in water to remove excess salt. Another technique relied on air drying to remove moisture from the meat thus eliminating favorable conditions for the growth of bacteria. Smoking fish was also effective as it prevented some bacteria from growing and removed moisture at the same time.

Most of the bacteria in the fish is present in the slime that covers the body of the fish and in its digestive tract. There are two reasons that fish spoils faster than other meat :

1. Its meat contains more water (bacteria need moisture)

Beef	-	60%	water
Veal, poultry	-	66%	water
Lean fish	-	70%	water
Fat fish	-	80%	water

2. Its meat contains very little salt (salt inhibits growth of bacteria). Both freshwater and saltwater fish have very low salt content in their meat (0.2-0.7% of salt). When salt is applied to fish, it removes water from the meat which inhibits the growth of bacteria. Heavy salting of the fish is practiced today only in most undeveloped nations and everywhere else we strive to give fish the best taste and flavor. And there is no doubt whatsoever that smoked fish tastes the best. Fish like other meats can be smoked by different smoking methods and the taste and shelf life will depend on smoke temperature and the length of smoking. The flesh of fish is delicate by nature and they have to be handled gently when hanging them on smokesticks or hooks. There are a few commonly used methods of securing fish for smoking:

- Placing fillets or smaller pieces of fish on a screen, making sure they don't touch each other.
- Inserting sharp pointed sticks through fish gills.
- Inserting "S" shaped hooks through the gills of the fish and hanging them on smoking sticks.
- Nailing fish directly to smoke sticks.

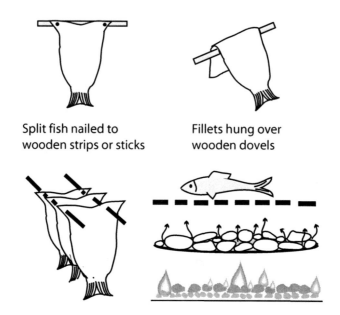

Split fish nailed to
wooden strips or sticks

Fillets hung over
wooden dovels

Fig. 7.1 Hanging fillets.

When hanging fillets it is advisable to leave the skin on otherwise the fillets may break apart.

Small whole fish hung on "S" shaped hooks

through the gills and the mouth

Whole fish strung on round wooden dovels

Small whole fish hung with butchers twine

through the eyes

Fig. 7.2 Hanging small fish.

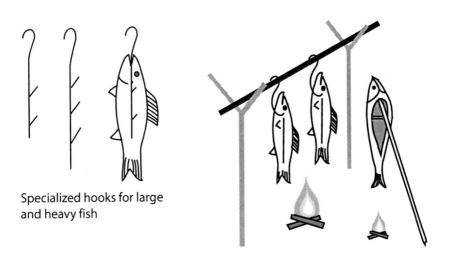

Specialized hooks for large and heavy fish

Fig. 7.3 Hanging large fish.

Fig. 7.4 Smoking over camp fire.

All fish may be smoked but the fatty ones absorb smoke better, stay moister during smoking and taste better. Fat content of different fish:

Lean fish	< 2.5%
Medium fat fish	2.5 – 6.5%
Fat fish	> 6.5%

The same species of fish, depending where they live (Europe, Atlantic or Pacific Ocean), may have a significantly different fat content in their flesh. Some of the *lean fish*: cod, flounder, grouper, haddock, hake, halibut, perch, pike, pollock, porgies, rockfish, snake eels, snapper, soles, tuna, whitting. Some of the *fat fish*: bluefish, carp, freshwater eels, herring, mackerel, mullet, sablefish, salmon, shad, trout, and whitefish.

The process of smoking fish consists of the following stages:

- Cleaning.
- Brining.
- Drying.
- Smoking.
- Storing.

7.1 Cleaning Fish

Unless a fish is of a very large size, it is not filleted but only gutted and cleaned on the outside. The gills and all traces of blood are removed, especially the blood line along the back of the fish. Then depending on the size, the fish is either cut across into 2" pieces, filleted or hung in one piece. After cleaning, the fish has to be washed again. Previously frozen fish can be thawed in a refrigerator or under cold running water and brined and smoked.

7.2 Making Brine

The stronger the brine the shorter time of brining. A large fish and fat fish absorb salt slowly. Only fine non-iodized salt can be used as the iodized salt can impart a bitter flavor to the fish. The best solution is to use a brine tester or to use the brine tables. The fish is normally brined with a heavy brine for the following reasons:

- Its meat contains very little salt and a lot of water. These are the ideal conditions for the development of meat spoiling bacteria.
- Fish is home to an unusually high concentration of bacteria.

By placing fish in a strong 80 degrees brine we are perfoming an all out attack on the bacteria preventing them from growing. Salt penetrates the flesh of fish very rapidly and the brining times are relatively short, between 1 and 2 hours. Brines stronger than 80 degrees can deposit salt crystals on the surface of the fish skin creating unattractive white patches that can be difficult to remove. We can get better and more uniform salt penetration if the brining times are longer but that will call for a 40 degrees solution. In such a brine fish may be left overnight.

Fish that will be smoked must be salted or brined first. Brining provides the following advantages:

- Improves the flavor and looks of the fish.
- Improves texture-makes flesh much stronger which is important when fish is hung.
- Prevents growth of bacteria.

Salt penetrates fish easier in places that are open or cut than through the skin. A medium size herring should remain in 80 degrees brine for about 4 hours. Fillets need to be submerged in the same brine for only 20-30 minutes.

Brine in degrees at 60° F	salt (gram/liter)	salt (lb/gallon)	% salt by weight
10	26.4	0.22	2.64
20	53.8	0.46	5.28
30	79.2	0.71	7.91
40	105.6	0.98	10.55
50	132.0	1.26	13.19
60	158.4	1.56	15.83
70	184.8	1.88	18.47
80	211.2	2.23	21.11
90	237.6	2.59	23.75
100	264.0	2.98	26.39

A typical 80 degrees brine:

- 1 gallon water
- 2.25 lbs salt (4 cups)
- 1 lb brown sugar
- 2 Tbs Cure #1
- 1/3 cup lemon juice
- 1 Tbs garlic powder
- 1 Tbs onion powder
- 1 Tbs allspice powder
- 1 Tbs white pepper

One gallon of brine is sufficient for 4 pounds of fish. Other ingredients like sugar and spices should be added to the solution after the correct brine strength has been established. Fish pieces should be completely immersed in brine and covered with a weight plate. The temperature of the brine should not exceed 60° F (15.5° C) at the start of the brining. If the brining time exceeds 4 hours, the solution must be placed in a refrigerator (38° F) or ice should be added to the brine. Adding ice will change the strength of the brine and a better solution is to add re-usable blue ice packs. Keep in mind that brine loses its strength in time as the water leaves the fish and increases the volume of the original brine. At the same time salt penetrates the meat leaving behind a weaker brine. When brining times are long the solution's strength should be periodically checked with a brine tester and readjusted accordingly.

Fish like any other meat is susceptible to food poisoning given the right conditions for the development of *C. Botulinum* spores into toxins. Those conditions (lack of oxygen, humidity, temperatures 40-140°F) always exist when smoking meats. Furthermore many times fish will be packed by the Reduced Oxygen Packaging Method that can create favorable conditions for *C.botulinum* to become toxin even after fish was hot smoked and cooked. To eliminate the possibility of such a danger Cure # 1 is added the same way it is used when smoking meats or sausages.

In order to eliminate nitrites (Cure #1) the salt concentration in the water should be high enough to inhibit the growth of *C. botulinum*, without making the product too salty to eat. A minimum concentration of 3% is considered to be effective for hot smoked fish. Also smoking and cooking temperatures should be kept above 180° F (82° C). For comparison in most smoked sausages the salt concentration is about 2%. People on a low salt diet who prefer low salt concentation in a product would be safer to include nitrites in the brine.

7.3 Brining Times

The brining time depends on the size of the fish and the salt concentration of the brine. It is hard to derive time for fish fillets, fish with the skin on, and little fish or pieces of fish. It is logical to expect that the fish fillet will be oversalted if immersed for the same time in the same brine as a large fish. When brining many types of fish of different sizes it will be a good idea to use separate containers and classify fish according to its species and size. When using a single container, place small pieces on top so they can be removed earlier.

Brining times for **cold smoking:**

80 degrees brine

½" fillets	-	½ hr
1" fillets	-	1 hr
1 ½" fillets	-	2 hrs

Brining times for **hot smoking:**

80 degrees brine

½" fillets	-	15 min
1" fillets	-	30 min
1 ½" fillets	-	1 hr

The whole fish will require a longer brining time than a fillet:

Brine strength	Brining time
30 degrees	10 – 12 hrs
50 degrees	3 - 4 hrs
80 degrees	1 - 2 hrs

7.4 Drying Fish

A fish that was properly dried would acquire color much faster than a wet one and would also develop a better taste. After brining the fish are carefully rinsed under cold running water to remove salt crystals and any traces of spices. The fish are then placed in a draughty area (fan works well) until they develop "pellicle" which is a type of secondary shiny skin. Pellicle helps in smoking and the final product has a nice glossy color. It is a good idea to place small fish pieces on smoking screens right from the begining of the drying process. Brush screens lightly with oil so the fish will not stick to them.

7.5 Smoking Fish

Cold smoking – fish is smoked below 80° F (26° C) from 1-5 days. Temperatures above 80° F (26° C) will cook the fish. If the temperature of the fish flesh exceeds 84° F (29° C) for longer than a few minutes the protein will be coagulated and parts of the fish will be cooked. Such fish will not have the elasticity and texture of the properly cold smoked product. Cold smoked fish is still considered raw meat as it was never submitted to high temperature. That is why it has to be heavily salted or brined at 16% salt (about 65 degrees brine) or higher to provide safety for the consumer.

The longer smoking period the more moisture is removed (30-50%) and the drier the product becomes with of course a longer shelf life. Its color also changes from gold to brown. This method of smoking can last up to a few weeks and the fish will have excellent keeping qualities. It should be noted that the final product will taste much saltier and its texture will be much harder. After prolonged cold smoking the fish has lost enough moisture not to be cooked at all. A typical fish done that way is salmon or sturgeon. Cold smoking requires heavy brine and longer brining times. Fish that were cold smoked hold well together and can be very finely sliced which can not be done if the fish were hot smoked. Because of the time and costs involved this method is rarely used today.

Hot smoking – fish are smoked and cooked at the same time. Hot smoking requires a lighter brine and a smokehouse temperature above 90° F (32° C). The fish are smoked/cooked from one to five hours. The fish can be smoked/baked in 30 minutes when the applied temperature is 300-350° F (150-180° C). Hot smoking is a commonly used method though the final product is tougher and more breakable than the fish that was smoked with cold smoke. The shelf life of the product is also shorter and the product must be kept under refrigeration. Hot smoking is basically performed in three stages:

1. A preliminary smoking/drying period at 86° F (30° C) during which the skin is hardened to prevent breakage. The air dampers are fully open for maximum air flow and moisture removal. This period lasts from 30-60 minutes.

2. A heavy smoke is applied for about 30-45 minutes with the exit smoke damper left at ¼ open position. The temperature is gradually raised to 122° F (50° C).

3. The temperature is raised to 176° F (80° C) and the fish is cooked to 145° F (63° C) internal temperature for a minimum of 30 minutes. Depending on the size of the fish this stage may last from 30–60 minutes. A light smoke may be maintained. When the temperature is raised to 176-194° F (80-90°C) we are smoking/cooking fish until its meat flakes out easily when pressed with a knife or a fork. The cooking process will be shorter but the fish will taste drier. Fish is considered done when cooked to 145° F internal temperature.

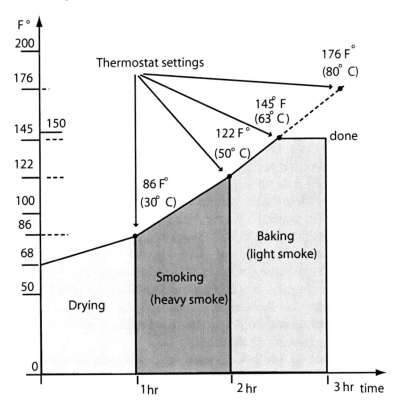

Fig. 7.5 Smoking small fish.

Typical fish fillets smoking times are 4-5 hours depending on the size. When smoking is finished, the fish should be cooled rapidly to the ambient (50° F, 10° C) and then to lower temperatures (38° F, 3° C) to prevent the growth of microorganisms. This cooling process should be accomplished within 12 hours. Smoking fish is a lot of trial and error and record keeping. Notes should be made for future reference.

In the open fire smokehouse, the rear of the chamber is receiving most of the heat and re-arranging smoke sticks is a welcome idea. If the fish feels moist it is a sign that there is too much wet smoke inside and the draft must be open more. The back of the fish or the skin of the fillet should face the back of the smoker. That allows for the better judgment of the fish color and protects the flesh from higher temperatures that are normally found in the back of the smoker. When using a few levels of smoke sticks place the upper row first, then after 5-10 minutes the lower one, then the lowest one. If all three levels were placed in a smokehouse at the same time, the upper most row will get the least of the available heat during drying. On the other hand it will get the most moisture which will gather from the smokesticks below.

7.6 Fish Meat Color

Meat color is determined largely by the amount of myoglobin (protein) a particular animal carries. The more myoglobin the darker the meat. To some extent oxygen use can be related to the animal's general level of activity: muscles that are used frequently such as a chicken's legs need more oxygen. As a result they develop a darker color unlike a chicken's breast which is white due to little exercise.

Fish float in water and need less muscle energy to support their skeletons. Most fish meat is white, with some red meat around the fins, tail, and the more active parts of the fish which are used for swimming. Most fish don't have myoglobin at all. There are some antarctic cold water fish that have myoglobin but it is confined to the hearts only (flesh of the fish remains white but the heart is of the rosy color. *The red color of some fish, such as salmon and trout, is due to astaxanthin, a naturally occurring pigment in the crustaceans they eat.*

Most salmon we buy is farm raised and as it is fed a prepared commercial diet that even includes antibiotics, its meat is anything but pink. The only reason that farmed raised salmon flesh is pink is that canthaxanthin (colorant) is added to the food the fish eats.

The pink color of the smoked meat is due to the nitrite reaction with myoglobin. As most of the fish don't have myoglobin the meat is not going to be pink and that explains why very few fish recipes include cure. In addition, nitrites are not allowed in all species of fish used for smoking. The Food and Drug Administration currently allows nitrites to be used in salmon, sablefish, shad, chubs, and tuna. Why out of millions of species of fish swimming in the ocean, only five species can be cured with nitrite?

What made those fish so special was the question that bothered me for a long time. Finally I had enough and the letter of inquiry was sent to the Food Safety and Inspection Service. And that was the answer to my intriguing question:

"The reason nitrite is approved for use in those species is because someone submitted a petition for its use in those specific fish. Other species can be added through additional petitions."

7.7 Storing

Fish can be eaten immediately after smoking though most people will say that it tastes better when cold. Fish should be wrapped up in wax paper or foil and placed in a refrigerator where it can remain for up to 10 days. To hold it longer we have to freeze it. Freezing fresh fish in a home freezer is not the best idea as it is a relatively slow process. As a result large ice crystals form inside and damage the texture of the flesh making it mushy. Fish that are commercially frozen at much faster times don't exhibit such symptoms.

7.8 More About Salt

For brining purposes both table salt and kosher salt will work equally well in terms of providing the desired effects, though kosher salt – and in particular Diamond® Crystal kosher salt dissolves more readily. What is important to remember is that kosher salts are less dense than ordinary table salts and measure quite differently from a volume standpoint. Kosher salt has larger crystals and is bulkier. For example a given weight of Diamond® Crystal takes up nearly twice the volume as the same weight of table salt.

The list below shows approximate equivalent amounts of different salts:

Table Salt	1 cup	292 g (10.3 oz)
Morton® Kosher Salt	1-1/3 to 1-1/2 cups	218 g (7.7 oz)
Diamond® Crystal Kosher Salt	2 cups	142 g (5 oz)

As you can see it is *always advisable to weigh out your salt.*

Photo 7.2 Snook. The first step to successful fish smoking is to catch them says the author Adam Marianski.

Photo 7.1 Smoked fish.

Chapter 8

Barbecuing And Grilling

8.1 Smoking, Barbecuing, And Grilling

There is a significant difference between smoking, barbecuing, and grilling. When grilling, you quickly seal in the juices from the piece you are cooking. Grilling takes minutes. Smoking takes hours, sometimes even days. Don't be fooled by the common misconception that by throwing some wet wood chips over hot coals you can fully smoke your meat. At best you can only add some flavor on the outside because the moment the outside surface of the meat becomes dry and cooked, a significant barrier exists that prevents smoke penetration. A properly smoked piece of meat has to be thoroughly smoked, on the outside and everywhere inside. Only prolonged cold smoking will achieve that result. Smoking when grilling is no better than pumping liquid smoke into it and claiming that the product has been smoked. Let's unravel some of the mystery. All these methods are different from each other, especially smoking and grilling. The main factor separating them is temperature.

Smoking – very low heat	52° - 140° F (12° - 60° C)	1 hr to 2 weeks, depending on temperature
Barbecuing – low heat	190° - 300° F (93° - 150° C)	*low and slow,* few hours
Grilling – high heat	400° - 550° F (232° - 288° C)	*hot and fast,* minutes

The purpose of **grilling** is to char the surface of the meat and seal in the juices by creating a smoky caramelized crust. By the same token a barrier is erected which prevents smoke from flowing inside. The meat may have a somewhat smoky flavor on the outside but due to a short cooking time it was never really smoked.

Barbecuing is a long, slow, indirect, low-heat method that uses charcoal or wood pieces to smoke-cook the meat. *The best definition is that barbecuing is cooking with smoke.* It is ideally suited for large pieces of meat such as butts, ribs or whole pigs. The temperature range of 190–300° F (88-150° C) is still too high for smoking sausages as the fat will melt away through the casings making them greasy.

Barbecue is a social affair, people gather to gossip, drink, have fun and to eat the moment the meats are cooked. On the other hand, *traditionally smoked meats are usually eaten cold* at a later date. As barbecue brings people together, it is not surprising that everybody loves the event. Although barbecue is popular in many countries, nobody does it better than Americans. There, barbecue is a part of tradition like American jazz. It has become the art in itself with constant cookouts and championships all over the country. Although barbecued meats can be placed directly on the screen and cooked, in many cases they are first marinated. Marinades consist of many flavoring ingredients such as vinegar, lemon juice, and spices whereas traditional curing basically contains only water, salt and nitrite, sometimes sugar is added as well. To make great barbecued products the understanding of the following steps is required: controlling fire and temperature, moisture control, smoking with wood and the required time for barbecuing.

8.2 Choice of Fuel

1. Wood is the best but it is heavy and a lot of it is needed. It is difficult to control the combustion temperature especially in small units. For those reasons only a few restaurants use wood to generate heat. In large barbecue restaurants the system is designed in such a way that a product is kept a safe distance from a wood burning fire pit. When barbecuing meats at home much smaller units are employed, very often just a kettle grill.

2. Charcoal briquettes are the choice fuel for backyard barbecue as they are light, burn slow, and are easy to control. They produce a hot, long-lasting, smokeless fire. When using charcoal briquettes it may seem that smoke is generated even without the addition of wood chips. This is due to fat dripping on hot coals which burst into flames but there is no smoke present. The resulting flavor is the flavor of burned fat. Charcoal is produced by burning wood in a low-oxygen atmosphere. This process removes the moisture, sap and volatile gases that were present in the original fuel. The final product is pure carbon.

Lump charcoal	Charcoal briquettes	Modified briquettes
Irregularly shaped charred lump charcoal pieces. Very light, they burn hotter and faster than other charcoal types, producing sparks and crackling sounds. Lump charcoal gets hot in about 10 minutes.	Lump ground charcoal mixed with natural starch and pressed into uniform size briquettes. Starch acts as a binder. They burn as fast and hot as lump charcoal. The advantage they offer is their uniformity which helps to create a smooth layer of coals.	Lump ground charcoal mixed with natural starch, hard and soft coal powder (to raise and prolong heat) and limestone (to create coating of white ash). They produce longer and more even heat than other types. This is the most common American charcoal briquette that should be pre-burned until covered with white ash.

Adding black briquettes directly into the fire will create off flavors.

3. Gas is predominantly used for grilling and it can supply a lot of heat instantaneously. It is hard to obtain a smoky flavor when grilling due to a short cooking time. Adding a few wood chips will not cut it. A lot of heavy smoke must be generated and it is feasible to construct a small smoke generator from a little metal pan, about 5-6" (12-15 cm) in diameter, preferably made of stainless steel. The pan is filled with wood chips or sawdust and is placed on a hot plate to ignite the wood chips. Once they start producing smoke, the pan can be placed inside of the grill and the cooking process can be started. If there is an available burner inside of the unit the pan can be placed on it. Needless to say the pan should produce smoke before the meat is submitted to a cooking chamber. The charcoal should extend 3-4 inches beyond the piece of meat on the screen above. Otherwise the food will not cook properly. When adding wood chips to generate smoke, it must be kept in mind that smoke penetrates meat much faster at high temperatures. A traditionally smoked meat piece at 120° F (50° C) for 4 hours may acquire an over smoked bitter flavor if smoked at 250° F (120° C) for the same length of time.

8.3 How Hot Is It?

The best method is to check the reading of the built-in thermometer if the unit has one. When barbecuing on an open fire you can use the "palm method". Hold the palm of your hand about 1" above the cooking screen and start counting seconds until the heat forces your hand away.

This pain tolerance method needs some refining in each individual case but once it is mastered it works quite well.

Heat	Temperature	Pain tolerance
High	288-260° C, 550-500° F	1-2 seconds
Medium	260-204° C, 500-400° F	3-4 sec
Low	204-150° C, 400-300° F	5-6 sec
Very low	150 - 94° C, 300-200° F	7-8 sec

8.4 Open Fire Barbecue

Cooking with open fire is normally accomplished with spits or placing meats on grill screens.

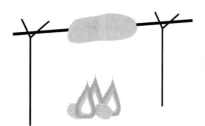

Fig. 8.1 Camp fire spit barbecue.

The horizontal spit is a skewer like metal shaft onto which the meat is inserted. The meat is turned around above the hot coals until it is cooked. When the horizontal spit is turned around it becomes the simplest form of the modern rotisserie. This can be accomplished by attaching a handle or a motor to the spit rod. The end of a spit bar can be heated and bent to form a handle. A practical solution is to use two sections of pipe as support bearings.

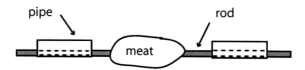

Fig. 8.2 Simple horizontal spit with pipe supports.

threaded connections

Fig. 8.3 There is a variety of ready to connect connections in a plumbing department.

Don't confuse small American spits with Argentinian asado spits which are used to hold large pieces of meat such as whole lambs, goats, or even cows. Argentinians have perfected spit barbecuing over open fires for centuries and the sight of 100 animals barbecued at the same time is simply breathtaking.

Photo courtesy Marta Mottirroni, Argentina.

Photo 8.1. Asado on an Argentinian street. Wood logs are burned about 4 hours earlier before the spits are embedded into the ground. Then the meat is secured to the spits. Fire tenders are walking between or outside the asado spits and using shovels or long pokers they keep control over the process.

3:00 AM - the logs are lit with fire to generate hot coals.
7:00 AM - the hot coals are moved towards the ribs, the bone side first.
10:30 AM - the spits are turned around and the meat side faces heat now.
It can be seen in the photo that the bulk of hot coals is situated in the spit alley. The smaller piles of coals on outside provide heat to already cooked meat. The photos were taken around that time.
1:00 PM "El asado" is ready to be served.

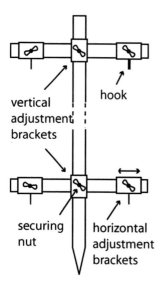

vertical
adjustment
brackets

hook

securing
nut

horizontal
adjustment
brackets

Fig. 8.4 Asado vertical spit. A vertical spit is made of cast iron or stainless steel with a high vertical post plus two horizontal cross-bars. The meat is attached to the crossbars with hooks which can be adjusted to the size of the meat. For extra security the meat is tied to hooks or crossbars (horizontal and vertical) with a steel wire. The simplest spit is hammered into the ground under an angle and after one side is cooked the spit is turned around to finish the meat. Better models have leg support and mechanisms that permit angle adjustment. In a most simple spits the horizontal bar is permanently welded to the vertical bar and meat is secured with a steel wire.

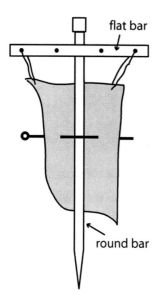

flat bar

round bar

Fig. 8.5. Very basic asado spit. The most important part of a spit design is that it is strong enough to hold the meat.

Photo. 8.2 Basic asado spit.

Photo courtesy of the Calitina Wine Resort, San Rafael, Mendoza, Argentina.

Backyard barbecuing is what we normally associate with this type of cooking and the first factory made unit which was widely accepted by the public is the kettle barbecue described below.

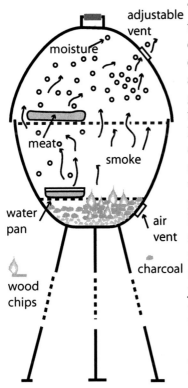

Fig. 8.6 Ever popular kettle grill.

The best approach for creating smoke is to periodically add pre-moistened wood chips into the hot coals. They will produce smoke and the meat will acquire a smoky flavor. Wood chunks are bigger than chips and may produce larger flames. Occasionally when fat drips on hot coals, flares will be produced but will do no harm. They will help sear the meat surface and will go away when the grease will burn out. When too many flares take place, the way to choke them down is by decreasing the vent opening. To keep meats moist you either place a water pan inside or open the lid and baste them. A marinade can be used to fill the pan. Meat juices and fat will drop into the pan. Then they will evaporate, mix with smoke and baste the meat. You should see smoke exiting through a vent at all times. Hot coals do not need to be spread evenly and it is better to keep them in a small pile away from the meat. This prevents flares that might be created by the dripping fat.

Pit in the ground method is sometimes used for cooking whole pigs. It is not easy and requires a lot of wood and heavy labor. The biggest drawback to this method is that you only get one chance without any room for correction. A hole, about 5 feet deep and about 6" longer and wider than the pig is made in the ground. A lot of hardwood, at least twice the weight of a pig is burnt to create 18" (45 cm) deep layer of hot coals. Then a pig is rested at least 12" (30 cm) above hot coals. The pit is covered with a metal sheet, the soil is spread over the metal cover and the pig is left in the ground to cook. Depending on the pig's size this may take 8 to 20 hours. If not enough hot coals were made, the pig would be under cooked. An interesting addition is putting large river gravel stones in a fire and then placing them inside of the animal. There is an abundance of tales regarding pit smoking method but no plans. The only design we have encountered comes from the 1936 book "Camp Stoves And Fireplaces" published by the Forest Service, United Stated Department of Agriculture. The plan has been redrawn by us and follows:

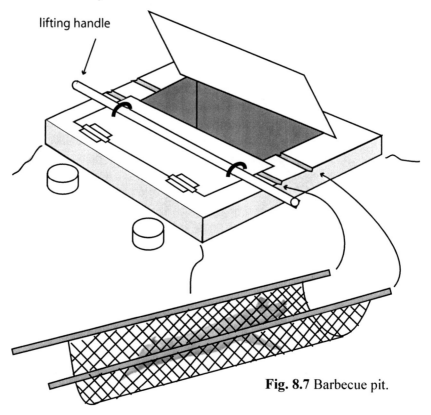

Fig. 8.7 Barbecue pit.

Description

This is a very large unit which will easily accommodate a fully grown pig and will provide enough food for a few hundred people. The unit can be scaled down to accommodate the needs of one or two families. The heart of the system is the fire pit and it must be lined with firebricks and stone. The idea is to confine heat inside of the fire pit and keep it there for as long as possible. This is the same principle which has been employed in massive wood fired brick ovens for making bread. Or in wood or coal fired masonry heating ovens that are used in Northern European countries like Sweden, Norway or Finland.

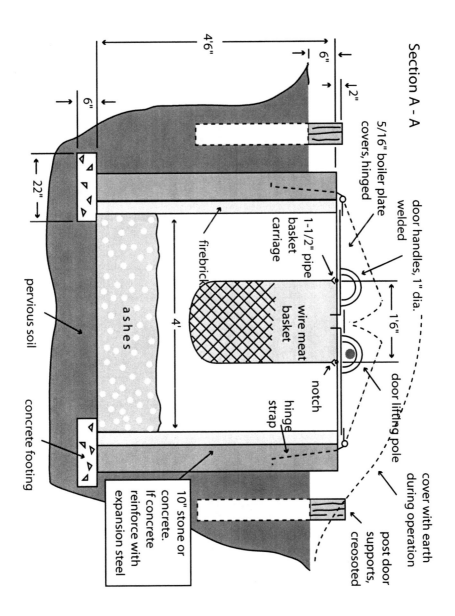

Fig. 8.8 Barbecue pit.

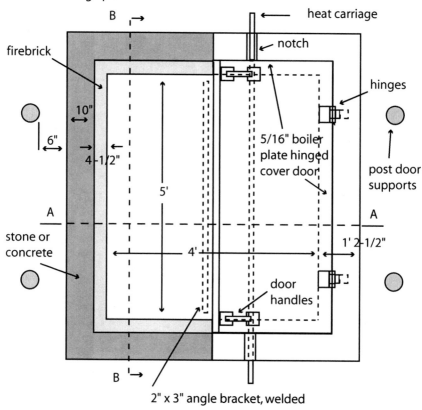

1/2 Plan through pit

B → heat carriage

firebrick

notch

hinges

10"

6"

4-1/2"

5/16" boiler plate hinged cover door

post door supports

5'

A — — — — — — — — — — — A

stone or concrete

1' 2-1/2"

4'

door handles

B →

2" x 3" angle bracket, welded

Fig. 8.9 Barbecue pit.

If we burn a large amount of wood directly in the ground, the heat will warm up the surrounding soil and will dissipate. As a result, the large piece of meat will end up being undercooked. On the other hand, the firebricks and stones will store heat inside and will radiate it back for a long time. This method results in a slow barbecuing process that will go on for a full day without any intervention on our part. After the animal is placed inside, the plates are closed and covered with soil.

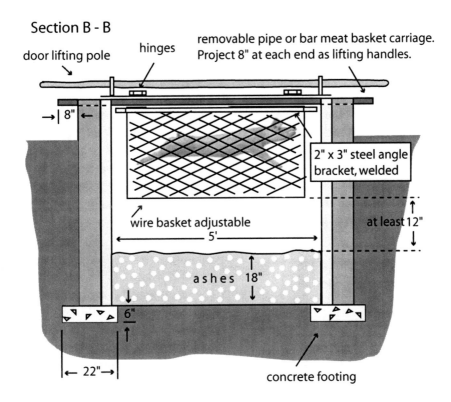

Section B - B

door lifting pole

hinges

removable pipe or bar meat basket carriage.
Project 8" at each end as lifting handles.

8"

2" x 3" steel angle bracket, welded

wire basket adjustable
5'

at least 12"

ashes 18"

6"

22"

concrete footing

Fig. 8.10 Barbecue pit.

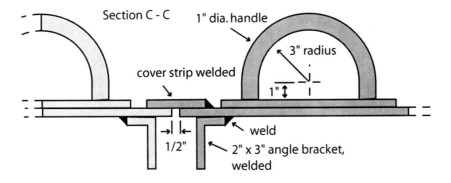

Section C - C

1" dia. handle

3" radius

cover strip welded

1"

weld

1/2"

2" x 3" angle bracket, welded

Fig. 8.11 Barbecue pit.

8.5 Building Your Own Barbecue

It will be futile to construct a gas powered grill at home as commercial units are well made in factories and carry reasonable prices. Thus the discussion is limited to building wood or charcoal burning units. If a lot of heat is produced these units work in a grilling mode, when low heat is applied they can cook meats for a long time in a true barbecue mode. Barbecuing one chicken and a few sausages can be easily accomplished with a few pounds of charcoal and may be accomplished with one load only. Charcoal briquettes will last about 30-45 minutes and more briquettes will have to be added when barbecuing for a number of hours. Our discussion is limited to the real slow burning barbecue which continues for a period of time and requires a steady supply of hot coals or charcoal briquettes.

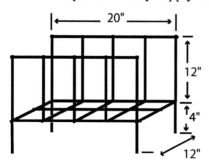

Fig. 8.12 Firebox for making hot coals.

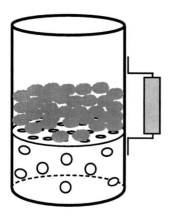

Fig. 8.13 Charcoal starter.

Solid wood logs must be preburned and an iron wood holding box can be made from 1/2" metal rebars. Simple weld tacks will hold it together. The unit should be placed on the fire pit side. The box is loaded with wood logs and as they burn they get smaller. When they become hot coals they will fall through the bottom of the grate and can be moved over to the fire pit.

Charcoal briquettes should be pre-burned until covered with whitish ash, otherwise meats may acquire a lighter fluid flavor. A simple starter can be made from a large metal can by removing the top and the bottom. Fresh charcoal is placed on a perforated plate, then a paper is ignited below. There are holes made on the outside in a lower part of the can for supplying air. The unit can be placed on hot coals too. When ready, the pre-burned briquettes are delivered to the fire pit.

Another method to light charcoal is to use an electrical wire starter like the one on page 15. Regardless of the type of charcoal starter used, the combustion of briquettes will greatly benefit by having an air space below. This will supply air from below and charcoal briquettes will burn easier. A practical solution is to have two charcoal pans with holes drilled in the bottom. The first pan provides heat in the unit and the second one pre-burns the new load of briquettes. Then the pans are switched over and barbecuing continues at a steady pace and temperature.

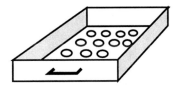

Fig. 8.14 Charcoal pan with drilled holes.

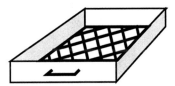

Fig. 8.15 Charcoal pan made from wire mesh.

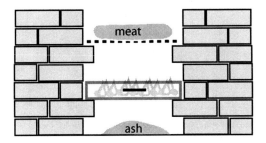

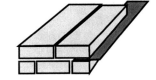

Fig. 8.17 Steel flat support.

Fig. 8.16 Charcoal pan resting on bricks. The holding supports can be made from offset bricks as shown in the drawing above or by inserting steel flats in fresh mortar joints.

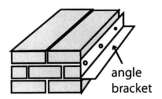

Fig. 8.18 Steel angle bracket support. Use long bolts and stick them into mortar when still wet. This way drilling can be avoided.

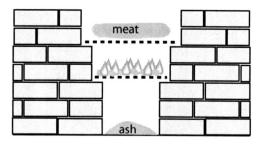

Fig. 8.19 Stepped down walls look attractive and allow for easier ash removal. Make sure that the ash pit is wide enough to accommodate a shovel.

The bottom of the unit should be sloped towards the front for rain water drainage. The grill screens should be slightly narrower for expansion of metal.

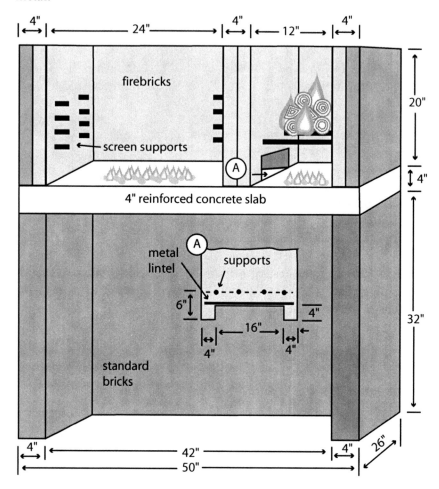

Fig. 8.20 Practical barbecue unit.

There is a hot coals producing firebox on the right which makes the unit friendlier to operate. As burning logs become smaller they fall down through the grate. Then they are pushed over to the left through the 16 x 4" opening in the side wall. The same system can be employed for pre-burning charcoal coals. It is possible to eliminate the partition wall "A" and place a free standing firebox as depicted in Fig. 8.12 drawing. The two supporting rebars could run from wall to wall (42"). If angle brackets are used for making a V-channel screen (Fig. 8.23) the rear support rebar should be installed slightly higher to facilitate the flow of grease toward the front. The aluminium collector can be attached to the screen to catch grease. To confine heat inside a top cover can be installed. The area below the slab can be used for storage or a propane tank can be placed there.

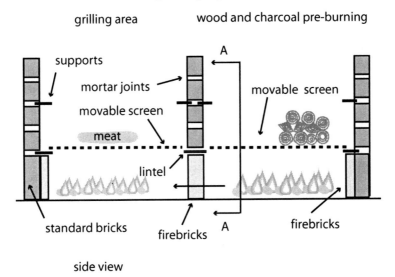

grilling area   wood and charcoal pre-burning

supports

mortar joints

movable screen

movable screen

meat

lintel

standard bricks   firebricks   A   firebricks

side view
section A - A

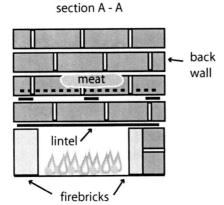

meat

back
wall

lintel

firebricks

Fig. 8.21 An easy to operate barbecue. Hot coals or pre-burned charcoal briquettes are moved towards the grilling area. If barbecuing for many hours, it is recommended to install front and top covers, with a provision for an exhaust vent.

It shall be noted that firebrick mortar joints are very thin, 1/8" or less. This does not leave enough room for placing round rebar between them. Increasing the size of a joint will weaken it and it may break in time. Making supports from 1/8" flat steel is a better idea. Installing any kind of metal which gets heated to high temperatures directly into masonry or stonework is a poor choice because metal will expand. This, in time will create damage to a brick or a stone. It is recommended to line the walls with firebrick for areas subjected to high temperatures. The floor of the unit and the reinforced concrete slab can withstand high temperatures. The concrete slab can extend to the left, right, or both, to create extra working areas. The support rebars should be placed into the mortar between the bricks.

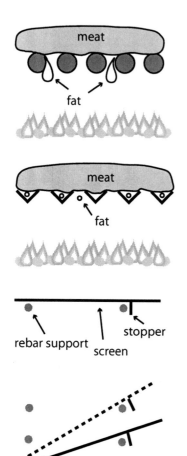

Fig. 8.22 Round bar screen.

Almost all factory made units employ screens made out of round bars. This does little to prevent grease from dripping down on hot coals and creating flames.

Fig. 8.23 V-channel screen.

Argentinian grills use angle brackets which are very effective in removing accumulating fat. The screens are slightly raised towards the back to provide an easy path for the grease to flow towards a removable collector tray.

Fig. 8.24 Screen adjustment.

By careful arrangement of supporting brackets/rebars, the screen can be placed at different angles. This helps to control heat. A steak can be seared on each side at the lowest screen setting. It is then placed higher to be cooked at lower heat. When done it may be moved even higher where it will be kept warm.

In many commercial establishments grill screens are suspended in the air by attaching them to adjustable chains. This is especially visible in Spanish speaking countries such as Argentina, Uruguay, Chile, Mexico or in Brazil.

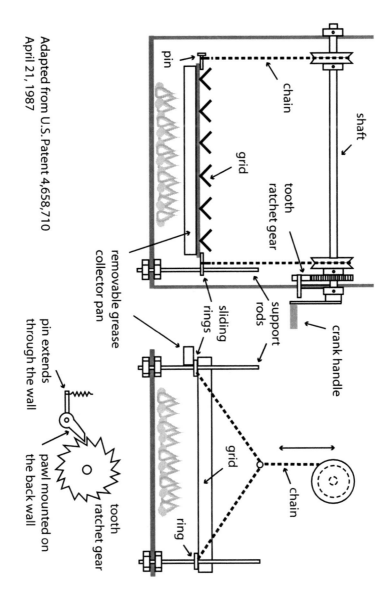

Fig. 8.25 Arrangement for raising or lowering grid.

A manually operated crank handle lifts up the screen to the desired height. To bring it down a pin is pulled which disengages the pawl in the ratchet gear. This allows the gear to turn the other way bringing the screen down. V-shaped channels are the norm and to have fat flowing to the collector, the screen must have a little tilt. It is easily accomplished by placing more meat in the front of the screen. The screen can not tilt too much as it is attached to the rings which ride on support rods.

This design offers great flexibility: it may be part of a movable barbecue or it may become a part of a masonry unit. The bottom plate can be eliminated and the sides may be secured to the permanent structure. In any case unit should be lined with fire bricks on inside.

Ratchet mechanisms are very useful devices to lift heavy weights. Ratchets consist of a gearwheel or linear rack with teeth, and a pivoting springloaded finger called a pawl that engages the teeth. Either the teeth, or the pawl, are slanted at an angle, so that when the teeth are moving in one direction, the pawl slides up and over each tooth in turn, with the spring forcing it back with a 'click' into the depression before the next tooth. When the teeth are moving in the other direction, the angle of the pawl causes it to catch against a tooth and stop further motion in that direction.

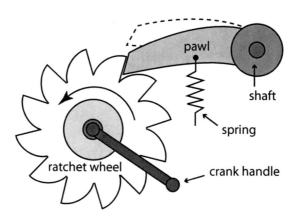

Fig. 8.28 Ratchet mechanism.

Chapter 9

Wild Game

The definition of wild game covers large animals such as dear, elk, moose, bear, mountain goat, and smaller animals such as squirrel, rabbit, opossum, and wild birds. Meat from wild animals is very lean, darker in color, and often has a gamey flavor which some people find objectionable. Fat is known to carry a lot of this flavor and as much of the fat as possible should be cut away. As the game meat contains very little fat to begin with, it is understood that smoking and cooking will produce a very dry product. The solution is to lace meat with pork back fat, add pork fat into sausages, cover smaller meat pieces with bacon strips or baste meat with marinade often. All meats will benefit from applying wet cure. The brine will not only tenderize the meat but will also remove any unpleasant gamey odors.

If smoking meats at low temperatures use sodium nitrite (Cure #1). You don't need nitrite when meats are smoked/cooked above 170° F (77° C). Note that wild game such as deer and bear are often infected with the trichinae parasite which is destroyed at 137° F (58° C). If present in pork, this parasite may also be destroyed by keeping meat frozen for a certain time (explained in the chapter on food safety). Latest research has demonstrated that meat coming from wild animals living in cold climates is resilient to cold treatment for trichinae and the only way to be safe is to cook the meat to 160° F (71° C) internal meat temperature.

9.1 Big Game

Large animals will be butchered into smaller cuts, noble cuts such as loins will be barbecued. Tougher cuts from older animals may be stewed. Other cuts may be frozen for later use. If no freezer is available, they can be preserved by careful application of preservation methods. Meat can be dry cured with salt (2.5%) and nitrite (Cure #1), ground, mixed with pork fat and made into sausages. Then the sausages can be smoked and cooked to 160° F (71° C). After that they can be stored at 10-12° C (50-53° F) losing more moisture and in time becoming dry sausages. If large cuts are to be smoked with preservation in mind, use the dry cure method, rub salt and

Cure #1 into the meat. By eliminating moisture (dry curing, smoking, cooking, drying) we create hostile conditions for the bacteria to grow.

9.2 Small Game

Small game parts require about 6-10 hours of curing, whole squirrel about 24 hours, and rabbit 24-36 hours. After curing rinse meats with cold water, allow to dry and then smoke.

9.3 Wild Fowl

The meat quality of wild birds is less predictable than farm raised chicken or turkey due to the different age of the birds that reside in different areas. They feed on an unknown diet which affects the flavor of the meat. What is predictable is that these birds are very lean and will benefit from curing. Cure birds as you would domestic poultry. Wild birds require frequent basting during smoking and cooking. Place an aluminum pan under the bird to catch drippings which may be utilized for making gravy later. A good approach is to cover the whole bird with bacon strips and secure the strips with wooden toothpicks. Keep in mind that meat areas covered with bacon strips are not exposed to smoke and will develop a pale color. For uniform color bacon strips should be removed during the last 1-2 hours of smoking. During the cooking stage, the temperature will be raised to 170° F (77° C) or higher and the meat should be frequently basted to prevent drying.

9.4 Jerky

Quality jerky is made from lean meats with as much fatty tissue removed as possible. Fats become rancid in time and the jerky's flavor will deteriorate. Wild game meat is very lean by nature so it is not surprising that great jerky is made from venison.

9.5 Barbecuing Wild Game

If meat preservation plays a secondary role, wild game can be successfully smoked/cooked (barbecued) with fire. Traditional method of curing meat with salt and nitrite may be replaced with marinating. Marinade may include strong herbs or spices such as juniper or rosemary which can offset the gamey meat flavor. As smoking/cooking will be performed at 200-225° F (93-107° C) there is little to worry about botulism (no nitrite needed) or trichinae. At these temperatures wild game lean meat will easily dry out and it should be frequently basted with oil rich basting marinade.

9.6 Larding Meat

Larding is a method used to add fat to very lean meat. It also helps to enhance the flavor of tougher cuts by internally basting and moisturizing them with fat. A strip of fat is cut from pork back fat or bacon and it should be chilled to harden it. All wild game, wild fowl included, will benefit greatly from this procedure.

A larding needle is designed to push fat into meat. Fat can be seasoned with herbs, or spices and the ingredients will fully penetrate the meat rather than remaining on the surface. A strip of fat or lard is forced into the larding needle, and then the needle is pushed through the cut of meat to be larded. As the needle passes through the meat, it leaves the strip of fat behind.

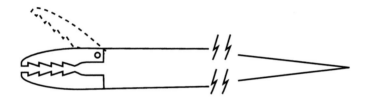

Fig. 9.1 A typical larding needle. The sharp point of the needle penetrates meat and exits on the other side. A serrated jaw swings outward to facilitate fat loading.

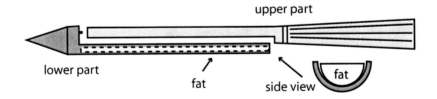

Fig. 9.2 Adjustable depth larding needle. A two part design, consisting of two separate interlocking half tubes. A fat strip is loaded into the bottom half tube. Both parts are locked and the needle is inserted through the meat. The sharp part of the needle is removed on the exit side, the upper pushing part is removed at the insertion point and the fat strip remains inside.

Drawing adapted from U.S. Patent 2,124,700, March 9, 1935.

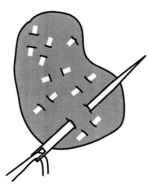

Fig. 9.4 Deep larding. Long, thin strips of fat are threaded through the whole piece of meat, following the grain.

Fig. 9.3 Surface larding. Thin strips of fat are threaded with the needle, just below the surface.

9.7 Barding Meat

Barding is a technique similar to larding that relies on the laying of fat over the meat rather than inserting it into the flesh. This method is more practical for fattening small pieces of meat and wild fowl. Commercially manufactured rendered lard (melted pork fat) can be spread on the surface of meat. A combination of larding and barding may be used as well.

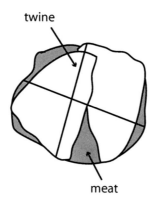

twine

meat

Fig. 9.5 Barding. Cut thin but wide sheets of pork fat and cover the entire piece of meat, for example the breast of the goose. Secure with twine.

Chapter 10

Recipes

A recipe is just a definition, it does not imply that one will produce an outstanding sausage. Making quality sausages has nothing to do with recipes, it is all about the meat science and the rules that govern it. All sausage making steps, especially temperature control, are like little building blocks that would erect a house. It is like the strength of the chain, which is only as strong as its weakest link. *Each step in sausage making influences the step that follows, and when performed correctly, as a final result all those steps create the quality product.* Let us quote Madame Benoit, the famous Canadian cookery expert and author who once said:

> *"I feel a recipe is only a theme, which an intelligent cook can play each time with a variation"*

We could fill this book with hundreds of recipes but that won't make you more knowledgeable. *There isn't one standardized recipe for any of the sausages.* The best meat science books, written by the foremost experts list different ingredients for the same sausage. Keep in mind that many of those wonderful recipe sites on the Internet are run by college educated kids or telemarketers who are good at writing. This is what they do for a living - they sit at home and nicely compile information that they think is relevant to their employer. How many do you think have made their own headcheese, blood sausage, cold smoked salmon or pork loin?

Most likely you will be making sausages for yourself, so use spices that you and your kids like, after all you will end up eating it. Basically a sausage is meat, salt and pepper. I will never forget when I made my first Polish smoked sausage that turned out very well and I proudly gave it to my friend - professional sausage maker Waldemar to try. I have included salt, pepper, garlic, and added optional marjoram. I also added nutmeg and other spices that I liked. Well my friend's judgement was as follows:

> *"Great sausage, but why all those perfumes?"*

For him it was supposed to be the classical Polish Smoked Sausage and all it needed was salt, pepper and garlic. The moral of the story is that putting dozens of spices into the meat does not guarantee the best product. Combining meat with salt and pepper already makes a great sausage providing that you will follow the basic rules of sausage making. It's that simple. Like roasting a chicken, it needs only salt, pepper, and it always comes out perfect. If you don't cure your meats properly, grind warm fat or screw up your smoking and cooking temperatures, all the spices in the world will not save your product. By adhering to the guidelines outlined in this book, you have to make a great sausage. By all means look at different recipes but be flexible and not afraid to experiment. Use ingredients that you personally like as in most cases you will make a sausage for yourself, so why not like it? When creating your own recipe remember the following facts:

- All meats will taste better when brined/cured first.
- All meats will taste better when smoked/cooked at lower temperatures.
- Theres is no smoking at low temperatures without curing first.

Although most of the information presented here pertains to making sausages, the reasoning behind it holds true for making any product, whether traditionally smoked or barbecued on the open fire. There is even more flexibility when barbecuing meats and there are countless recipes for making ribs, loins, or other products. Not forgetting dozens of marinades and sauces standing on the shelf in a supermarket. *A recipe is just a recipe and let your palate be the final judge.* But there is one rule which is obeyed by professionals who keep on winning barbecue contests: *cook it low and slow.* The same principle applies to traditional methods of smoking meats and sausages. It is all about temperatures and patience, other factors such as marinades, sauces, different woods are just a dressing.

10.1 Sausage Recipe Secrets

1. Fat. The meat needs about 25 - 30% fat in it. This will make the sausage tender and juicy, without fat it will feel dry.

2. Salt. You need salt. The proper amount of salt in meat (tastes pleasant) is 2–3%, though 1.5–2% is a usual average acceptable level. About 3.5-5% will be the upper limit of acceptability, anything more and the product will be too salty. Get the calculator and punch in some numbers. Or if you use the metric system you don't even need the calculator: You need 2 grams of salt per 100 grams of meat. If you buy ten times more meat (1 kg) you will also need ten times more salt (20 grams). Now for the rest of your life you don't have to worry about salt in your recipes. If you want a consistent product weigh out your salt. Estimating salt per cups or spoons can be deceiving as not all salts weigh the same per unit volume. *Salt perception can be an acquired taste.* If you decide to go on a low sodium diet and start decreasing the amount of salt you consume, in about three weeks time you may reach a point when your food tastes enjoyable, though you use less salt than before. This is fine as long as you prepare those meals for yourself. When smoking meats for your friends, try to adhere to the amount of salt the original recipe calls for, as other people might like a different amount of salt. When smoking large amounts of meat that will be kept for a week or longer, remember that *it will keep on drying out* (losing moisture). *Salt will, however, remain inside and your sausage will now taste saltier and will be of a smaller diameter.* The meat flavor will also be stronger now. In such a case you may use less salt than originally planned for, let's say 15 g/kg. That will not apply when making a fresh sausage which will be consumed in a matter of days, and 18 - 20 g (1.8-2%) salt per one kilogram of meat will be fine.

3. Pepper

- Black pepper - unripe seeds of the plant with the skin left on.
- White pepper - ripe seeds with the skin removed.

It is available as whole seeds but you have to grind it. Like in a case of coffee beans, the advantage is that you get a fresher aroma when grinding seeds just before use. It is available as coarse grind, sometimes called butcher's grind or fine grind. A recipe will call for a particular grind but the final choice will be up to you. Black pepper is normally used in fresh sausages and blood sausages, and white pepper is used in others. Polish sausage might need black pepper of a coarse grind but a hot dog, Bologna or Krakowska sausage will call for white pepper. The dividing line is whether you want to see the pepper in your product or not. Otherwise it makes no difference and you can replace black pepper with the same amount of white pepper, although the black pepper is a bit hotter.

4. Sugar. Less crucial, normally used to offset the harshness of salt. Amount used is about 10% of the salt used in the recipe. Sugar is normally used with salt when curing meat with nitrate. As a flavoring ingredient, sugar plays a little role in making sausages. No more than 3 g of sugar is added to 1kg of meat otherwise it can be noticeable. Chinese are very fond of sweet sausages so they might be an exception to the rule. Adding sugar was very important when making fermented sausages with nitrate as it provided food for bacteria and helped to form the lactic acid. Now we have commercially prepared and ready to use starter cultures and adding sugar is less important. Sugar also helps to preserve the red color of meat. In Europe beet sugar is commonly used, in the USA cane sugar is readily available. Often dextrose is used, but keep in mind that it is only 70% as sweet as sugar. Dextrose is the sugar of choice for making fermented sausages as it can be immediately consumed by lactic acid bacteria but other sugars must be broken down to glucose first.

5. Spices. Guidelines for spice usage as practiced by commercial sausage manufacturers.

Spice	Dosage in g/kg
Allspice	1.5
Cardamom	2.0
Chillies	0.5
Cinnamon	2.0
Cloves	1.5
Coriander	2.0
Fennel	2.0
Garlic paste	5.0
Garlic powder	1.5
Ginger	2.0
Juniper	2.0
Marjoram	3.0
Mace	1.0
Nutmeg	1.0
Onion (fresh)	10.0
Onion powder	3.0
Paprika	2.0
Pepper-white	2.0
Pepper-black	2.0
Thyme	1.0

How many grams of spice in one flat teaspoon	
Allspice, ground	1.90
Bay leaf, crumbled	0.60
Basil, ground	1.40
Caraway, seed	2.10
Cardamom, ground	1.99
Cinnamon	2.30
Cloves, ground	2.10
Coriander, seed	1.80
Fennel, whole	2.00
Garlic powder	2.80
Ginger, ground	1.80
Mace, ground	1.69
Marjoram, dried	0.60
Marjoram, ground	1.50
Mustard seed, yellow	3.20
Mustard, ground	2.30
Nutmeg, ground	2.03
Onion powder	2.50
Oregano, ground	1.50
Paprika, ground	2.10
Pepper-black, ground	2.10
Pepper-white, ground	2.40
Thyme, crumbled	0.60

1 tsp of sugar = 5 g,
1 tsp of table salt = 6 g,
1 tsp of Cure #1 = 6 g,
1 tsp of juniper berries = 1.53 g, 1 Tablespoon = 3 teaspoons.

Ground spices lose their aroma rapidly so make sure they are as fresh as possible. The most popular spices in the manufacture of sausages are pepper and garlic, sage, allspice, marjoram, thyme, rosemary, fennel, anise, cinnamon, mace, mustard, nutmeg, ginger, cardamom, coriander, oregano, and are normally added at around 0.1-0.2% (1-2 g/kg).

If a recipe involves 10 kg meat, just multiply the above numbers by a factor of 10. Remember those data are a point of reference for your calculations and you can adjust the amount of spices the way you like. To weigh spices and starter cultures accurately, specialized digital scales are recommended. They are small, up to 1/100 g accurate and inexpensive.

10.2 Recipes

To get the reader started there are twenty-two recipes listed below:

Kindziuk - known in Poland as Kindziuk and in Lithuania as Skilandis, it is an almost legendary product, famous for its long keeping properties. The sausage made from pork and beef is smoked and dried, but not cooked. It may be considered a traditionally fermented product.

Materials:
Lean pork (ham, loin), 85%, 4.25 kg (9.35 lbs)
lean beef chuck, 15%, 0.75 kg (1.65 lb)
Meat total: 5 kg (11 lbs)

Ingredients:
Salt, 3.5% (Cure #2 accounted for). 165 g (9 Tbsp)
Cure # 2, 12 g (2 tsp)
Sugar 0.05%, 2.5 g (1/2 tsp)
Herbal pepper * (see note below), 5 g (2 tsp)
Finely minced garlic, 15 g (5 cloves)

Instructions:
1. Cut meat into 1.5" (300-400 g) pieces. Rub in salt, Cure # 2 and sugar and leave on a screen for 3-4 days at 3-4° C (37-40° F).
2. Cut pork into 20-30 mm (3/4-1-1/4") by 10-15 mm (3/8-5/8") pieces.
3. Grind beef through 2-3 mm (1/8") plate.
4. Mix beef with all spices. Add pork and mix everything together.
5. Stuff firmly into pork stomach, bladder, 60 mm beef middles or 60 mm

fibrous casings. Reinforce with butcher's twine: two loops lengthwise and loops across the casings every 2" (5 cm). Form 10-12 cm (4-5") hanging loop on one end.

6. Hang for 2 months at 2-4° C (35-40° F).

7. Apply cold smoke 18-22° C (64-72° F) for 8 hours.

8. Hang in a cool place for 2 weeks.

9. Apply cold smoke again at 18-22° C (64-72° F) for 8 hours.

10. Dry for 2 months at 8° C (46° F) and 75% humidity. The sausage should lose about 35% of its original weight.

11. Store in a dark, cool and dry place.

Notes:

Meat should come from mature animals. Remove all sinews, glands and gristle. Originally all ingredients were stuffed into pork stomach or bladder. The stomach was sewn and the bladder was tied off with butcher twine. Traditional Kindziuk was smoked with alder wood. Don't decrease the amount of salt. Salt and nitrite are the first line of defense against spoilage and pathogenic bacteria. Then, as the sausage dries out it becomes microbiologically more stable every day.

* Herbal pepper is a combination of spices which is used in many countries such as French Quatre-epices (pepper, nutmeg, cloves, cinnamon) or Indian curry powder (turmeric, coriander, fenugreek, cumin and other spices). Italian seasoning (marjoram, thyme, rosemary, savory, sage, oregano and basil) is another known combination of herbs. In East European countries such as Poland or Lithuania herbal pepper is commercially made and available in supermarkets. A typical Polish herbal pepper contains: white mustard seed, caraway, marjoram, chili, hot and sweet paprika and bay leaf. You can buy pre-mixed spices or use your imagination for creating your own version. If you decide to go without herbal pepper, use 10 g (5 tsp) of black or white pepper.

Smoked Pork Butt

    5 lbs pork butt
    5 tsp (30 g) Cure # 1
    1 ½ oz (45 g) salt
    1 qt water
    seasonings

Mix all ingredients in 1 qt of cold water (40° F, 4° C), then spray pump pork butts to 10% of the green (original) weight. Then leave them in the remaining brine for 3 - 4 days in a refrigerator. Take them out, wash briefly with cold water and let drain. Place them in stockinette bags. Hang them in a preheated to 130° F (54° C) smokehouse for 2-3 hours until dry. Then apply a medium smoke increasing temperature to 150° F for about 3 hours. Then raise the temperature to 160–165° F and continue smoking until an internal temperature of 154° F (68° C) is obtained. Shower with cold water and hang them at room temperature to start cooling. Store in the refrigerator.

Smoked Back Fat

Another old Polish classic that you can't buy unless you make it yourself. It can be used for flavoring other dishes.

11 lbs (5 kg) back fat pork (not salted)
12 oz salt (350 g)

Instructions:

Pork fat slabs, with or without skin, about 9-11" (24-28 cm) long and 3- 6" (8-16 cm) wide and at least 1¼" thick (pork with the skin on) or 1" thick (pork without skin). Keep salt pork at 40-42° F (4-6° C). When cutting slabs you can choose your own length but make it 3-6" wide. Trim out all remaining pieces of flesh and blood, until you have a clean piece of pork. Find a suitable curing container and spread salt on the bottom. Rub the salt into the pork on all sides and place in the container skin down. Cover the pork with salt on top, rub salt into the next pork piece and place it on top of the first one, skin down. Put more salt on top. Don't go any higher than 20" (50 cm). After 7 days remove the pork pieces, rub in more salt and add more salt between them and on top. The pork should be well covered with salt all over. The container should remain in a cool 40-42° F (4-6° C) and dark place for 1-2 weeks. Total salt curing time 2-3 weeks. After 1 week of curing when rearranging the pieces, you may rub in some favorite spices of yours - sweet Hungarian paprika works great. Shake off salt from the pork pieces, rinse in warm water, 100-104° F (38-40° C), check that they are clean on the outside and hang for 12-24 hours to dry them out. Make 4-5" (10-12 cm) long loops of butchers twine.

Salt pork is cold smoked below 70° F (22° C) with thin smoke for 2-3 days until a light brown or brown color is achieved. Cool to below 64° F (18° C). Store in a refrigerator. No Cure #1 or nitrates used. Product not cooked but ready to eat.

Smoked Pork Loin (Canadian Bacon)

This is one of the easiest products to make, one with a great flavor and known all over the world. No grinding, no mixing and no stuffing involved.

  4.4 lbs (2 kg) pork loin without bone
  4 Tbsp (80 g) salt
  1 tsp sugar (6 g)
  5 tsp (30 g) Cure #1
  1 liter water

Instructions:

1. Wet cure method. Mix all ingredients with cold water. Using a needle syringe, pump the loin to 3-4 % of its green weight. That means you are taking the amount of brine that equals 3-4% of the loin meat weight. In this case it comes to 60-80 g (2.1 - 2.8 oz) or 1/3 cup. The loin then is placed in the leftover brine and placed in a refrigerator for 24 hours. Then wash the outside of the loin briefly with tap water. It is wise to taste it now and if it is too salty place in cold water (refrigerator) for a few hours. If you want it saltier, stick it back into the brine for a few hours. This curing time is for one loin only, in case you will make more loins, increase curing time to 3 days. Turn loins over once a day. Loins must be covered with brine, use some kind of weight on top of them.

2. Let it drain and dry for 6-8 hours at room temperature. Rub the dry loin all over with the yolk of an egg. That will give the loin a beautiful gold color on the outside after smoking.

3. Preheat the smoker to 130° F (54° C) and if the loin is dry, introduce smoke with dampers 1/4 closed and smoke for 1 hour at 122-140° F (50-60° C). Increase smoking temperature to 150° F (66° C) and stop when the meat's internal temperature reaches 142° F (61° C). Trichinae, almost non-existent in American pork, dies at 137° F (58° C).

4. Shower with cold water until the internal temperature is reduced to 110° F (44° C). Hang at room temperature for 1 hour then place in a refrigerator.

Notes:

Cooking is optional. The smoked loin was never submitted to high temperatures and has a characteristic color, taste and flavor. Try it; most people love it that way. Nothing prevents you from increasing smoking temperature (keep the smoke on) to 160-170° F (71-77° C) until the meat's internal temperature reaches 154° F (68° C). There will be a noticeable difference in flavor between the cooked and uncooked version.

Mysliwska - Hunter's Sausage

Hunter sausages were carried in bags by hunters who stayed away from home for a number of days. They were small, nutricious and kept well for a long time.

Pork butt, 90%, 4.5 kg (9.90 lbs)
Beef, 10%, 0.5 kg (1.10 lb)
Salt 90 g (5 Tbs)
Cure #1, 12 g (2 tsp)
pepper, 10 g (5 tsp)
sugar, 10 g (2 tsp)
garlic, 5 g, (2 cloves)
juniper, 5 g, (20 dry berries)

Instructions:

1. Cut meat into 2" (5 cm) cubes, mix with salt and cure #1 and place in container. Avoid creating air pockets, cover meat with a cloth, and leave in refrigerator for 48 hours.

2. Grind pork through 3/8" (10 mm) plate. Grind beef through 3 mm (1/8") plate. Refreeze beef and grind again adding 1/2 cup cold water.

3. Mix pork, beef and everything else together.

4. Stuff firmly into 32 mm hog casings. Form 8" (20 cm) long links. Make pairs.

5. Hang on smoke sticks for 60 min.

6. Hot smoke for 90 minutes. Increase temperature and cook in smokehouse for 30 min until the internal meat temperature reaches 68-70° C (154-158° F). The total smoking and cooking time around 2 hours.

7. Shower with cold water

8. Store in refrigerator or hang in a dry, cool place at 12° C (54° F).

During the last stage of smoking, juniper twigs or branches were often added to wood chips for an extra flavor. This also darkens the sausage to some extent. When a sausage exhibited heavier juniper flavor it was known as "Juniper Sausage".

Polish Smoked Sausage (Cold Smoked)

This is the original recipe for the famous Polish Smoked Sausage as it has been made for centuries.

    11 lbs (5 kg) pork butt,
    5 Tbsp salt (90 g)
    3 tsp black pepper (7.5 g)
    3 cloves fresh garlic (9 g)
    2 tsp marjoram (3 g)
    2 tsp sugar (10 g)
    Cure #2, 2 tsp (12 g)

You can see that there is no cooking involved and in order to eliminate any possibility of Trichinae occurance, the meat should be deep frozen for the prescribed time (see page 64). It is worth the effort as it is almost impossible to buy this product anymore.

Instructions:

1. Cut meat into 2" diameter pieces, and add 2 tsp Cure #2, 1 tsp of sugar and 4 Tbsp of salt. Mix well together; pack tightly in a container leaving some space on top and cover. Place in refrigerator for 72 hrs. Grind all meat with ½" plate. Add remaining 1 Tbsp of salt and all other ingredients and mix thoroughly with ground meat. Continue mixing until the meat becomes glutinous.

2. Stuff mixture into 32-36 mm hog casings and form 30-35 cm links (12-13"). Prick any visible air pockets with a needle. Keep the total number of links an even number, as it will be easier to divide them later into pairs. Leave it hanging on smoke sticks in a cool place at 35-42° F (2-6° C) for 1-2 days at 85-95% relative humidity.

3. Smoke with cold smoke at 60-72° F (16-22° C) for 1 - 1.5 days until brownish - yellow color is achieved. Rotate smoke sticks during smoking unless your smoker is capable of very even smoke distribution.

4. Divide sausages into individual pairs. Store at 50-54° F (10-12° C) with a relative humidity of 75-80% until a weight loss of 23% is achieved, which may take approximately 2 weeks.

Polish Smoked Sausage (Hot Smoked)

This is the hot smoked version, much easier and faster to make than the "real" cold smoked one, which is listed above.

    11 lbs (5 kg) pork butt,
    5 Tbsp salt (90 g)
    3 tsp black pepper (7.5 g)
    3 cloves fresh garlic (9 g)
    2 tsp marjoram (3 g)
    2 tsp sugar (10 g)
    Cure #1, 2 tsp (12 g)
    2 cups ice water

Instructions:

1. The ingredients remain the same except that Cure #1 is used and water is added. Cut meat into 2" diameter pieces, and add 2 tsp Cure #1, 1 tsp of sugar and 4 Tbsp of salt. Mix well together, pack tightly in a container and cover with fabric. Place in a refrigerator for 72 hrs.

2. Grind the lean meat with a 3/8" grinder plate and the fat meat through 3/16" plate.

3. Add remaining 1 Tbsp of salt and all other ingredients including ice water. Start mixing until the meat becomes glutinous.

4. Stuff mixture into 32-36 mm hog casings and form 30-35 cm links (12-13"). Prick any visible air pockets with a needle. Keep the total number of links an even number, as it will be easier to divide them later into pairs. Leave it hanging on smoke sticks until casings are dry or feel tacky to touch. By the time you are done stuffing the sausage, most of it is already dry. If unable to start smoking now, place sausages in a refrigerator where the casings will dry overnight.

5. Place sausages in a preheated smoker at 130° F (54° C) with draft dampers fully open. When the casings are fully dry apply heavy smoke and keep the draft dampers 1/4 open. When smoking, keep on increasing the smoking temperature until you reach the 160-170° F (71°-76° C) range. The sausage is done when the internal temperature reaches 154° F (68° C). Rotate smoke sticks during smoking.

6. Remove sausages from the smoker and shower with cold water. When the internal temperature has been reduced to 110° F (44° C) it is safe to hang the sausage at room temperature for 0.5-1 hr. This will allow for more moisture to escape from the inside of the sausage and will also develop the final color and shine. Store in refrigerator.

Kabanosy (Meat Sticks)

Very famous Polish Meat Sticks known by this name in all Eastern Europe.

11 lbs (5 kg) Pork butts,
5 Tbsp (90 g) salt
3 tsp (7.5 g) pepper
1 ¼ tsp nutmeg (3 g)
1 tsp ground caraway (2.5 g)
2 tsp sugar (10 g)
2 tsp Cure #1 (14 g)

1. Cut meat into 2" diameter pieces, and add 1 tsp Cure #1, 1 tsp of sugar and 4 Tbsp of salt. Mix well together; pack tightly in a container leaving some space on top and cover. Place in refrigerator for 72 hrs. Grind lean pork with 3/8" plate, fatter pieces with 3/16" plate. Add remaining 1 Tbsp of salt and all other ingredients and thoroughly mix with ground meat.
2. Stuff mixture into 22 mm diameter sheep casings. You may use 24-26 mm sheep casings; anything bigger will not be a meat stick but a sausage. It will also need different smoking and cooking times. Link sausage into 60-70 cm (24-27") links so when hung in the middle each individual link (half of the meat stick) will be about one foot long. Prick any visible air pockets with a needle. Leave it hanging on smoke sticks for 30-60 min.
3. Smoke with hot smoke 104-122° F (40-50° C) for 50-60 min.
4. Cook for about 20 min at 140-190° F (60-90° C) until the meat reaches the temperature of 154° F (68° C) inside. The color of the casings should be dark brown. Total smoking and cooking time about 70-90 min. This is a rather short time due to the small diameter of the meat sticks.

Notes:

Traditionally made Kabanosy were placed for 5-7 days in a room at 54-64° F (12-18° C), relative humidity of 75-80%, until the weight was reduced by 45%. If during this drying period you will see a slight accumulation of mold on the outside surface, just wipe it off, this is normal. Kabanosy are ready to eat immediately after cooking but the taste will continuously improve as they are drying out.

Hot Dog

Hot dogs, frankfurters, and wieners all belong to the emulsified group of sausages. What this means is that they are ground to a consistency of a very fine paste which is accomplished commercially in bowl cutters or at home with food processors. We have successfully made those sausages even before food processors were invented and the same effect can be somewhat achieved by grinding meat a few times through a very fine grinder plate. Such a process generates a significant amount of heat and finely crushed ice is added into the meat during grinding.

Originally meat was stuffed into edible sheep casings but as the demand for the product grew enormously, cellulose casings were introduced. As the natural casings vary in quality and diameter it would be impossible to produce a product of a constant weight in relation to its length.

It may come as a surprise to many but a hot dog or frankfurter is a lightly smoked product. In order to keep costs down, commercial manufacturers spray sausages with atomized liquid smoke. During smoking and then poaching a sausage in hot water, its surface hardens and holds its shape even after removing the cellulose casing. Of course there is no need to do it when using a sheep casing.

There was no way to predict what went into those sausages before but now with better government control we get a better product and certain parts like brains or lungs are not permitted anymore.

A basic recipe:

About 30% beef, 25% pork, 30% back fat (fat pork, jowls, bacon) and 15% crushed ice. In other words for making 1 kg hot dogs you will need:

> 300 g beef
> 250 g pork
> 300 g fatback
> 150 g crushed ice
> 2 g (1/3 tsp) Cure #1
> 16 g salt (1 flat Tbsp)
> 1 g white pepper (1 tsp)
> 0.6 g mace (1/3 tsp)
> 1.0 g sweet paprika (1/2 tsp)
> 0.5 g garlic (1/2 clove)

Instructions:
1. Cut the meat into 1-2" cubes, partially freeze and grind through a fine plate (1/8 – 3/16").

2. Cut the meat into 1-2" cubes, partially freeze and grind through a fine plate (1/8 – 3/16").

3. Dissolve all other ingredients in a little water and stir well. Mix all ingredients with meats

4. Grind mixed meat in a food processor adding crushed ice (place some ice cubes in a towel and hit them a few times with a heavy object). Grind until the meat is emulsified. Depending on the size of the food processor you might have to do two separate batches.

5. Stuff into 6" sheep casings.

6. Smoke for about 1 hour at 140° F (60° C) until sausages develop red-brownish color.

7. Poach in water at 158-162° F (70-72° C) until the internal temperature reaches 154–158° F (68–70° C). That will take about 15 minutes.

8. Shower with cold water.

9. After sausages cooled down shower them briefly with hot water to remove any fat that might have accumulated on the surface. Wipe them dry and store in refrigerator.

Using a manual grinder

Grind beef and pork with 3/8" (10 mm) plate 2-3 times.

Grind fat pork with 1/8 (3 mm) grinder 2-3 times but keep fat separate

Add about 400–500 g of icy cold water to ground beef and pork and mix together until water is fully absorbed by the meat.

Add fat and all ingredients and mix everything well together. Then continue the recipe above.

Notes:

You could cure meats before grinding. In such a case mix meat cubes with salt and Cure #1, pack tightly in two containers (one for beef and one for pork), cover with clean cloth and leave for 72 hours. Then proceed to grinding as above.

You can use all beef (25% fat) or different combinations of meats; pork, veal, chicken, and beef.

About 5 g, 1 tsp phosphate may be added to effectively bind water with meat.

Smoked Chicken

Place chicken (2 lbs) overnight (10 hrs) in the refrigerator in the following brine (22 degrees):

> 1 gal of cold water
> ½ cup (146 g) of salt
> 3 oz (85 g) of Cure #1 – corresponds to 79 g of pure salt
> 3 oz (85 g) sugar (brown or white).

Rinse the chicken under cold running water for 5 minutes to remove any salt crystals from the outside that may interfere with smoke accumulation. Dry the chicken for 30–60 minutes. When the birds are dry or tacky to touch, they should be placed in a preheated smoker and if they are still wet, hold them at 130° F (54° C) for one hour or more until dry. Keep the damper wide open to allow moisture to escape.

Once the birds feel dry, leave the damper in ¼ open position and smoke at 130° F (54° C) for about five hours. Then continue smoking, slowly raising the temperature to 165-170° F (74-76° C) and hold until the inside temperature in the thickest part of the breast is 154° F (68° C). You could also insert a thermometer close to the ball and socket joint of the thigh as this is also the last place the meat becomes fully cooked. If a thermometer is not available, you can check the turkey by twisting the leg slightly. If it moves easily, the cooking is done. Small birds like Cornish Game Hens or Small Chicken will need shorter smoking and cooking times.

Smoked Trout

Gut and clean fish (1 lb in weight) and place in 80 degrees brine for 2 hours. You may leave fish overnight in 30 degrees brine. Rinse and dry for 2 hours. Start applying smoke and hold at 90° F for 15 minutes. Continue smoking increasing temperature and hold at 150° F (66° C) internal temperature for 30 minutes. Bigger fish will require longer smoking time. You can smoke/bake trout at 300–350° F (150–180° C) which will take only 20 minutes.

Smoked Salmon

Place salmon fillets for 2 hours in 80 degrees brine. Remove the fish from the brine and rinse it quickly under cold running water. Place the fish on a rack and dry for two hours. Apply smoke gradually increasing the temperature and hold at 150° F (66° C) internal temperature for 30 minutes. To achieve this your smoker's temperature will have to be higher, around 170° F. Remove the fish from the smoker and cool it.

Cold Smoked Salmon

Place salmon fillets in 80 degrees brine for 12 – 24 hours, depending on the size of the fillets. Remove fish from the brine and rinse for 1 hour under cold running water. Place on smoking rack and dry the fish (3 hours). Place in a smoker and smoke below 70° F (22° C) for about 16 hours. Remove the fish from the smoker and cool it.

Barbecued (Smoked/Cooked) Meats

Instead of traditional curing techniques which rely on salt and nitrite, barbecuing employs dry rubs, liquid marinades and sauces. Rubs and marinades tenderize and flavor meats, sauces may be compared to salad dressings, it is the final culinary touch given to the process. Sauces which contain sugars and honey are usually applied in the last minutes of the barbecue to create a caramelized crust and shiny surface on the product.

Dry rub commonly consists of:

- Salt.
- Sugar, honey, maple syrup. Sugar burns easily on the surface of the food.
- seasonings-lemon pepper, pepper, dry mustard, oregano, thyme, marjoram, sage.

There are three basic components of a marinade:

Acid	Oil	Seasonings
Vinegar, wine, lemon juice, orange juice, pineapple juice, Worcestershire sauce, tomatoes or ketchup.	Vegetable, olive or other oils. The leaner the food, the more oil it will need. Keep in mind that butter becomes solid in the refrigerator.	Spices, sugar, honey, flavorings

Look at the label of any commercially made product and you will see that the above ingredients are always present. Basting marinade is lighter and used on meats which are leaner. The amount of oil can be adjusted accordingly and will be higher in marinades used for lean wild game. Beer makes an excellent basting marinade.

Originally, they were two distinct barbecue sauces:

- Vinegar based sauces (no ketchup or tomato paste added), which were popular in the Eastern parts of the Carolinas and Virginia.

- Tomato ketchup based sauces more popular in the Western parts of the Carolinas, Virginia, Tennessee, Kansas, Kentucky and Texas. Texas sauces contained more hot peppers.

Today, there are dozens of marinades in every store. A typical dry rub and marinade:

Dry rub	Marinade
4 Tbsp salt, 2 Tbsp sugar, 2 Tbsp powdered garlic, 2 Tbsp paprika, 2 Tbsp sugar, 2 Tbsp ground celery seed, 1 Tbsp black pepper, 1 tsp cayenne.	1/2 cup oil, 1/2 cup lemon juice, 1 Tbsp salt, 1 tsp paprika, 1/2 tsp garlic powder, 1/2 tsp onion powder, 1 Tbsp lemon peel (zest).

Basic barbecue sauce:

2 cups ketchup, 1/4 cup oil, 1/3 cup honey, 1/4 cup Worcestershire sauce, 1/2 cup soy sauce, 1/4 cup vinegar, 1 tsp granulated garlic, 1 tsp granulated onion, 1/2 tsp liquid smoke, 1/2 tsp Tabasco sauce.

Keep in mind that acidic foods react with most metals such as common steel, copper, aluminum and it is best to use containers made of glass, food grade plastic or stainless steel.

Pork Spare Ribs

Remove membrane from back of ribs. Refrigerate ribs overnight in marinade. Smoke/cook ribs at 225° F (107° C) until meat starts to pull away from bones. Keep water pan in smoker. Coat ribs with sauce on upright side during final hour of cooking. You can finish them off with honey. Remove ribs when glazed in appearance. This might take 5-8 hours.

In many restaurants ribs are first boiled in a solution of water, ketchup, liquid smoke, then covered in foil and placed in a cooking tunnel. They then travel through the cooking chamber and exit fully cooked on the other side about 20 minutes later. Then they are passed as smoked or barbecued ribs, although they were only cooked. The resulting smoky flavor has been obtained due to the addition of liquid smoke.

Pork Shoulder With The Bone In

Marinate shoulder overnight. Use covered unit such as kettle barbecue unit and the water pan. Sear the shoulder on high heat (> 300° F, 149° C) by turning it around until all areas are sealed. Decrease temperature down to about 225° F, (107° C), and turn meat around every 30 minutes, basting with basting marinade or beer. Cook to 170° F internal meat temperature.

Although 160° F (71° C) is accepted as the safe temperature standard, slow cooked meat products such as pulled pork exhibit better texture when cooked to slightly higher temperature.

Smoked Chicken Teriyaki

Teriyaki marinade: 1/2 cup soy sauce, 1/4 cup sugar, 1/4 cup rum, gin or dry sherry, 1/2 tsp ginger, 1/2 tsp garlic powder. Marinate meat overnight in refrigerator. Smoke/cook on low fire.

Barbecued meats are smoked/cooked at temperatures which kill bacteria and no sodium nitrite is needed. As a result they will not exhibit the pink color so typical of nitrite cured meats.

All purpose marinade	Basting marinade
1 cup oil, 1/2 cup vinegar, 1/4 cup lemon juice, 1/4 cup soy sauce, 1/2 cup Worcestershire sauce, 1 Tbsp dry mustard, 1 Tbsp black pepper, 1/2 tsp cayenne	1 cup olive or salad oil, 1 cup vinegar, 1/2 cup water (or red wine)

Wild Game Recipes

Marinades

Basic marinade includes water, vinegar, oil and flavorings. Often orange, lemon or pineapple juice are added. Don't add too much sugar as it tends to brown and caramelize the surface of the meat. Keep in mind that a basting marinade is thin, it is not a sauce. *The oil is always used in wild game marinades.* Spices such as allspice, onion or garlic powder, ground celery, thyme, ginger, juniper, rosemary, sage, parsley, marjoram, and dry mustard are often added. Use 1 tsp each except 1/2 tsp for ginger, rosemary and ground juniper. Curry powder imparts a characteristic flavor to food and may be used with wild birds. In the wet smoking method marinade can be used instead of water when filling the pan. The pan should be placed under the meat to catch the meat juices dripping down. Then as the liquid evaporates, the marinade will baste meat with its own juices. If meat was marinated overnight, the marinade has picked up gamey odors and should not be used for basting purposes. Smaller parts may be marinated in wine marinade for about 6 hours. Then they are submitted to the smoking and cooking steps according to established rules.

Barbecued Rabbit or Squirrel

Place dressed squirrel in a roasting pan (aluminium foil tray is fine) and cook at 200° F (93° C) until the meat is tender (160° F, 71° C internal meat temperature). Add presoaked wood chips to generate smoke. Baste often with marinade and meat juices.

Venison Ribs

Marinate ribs with the above all purpose marinade for 3 days. Turn every 12 hours. Use covered pan. Drain ribs and discard the marinade. Cook at 200° F (93° C) basting often with a basting marinade until ribs separate easily. Add presoaked wood chips to generate smoke.

Wild Birds

Marinate bird overnight. Drain and discard marinade. Cook at 200° F (93° C) until the meat is tender (165° F, 74° C internal meat temperature). Add presoaked wood chips to generate smoke. Baste often with marinade and meat juices.

Deer Sausage

Deer meat, 3.5 kg (7.7 lbs)
Bacon slab (pork), 1.5 kg (3.3 lbs)
Salt, 90 g (5 Tbsp)
Cure #1, 12 g (2 tsp)
Salt total 100 g (2%, Cure #1 accounted for)
Pepper, 10 g (5 tsp)
Ground mustard 10 g (6 tsp)
Marjoram 10 g (6 tsp)
2 garlic cloves
1/2 cup, 125 ml water

Instructions:
1. Cut meat and bacon into 1" (2.5 cm) cubes, mix with salt and Cure #1 and leave for 1 day in a cool place or preferably for 2 days in refrigerator.
2. Dice meat with knife or grind through coarse plate (3/8-1/2", 9-12 mm).
3. Mix well with all spices and finely diced garlic. Add water and knead well until mixture becomes gluey.
4. Stuff into 36-40 mm hog casings.
5. Hang on smokesticks for 1-2 hours. The sausage may be cooked in water and consumed or continue to step 6.
6. Smoke with hot smoke for 3-4 hours. Keep increasing temperature slowly until meat reaches 160° F (71° C) internal temperature.
7. Store in a cool and dry place at about 12° C (53° F).

Wild Boar Sausage

Boar butt, 3 kg (6.6 lbs)
Pork butt or fat trimmings 2 kg (4.4 lbs)
Salt, 90 g (5 Tbsp)
Cure #1, 12 g (2 tsp)
Salt total 100 g (2%, Cure #1 accounted for)
Pepper, 10 g (5 tsp)
2 garlic cloves
5 dry juniper berries

Follow instructions for Deer Sausage.

Rabbit Sausage

Rabbit meat, 4 kg (8.8 lbs)
Pork back fat, 1 kg (2.2 lbs)
Salt, 90 g (5 Tbsp)
Cure #1, 12 g (2 tsp)
Salt total 100 g (2%, cure #1 accounted for)
Sugar, 10 g (2 tsp)
Pepper, 10 g (5 tsp)
Allspice, 10 g (5 tsp)
Nutmeg, 4 g (2 tsp)
Non fat dry milk, 4%, 200 g (7 oz)
Water, 2 cups (500 ml)

Instructions:
1. Cut meat and bacon into 1" (2.5 cm) cubes, mix with salt, sugar and Cure #1 and leave for 1 day in a cool place or preferably for 2 days in a refrigerator.
2. Grind meat and back fat through 3 mm (1/8") plate. Refreeze and grind again.
3. Mix well with all spices adding water. Knead well until mixture becomes gluey. This is an emulsified sausage like frankfurter or bologna.
4. Stuff into 36-38 mm hog casings or beef middles.
5. Hang on smokesticks for 2-3 hours.
6. Smoke with hot smoke for 3-4 hours.
7. Place sausages in boiling water, lower temperature to 80° C (176° F) **and poach for 30 min.**
8. Store in refrigerator.

Wild game meat is too lean for making sausages and pork fat should be added. Around 30% of back fat or fat pork trimmings may be added.

Chapter 11

Smokehouse Design Principles

11.1 Old Smokehouses

Old smokehouses were impressive structures that served both as smokers and as storage facilities. Communal smokers were responsible for supplying meat for many families. The same was true of bread ovens. They were far too expensive for one household to own, so many shared the same one.

The main purpose of the smokehouse was not to produce cold smoke to improve taste, but to preserve it so it will last for a longer period of time. Preservation was achieved by salt curing and prolonged cold smoking which took about 2 weeks or more. The product continued to hang in a different area of the smoker, sometimes up to two years, and during that time it lost more moisture and acquired more smoke, although at smaller rates. The meats were not cooked to a high internal temperature as done today (160° F, 72° C), because that would require strengthening the fire and the smokehouse could go up in flames. Besides, meat science was still in its infant stage and there were no established rules for cooking temperatures. Food poisoning due to *Clostridium botulinum* (botulism) or problems associated with *Listeria, Salmonella* or *E.coli* were not known yet. During that time, the lack of refrigeration promoted smoking to state of the art meat technology. Given cooling facilities, sausages would have been cooked quickly, similar to how they are done today. There would be no need to worry about the meat spoiling, and therefore no need to develop smoking techniques for preservation purposes.

It is not easy to improve the simple but practical design of the XV-century smokehouses. They were square chambers, with a steep chimney in the shape of a pyramid. There were no windows, just a door and screened openings below the roof to stop insects, provide ventilation and a route to allow smoke to escape. The door had a lock to safeguard the meats from thieves and animals. Below the roof there were beams with hooks where the meat was hung. The dimensions varied from 10-100 sq feet of floor space and 10-18 ft in height. The eastern part of Poland (what is now Lithuania) became very famous for its smoked products. There was a popular square tower shaped smokehouse with a side of 6.5 foot (2 m) and 20 ft (6 m) in height.

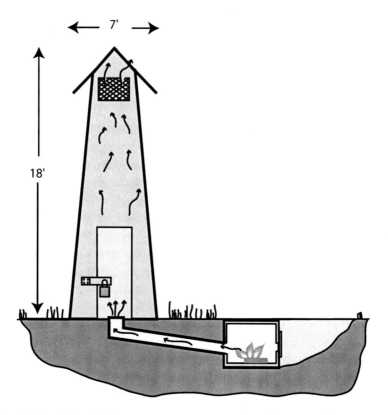

Fig. 11.1.1 Old Polish smokehouse.

The fire pit was located outside and a trench was delivering smoke into the smokehouse. The top part of the tower contained screened openings that provided ventilation and a means for the smoke to escape. Those openings had hinged covers on the outside and allowed smoke control by serving as a damper. Due to its height and a separate fire pit, the smokehouse was able to provide natural cold smoke. This is the best possible design for a smokehouse, and is reflected in hundreds of home made smokers or industrial units. They all employ a separately standing fire pit/smoke generator. In the USA, smoking was more popular in the Eastern parts of the country where there was a great availability of hogs running around. During the winter in Virginia, there were so many smokehouses puffing smoke around the clock that the sight looked like a stream of locomotives ready to take off at the station. Smokehouses used in XVIII Century Colonial USA were very similar to their European cousins. However, the fire pit was situated in the central part of the smokehouse, sometimes right on the ground. The fire was started every morning and left unattended for most of the day. Nobody worried if it went out, as it would be restarted again the following morning.

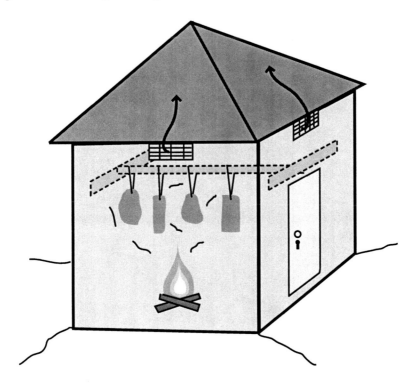

Fig. 11.1.2 American XVIII century smokehouse.

Such a simple design did not permit temperature, air speed, or smoke density control. There was an uneven smoke and draft distribution and blind pockets were created. To compensate for that the smoke sticks and screens had to be periodically re-arranged and hung at least 5 feet above the fire. After meats were smoked for about two weeks, they were hung in a different area of the smokehouse where they remained for up to two years. Thus the smokehouse functioned as a storage facility at the same time.

Humidity control was of little importance as the products were smoked and not air dried as was the case in Southern Europe. In countries such as Italy or Spain, humidity control was a highly desired and guarded skill. It was accomplished by placing water filled containers inside of the smoking/drying chamber and by placing wet towels on incoming air screens. In some European homes the meats were hung on top of the chimney. The serious drawback was that the meat had to accept any kind of smoke produced by the kitchen stove. Two strong nails were hammered into the walls of the chimney and a strong wire was stretched between them.

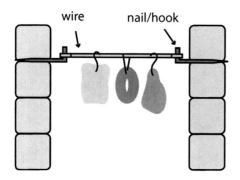

Fig. 11.1.3 Hanging meats in the chimney.

Another solution was to attach a wooden box to the bread stove or any wood burning appliance.

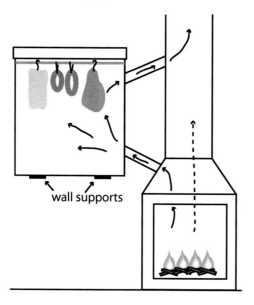

Fig. 11.4 Box on the wall.

A much better design was attaching a smokehouse to the chimney on the second floor. Two holes were made in the chimney: one for the smoke to enter the chamber and another to allow it to escape. On the other side a flat damper was pushed in or out of the chimney allowing the smoke to go straight up or forcing it to flow into the smokehouse.

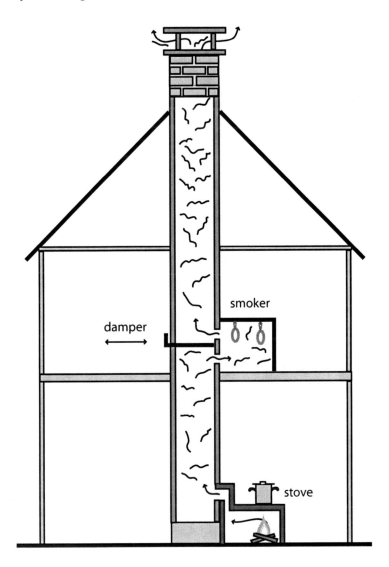

Fig. 11.1.5 Home chimney smoker.

Old Commercial Smokehouses

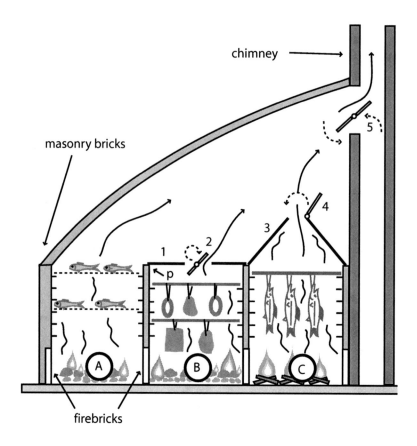

Fig. 11.1.6 Multi-chamber smokehouse.

Unit A - first generation multi-chamber smokehouse

Individual smokehouses were constructed on both sides of the chimney. That was a rather inefficient design as it required heating up not only each of the units (A) but the entire smokehouse chamber as well. Needless to say the wood usage was huge. The exiting smoke was controlled by a common to all chimney damper (5).

Unit B - improved design

A metal plate (1) was placed on top of each unit. This metal ceiling had an adjustable opening that was controlled by a flat metal damper (2). The weakness of this design was moisture gathered in the corners under the ceiling (p) which was dripping down on hanging products decreasing their looks and quality. The chimney damper was not needed anymore.

Unit C - second generation multi-chamber smokehouse

The next improvement was a design where each unit was independent of the others. It had a steep sloping conical ceiling (3) that provided an easier exit path for the smoke eliminating the problem of moisture pockets. The top of the ceiling was covered by an adjustable metal plate (4) that was controlled by a pull chain.

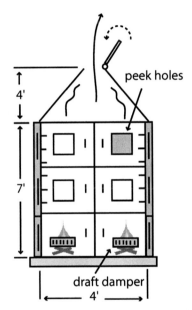

A few units shared smoke exit channels that led into a common chimney. Some units could be dedicated to cold smoking and some to hot smoking as the areas were physically separated which allowed for finer temperature control. In some smokehouses each unit had its own exit channel that would enter a common chimney. The size of the chimney was dictated by the size and the number of the individual units that shared that chimney. In most cases the front door consisted of three parts as shown in the drawing on the left.

Fig. 11.1.7 A typical door.

Double-sided door was divided into three parts:

1. Bottom door-provided access to the fire pit. It had built-in dampers for air supply control.
2. Middle door-used for loading the fish. It had peek holes for checking progress of smoking.
3. Top door-used for loading the fish.

Both sides were hinged and swung wide open for easy operation of the unit. Another interesting innovation was the design of a smokehouse consisting of two traditional smokehouses that shared a common and movable divider wall. The bottom section of the divider wall was built from firebricks (3' high) and a metal plate rested on top of them. This plate would be pulled up to allow the fish cart to travel from one unit to the other. One unit was dedicated to drying/cooking fish without applying smoke and the second one was for smoking only. There was hardly any fire in the second unit (smoke producer) and only little occasional flames were seen on top of the wood chips.

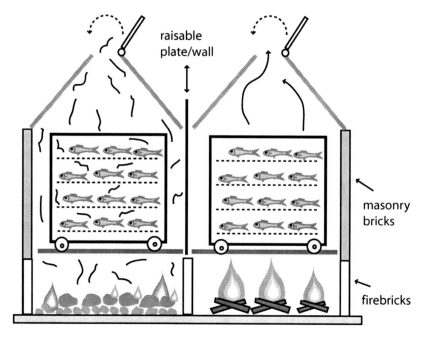

Fig. 11.1.8 Separate smoking/cooking smokehouse.

It should be noted that some 100 years ago a preferred method of hot smoking consisted of three stages:

1. Drying – 140-194° F (60-90° C).
2. Baking – up to 250° F (122° C).
3. Smoking – real smoking with a heavy smoke and dropping temperatures.

A relatively strong and steady fire would be burning at 140-250° F (60-122° C) to dry/bake fish which would normally take 1-2 hours. Then the metal divider plate/wall would be raised and the cart would travel into the smoking chamber. The purpose of this unit was to produce heavy smoke which was accomplished by burning wood chips. This process would normally last about two hours and the final temperature would be about 140° F (60° C). That design saved fuel, time, and permitted cleaner and safer conditions in the plant. It also created well defined and separate areas of operation:

- Fresh fish preparation-cleaning, washing, brining, loading.
- Drying/baking- steady fire allowing for easier temperature control.
- Smoking- constant smoke generation by burning wood chips.
- Cooling/packing-easier temperature control by controlling draft and using motor-driven fans.

Multilevel Smokehouses

Many three story buildings were converted into commercial smokehouses for smoking fish. A typical smokehouse would consist of:

- Basement-where a firebox/smoke producer would be located.
- First floor- smoke chamber.
- Second floor-smoke chamber.

A typical smokehouse consisted of 3-10 individual smoke chambers. These chambers were divided by a masonry brick wall going all the way from the basement to the roof. The smoke would exit through an adjustable hinged door or through rotating wind turbines. The units were about 3'6" wide and up to 15 feet long. The width was more critical as the worker was using corbells (bricks) that protruded from the wall as a ladder. He was climbing up them to hang the smoke sticks that were passed to him from another worker standing below.

On each wall there were about 20 corbells separated from each other by about 5 inches. Each unit on the second floor had its own door that gave access to the smoke chamber. After opening the door a wooden board was placed on top of the beams to provide a walkway for hanging more fish inside.

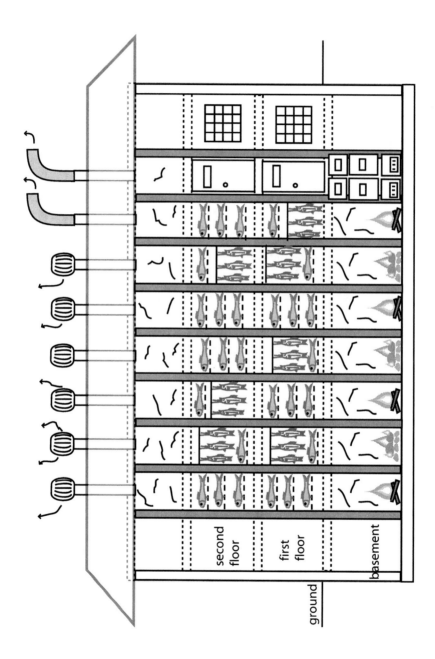

second floor

first floor

basement

ground

Fig. 11.1.9 Multilevel smokehouse.

142

Torry Kiln Smokehouse

Until 1939 most smokehouses were always built the same. They depended on a natural draft movement (air going up) to control the flow of heat and smoke without any means of humidity control. The majority of these smokehouses smoked meats for preservation purposes and the temperature was of little concern as long as the smoke was cold. Torry Kiln was the first design that employed an independent means of draft and temperature control. It was a mechanical kiln that used blowers to push smoke and electrical or steam heaters to generate heat.

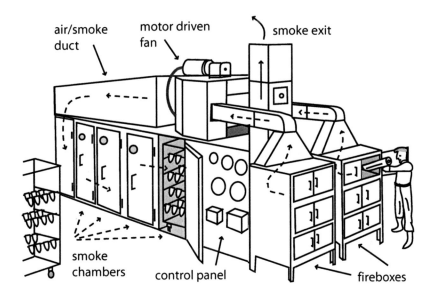

Fig. 11.1.10 Torry Kiln smokehouse.

The Torry Kiln design allowed for precise control of smoking parameters such as air temperature, its speed, and humidity. As a result the finished product was always of a consistent high quality. The Torry Kiln design incorporated a motor-driven fan, electric heaters, temperature sensors, air-diffusers, and even a photo-electric eye for smoke density control.

The inlet and outlet diffuser walls allowed for a very uniform air flow in all areas of the smokehouse. At the bottom part of the channel there was a recirculation damper (12) that controlled how much air was going out to the chimney (13) and how much air was returning back towards the fan (5). Fresh air was brought into the same area (14). Temperature sensors (15) controlled heaters (4 and 10).

Smoke was generated by three independently controlled fireboxes (1) that were standing above each other. Each had its own loading door and smoke damper. That provided a large smoke generating area without taking up much space. It also prevented soot and other large unburned particles from reaching hanging fish. The smoke would enter a common duct (2) and would be deflected by aerofoils (3) towards the electric heater (4). The motor-driven fan (5) would blow the heated air through the adjustable vertical blinds (6) towards aerofoil plates (7). At the bottom of the diffuser channel the air had to pass through the inlet diffuser wall (8) that contained many individually adjustable openings for the air flow adjustment. From there the heated air or smoke would pass through loaded with fish trolleys (9). Inside the smoke chamber there was an additional booster electric heater (10). The air/smoke leaving the chamber had to pass through the outlet diffuser wall (11) that consisted of fully adjustable openings.

As technology evolved, the brick and cinder block smokehouses were replaced with insulated stainless steel units. Electrical blowers and metal ducts were supplying smoke and the rotating dampers distributed heat precisely to all areas of the smokehouse. This second generation of smokehouses was called the batch oven type. In batch smokehouses, the meat is hung on smoke sticks or placed on stationary racks for the entire smoking process.

Then came smokehouses where meat traveled through the various zones (smoking, heating, chilling) within the smokehouse. The product was packaged and stored or shipped.

Drawings: Fig. 11.1.10 and Fig.11.1.11 courtesy The Food and Agriculture Organization of the United Nations. 11.1.9-doc.source: Kippers www.fao.org/wairdocs/tan/x5925E/x5925e01.htm 11.1.10-doc.source: Notes on Fish Handling and Processing www.fao.org/wairdocs/tan/x5927E/x5927e01.htm

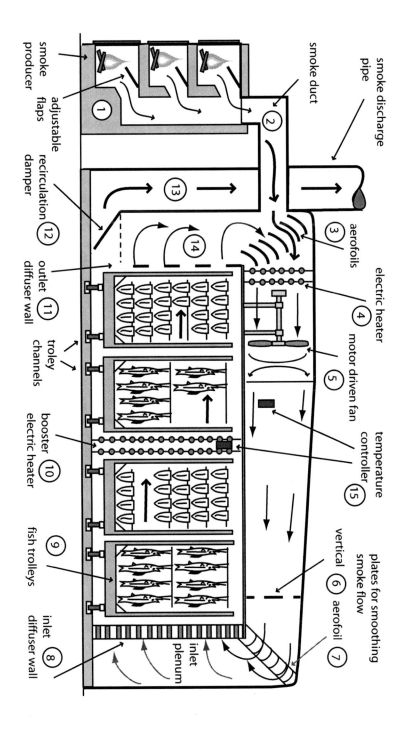

Fig. 11.1.11 Torry Kiln cross-section view.

145

11.2 Design Criteria

Understanding Smoking Process

Smoking meat is exactly what the name implies: *flavoring meat with smoke. Anyway you can and using any kind of improvised device* will do a splendid job as long as your creation is made from environmentally safe material. As long as smoke contacts the meat surface it will impart its flavor and the strength of the flavor depends mainly on the time and density of the smoke. *Smoking may or may not be followed by cooking.* Generally we may say that smoking in most cases consists of two steps:

1. Smoking

2. Cooking - this step determines the design and quality of your smokehouse as it needs temperature controls, reliable heat supply and good insulation to hold the temperature when the weather gets cold. *If cooking is performed outside the smokehouse, the unit can be incredibly simple*, for example an empty cardboard box.

We know now that the smoked meat must be cooked, but *where in the world does it say that it must be cooked inside of the smokehouse?* Don't we have wonderfully designed and factory built electrical or gas stoves inside every kitchen? They are insulated, have the built-in temperature controls and are almost begging for these smoked sausages to be baked inside. How about putting your smoked meats or sausages into a pot full of hot water and cooking these products on top of the stove? People seldom realize that about 50% of sausages are poached in hot water (around 80° C, 176° F) until fully cooked, which on the average takes 15-60 minutes, depending on the diameter of the product. Smoked sausages, hams, liver and blood sausages, head cheeses are all cooked in water.

A smokehouse is just a tool but smoking is time, temperature, and humidity, and how you control those parameters. The tool does not make a quality product - YOU DO! *If you understand the smoking process you will create a top quality product in any smoker and in any conditions.* And making quality products depends on meat selection, curing, smoking, cooking temperatures and other processing steps. Each step influences the step that follows, and all those steps when performed correctly will, as a final result, create the quality product. Almost any smokehouse will do for home production.

If you see smoke sipping through your cardboard box, you are smoking meat, its that simple. It does not have to be perfectly tight if the cooking process will be performed somewhere else. Commercial manufacturers make thousands of pounds of product an hour and they work by different rules to be cost effective. They have to produce a constant quality product that will be accepted every day by the supermarkets. They need fancy computerized equipment which costs millions of dollars. A hobbyist is not bound by those rules as he has plenty of time to watch smoke going out of his paper box smoker.

Design Notes

The presented information is aimed at home made smokers or smokehouses. The smokehouses used for commercial applications will be of course much bigger in size and the economy of running efficient day to day operation will play the major role in their design. Those factors are of lesser importance for a home sausage maker who smokes meats for himself a few times a year. It doesn't make much sense to blindly build a smoker to impress your friends and then later find out that it is ill suited for a particular climate because it can not generate enough heat to cook your products. It can look extremely sophisticated, but if it isn't effective, your friends won't be impressed.

It helps to first get familiar with the smoking process by using the simplest and the cheapest smoker available. That way you can develop the feel for what is expected from a smoker and most importantly gain valuable experience. After the first few smoking sessions you will be in a position to draw your own conclusions. The next step is to write down a few design notes:

Main purpose of the smoker – what climate are we in, can we create cold smoke all year round or only in winter months? Do we intend to fully cook our product in a smoker or only smoke it and cook it at home?

Cold smoke – do we want to cold smoke our products ? If yes, we may need a separate fire pit.

Location – where do we physically place the smoker, do we have a ground with a slope, can we sense prevailing winds and in which direction are they blowing? Do we need a support base, do we need to dig a trench for the pipe and how long should it be? Do we have water access?

Type and shape of the smoker – do we want a common metal barrel or a wooden box, steel, concrete blocks or bricks?

Materials needed – wood, metal, concrete block, brick, firebrick. What about insulation?

Smoker's size – how much meat do we intend to smoke at one time? Just for ourselves or for the whole block party?

Fire pit design – how big, what kind of bricks, cover, air draft. Do we want a fire pit inside of the smoker or free standing but connected with a pipe? De we want to cook the meat inside the smoker? Do we need secondary combustion to create higher temperatures?

Pipe – what material, what diameter, what angle, and how long?

Baffles – what kind, how many, diameter of holes, how thick.

Doors – how many, what material, do we want a built in draft control?

Screens – how many? What kind of supports?

Smoke sticks – how strong, what diameter, and how long?

Draft and its control – incoming air adjustment.

Smoke stack and damper control - how do we adjust and control the smoke exhaust?

Thermometers - how many and what type?

Maximum temperature and its control - do we want to only smoke meats or cook them as well? How can we control the temperature when using only wood for fuel?

Hardware - how do we connect all those parts and pieces? Do we need a welder or just a drill and saw?

Ash removal and cleaning - what about ashes and general cleaning?

Fuel type - wood only, electricity, gas, or a combination of the three?

There are basically three types of smokers and your design will be based on one of them:

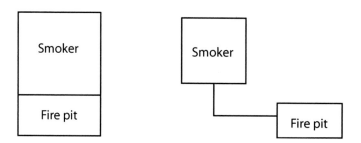

Fig. 11.2.1 Smoker and fire pit are one unit. Located at the bottom, the fire pit serves as a smoke generator and a heat supply.

Fig. 11.2.2 Smoker with separate fire pit. Free standing fire pit serves as a smoke generator and a heat supply.

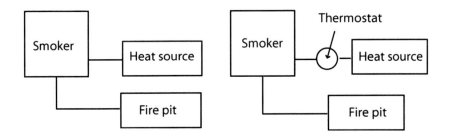

Fig. 11.2.3 Smoker with a separate fire pit and an independent heat supply.

Fig. 11.2.4 Smoker with a separate fire pit and an independent heat source controlled by a thermostat.

11.3 Smokehouse Design Principles

There is very little written information about constructing smokers. Old government designs exist on the Internet, and some have redesigned them as technical guides for building smokehouses for profit. However, the basic problem remains; these are just copied drawings and there is very little input on how and why a smoker should be built. The variety of smoker designs is certainly amazing, as is the imagination and ingenuity of those who built them. There are smokers made from plywood boxes, old refrigerators, metal drums and barrels, welded metal sheets, bricks and concrete blocks, *and they are all good as long as they produce smoke.*

Smokers are sold at popular department stores, garden centers, and on the Internet. Some are vertical, some horizontal, but they all perform the same basic function, to supply smoke. It doesn't matter how pretty it looks or what type of a device is being used to produce the smoke. What's more important is that it will be practical and easy to operate; many smokers require continuous baby sitting on the part of the operator. The properly designed smokehouse must:

- Generate smoke.
- Be able to achieve and maintain desired temperatures inside.
- Be able to cook the product to the required inside meat temperature, most often 154-160° F (68-72° C).

This last cooking requirement can be performed outside of a smoker by poaching meat in hot water or baking it in the oven and that will simplify the design greatly. Some meats are cooked in a smoker to make them ready to eat, while some will only receive a smoky flavor and will be taken out for prolonged periods of air drying.

The majority of so called smokers that can be bought in large department stores are either grills or barbecue cookers. On many of them the built-in thermometer starts indicating temperatures from 200° F (93° C) and higher, and such high temperatures have nothing in common with traditionally smoked meats. Moreover, they are all of a horizontal design but the real smoker is a vertically standing unit. Wherever meat or sausage comes in contact with any surface (a rack or a screen) or touches one another, the area of contact will remain pale and will not develop the right color. Customers will not buy such a product. The only difference applies to small fish or fish fillets which are very delicate and if not placed on a screen, they will fall apart. Nevertheless there are some companies that make combination units that perform a dual function of being a grill and a fully functioning smoker.

Photo. 11.3.1 Well designed grill-smoker.

Photo courtesy Tejas Smokers, Houston, TX.

The firebox is on the right, the grill in the middle and the smoker on the left. Smoke/heat flows from the firebox and through the barbecue/grill section into the smoking chamber. The smoking chamber contains screens resting on adjustable brackets. Screens can be removed and smokesticks can be placed on the brackets.

The adjustable smoke stack on top of the smoker controls the draft and the barbecue/grill section becomes the smoke delivery pipe. The screens are removable and the smokesticks can be hung instead.

Photo. 11.3.2 Inside view.

Photo courtesy Tejas Smokers, Houston, TX.

When smoking with a separate fire pit, we have more time to enjoy ourselves because we don't have to check the temperature so often. The sausage can be subsequently cooked in the kitchen. However, we are playing a completely different game if we want the smoker to cook the meat. Now outside temperatures become important factors. The smoker may need some insulation to maintain appropriate temperatures, especially during the colder months.

Holding internal temperatures of 152-160° F (67-72° C) can be difficult in cold climates when the smoker is situated outside. Maintaining temperatures by burning wood in a 55 gallon metal drum is a hit or miss proposition. The best solution, which is incidentally used in commercial smokers, is to rely less on the smoke generator or fire pit as our only heating source, but to install a second independent heat source.

The heating process is now shared by two separate components:

- A fire pit to generate smoke.
- An electrical heating element or gas burner to generate heat.

By using two components we can produce a quality product in any climate. A metal drum, unless insulated, is still a poor choice in hard winters, but anything built with brick or thick wood is fine. It should be noted that the whole design changes drastically when there is a supply of electricity. With a stand-alone fire pit, we can use a barbecue starter wire for heating wood chips or sawdust until they start producing smoke. Inside the smoker we can place an electric heating element to supply heat with a turn of the dial. By adding a thermostat to the arrangement, we can preset the temperature of a smoker. A gas burner can also be used as a source of heat.

Basic parts of a smoker

Every smoker, no matter how simple or sophisticated, consists of the following parts:

- A source of smoke (fire pit).
- A smoking chamber (enclosure that will confine smoke inside).
- Smokesticks, hooks or screens.
- Draft controls (dampers).

The most important parts are the smoke generator (fire pit) and the smoke chamber. They could be part of the same unit or they could stand separately. With smaller smokers it is difficult to control the heating process by burning wood unless an electrical heating element or a gas burner is used.

Smoker with a fire pit inside

Photo 11.3.3 Drum smoker. It can accommodate an electrical heating element as shown on the photo (note the cord). Note a stem thermometer on top cover.

Wood fired smoker

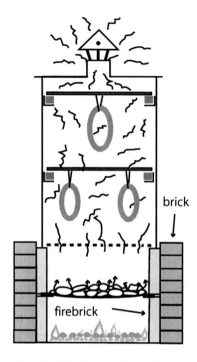

Using firewood to slowly bring the temperature to 170° F (76° C) and maintain it at that level for about 30 minutes is extremely difficult. Irregular sizes of wood need to be constantly added on. One moment of negligence and the temperature soars over 200° F. Without a safety baffle, this can be disastrous for a smoked product. The fat inside the sausage will melt, leak through the casings, and drop on the small flames in the fire pit below. These little flames will not be little anymore. If left unattended, a small controlled flame will turn into a raging fire. The sausage casings will become so dry and brittle that the sausages themselves will fall down into the fire pit.

Fig. 11.3.1 One unit smoker.

Smokers with a separate smoke generator

When the amount of air is limited severely, the resulting smoke is very dark as it contains a large number of unburned particles. Such smoke is generally undesirable for smoking meats and it can produce a bitter flavor. The design of a good smokehouse should provide for ample air supply during combustion. To fully utilize the little space small smokers have at their disposal, a separate smoke generator should be used. The benefits of a separate smoke generator are numerous:

- Ability to provide cooler smoke.
- Better flame control.
- Easier control of a smoking/cooking process.

In the woods, simply dig a trench. The sides and top must be supported somehow with rocks or pieces of plywood. Use caution, as these can collapse when stepped on. Any small heat fluctuation coming from the smoke generator will not have much effect on the temperature inside the smoking chamber.

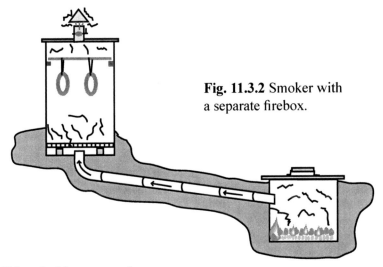

Fig. 11.3.2 Smoker with a separate firebox.

Traditional chimney smokers

It is hard to beat the effectiveness of a smoker that is connected to a fire pit with a pipe or a trench in the ground. The distance between them should be about 4-7" (1.2-2.1 m) and they should stand on a different level, with the smoker obviously higher than the fire pit. The connecting trench must be covered with at least 2" (5 cm) of soil to provide insulation. The rest depends on the imagination and technical skills of the builder and can involve dozens of different arrangements. Two metal drums can be used (one for the smoker and the other for the fire pit). For the smoker, a simple wooden box will do. The fire pit can be built from bricks, stones, or some other elaborate design.

Smoke delivery pipe

There is no fixed rule for the length of the pipe. A 4 –7' (1.2–2 m) pipe seems to be the preferred length in most installations. This figure is based on the fact that in a confined area with an adequate supply of air, the flames can shoot up as high as 5 feet. An important thing is that it has sufficient draft for the smoke to flow freely. The pipe connecting the fire pit and the smoker should be 6" (15 cm) in diameter and made of suitable materials such as stainless steel, metal stove pipe, sewer clay pipe, or a concrete pipe, but never plastic. For smaller smokers a 4" diameter pipe is acceptable. A little incline of 5–10 degrees will help direct the smoke into the chamber. Increasing the angle even more is not practical because it will require digging a very deep hole to accommodate a fire pit. Placing smokers on a very high base is inconvenient for loading. It is amazing how many designs call for a 12 foot long pipe, yet, they do not provide any reasons for such a length. The feasible explanation would be to cool the smoke down but how can you bring the smoke temperature down to 70° F (21° C) when it's a baking hot 95° F (35° C) in the shade in Florida? The hot smoke enters the pipe where it will remain for a few seconds. Even submerging it in the Gulf of Mexico will not help because the average water temperature is 85° F (30 °C) for about 6 months out of the year. At best you can generate cold smoke at night time in December, January and February when at night the temperatures drop down to 50° F (10° C).

The same pipe (if made of metal) will be effective in cooler climates allowing cold smoke generation for most of the year. What about those who smoke in the Northern States, Canada, and Northern Europe? They don't need a long pipe to cool down the smoke; they may have problems generating sufficient heat to cook the product. An exposed long metal pipe will lose so much heat in winter months that it will have to be insulated. Before we decide on the length of the pipe it would be wise to answer the following questions:

- Do we need cold smoke?
- Do we want to cold smoke the whole year or just in winter months?
- What temperatures can be expected at night time?

In the past the cold smoke problem was solved by building high smoking towers that were 18' tall. The smoke would come in through a trench from a free standing fire pit outside. The height of the tower induced a lot of natural draft and the smoke was quite cold before escaping the smoking chamber. Bear in mind that the countries in Europe where most serious smoking is done lie in the latitude of Quebec, Canada, where the climate is much cooler than the rest of continental USA. If you like to use cold smoke, then wait for the winter months. In the summer, you are better off to smoke products with hot smoke.

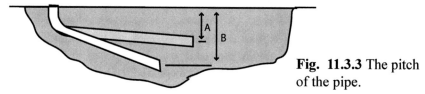

Fig. 11.3.3 The pitch of the pipe.

In the above drawing, pipe B is shorter than pipe A but it has a bigger angle and induces more draft. For instance, to achieve a 30 degree angle with a 10' (3m) pipe, the smoker's base has to be placed 5 ft (1.5 m) higher than the firepit. It is possible, however, to achieve a bigger angle and more draft by taking advantage of a mountainous terrain.

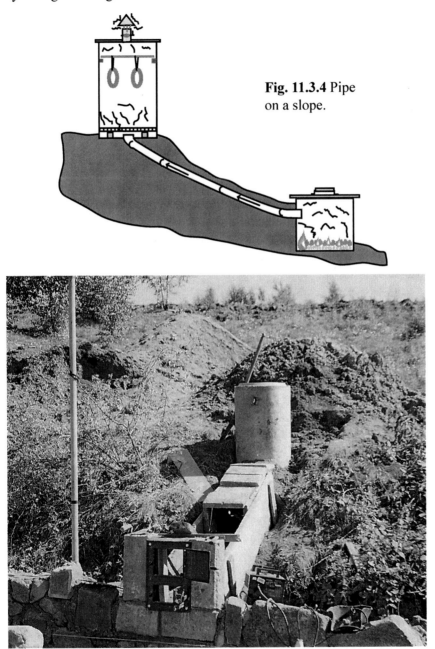

Fig. 11.3.4 Pipe on a slope.

Photo 11.3.4 Taking advantage of a mountainous terrain.

The pipe does not have to run straight and it can incorporate one or two elbows to change directions. Too many turns will decrease the draft.

Pipe material

Any environmently friendly material could be used for making pipes, and some of the best ones are listed. Stainless steel, metal, concrete, sewer pipe, clay pipe and stove pipes are all good materials. Air conditioning duct pipe is also good, and it comes in different sizes. There is a wide assortment of elbows, reducers, as well as other connectors made of galvanized steel. They are inexpensive, very easy to work with, commonly available, but there is one drawback.

To tell if galvanized steel is good for smoking is like trying to decide which came first, the chicken or the egg. Galvanized sheets are made of metal sheets that are dipped into a hot bath of melted zinc and other chemicals. Zinc melts at 787° F (420°C), and boils at 1,665° F (907° C). Although zinc presents no danger, a metallic element such as cadmium is bad for our health.

Determining the exact composition of a particular pipe is difficult. This is why the Food Safety and Inspection Service of the United Stated Department of Agriculture says *'Don't smoke foods in makeshift containers such as galvanized steel cans or other materials not intended for smoking'*. With every puff of a cigarette, we probably inhale more chemicals than if we had smoked meat for 100 hours with a galvanized pipe. But to keep our conscience clear, we decided to present the official view of our government.

Before smoking for the first time, any section of pipe that makes direct contact with burning wood in the fire pit should be burned with hot fire. This takes care of initially burning away any deposits. The rest of the pipe is exposed to such low temperatures that it can not possibly react with any chemicals that were deposited on its surface during the manufacturing process. Better still, break your pipe into separate sections. The section that makes direct contact with a fire pit can be made of steel, tile pipe, or reinforced concrete, and the rest can be made of galvanized duct.

A flexible dryer pipe

A very original solution is to use a flexible dryer exhaust pipe. It is made of aluminum and it stretches like an accordion. Though it is not a very strong material, it is perfect for above the ground solutions. It can be combined with air conditioning duct accessories such as couplers, elbows, and reducers to create almost any configuration.

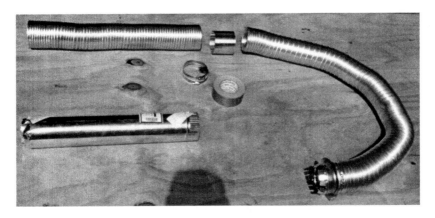

Photo 11.3.5 Flexible dryer pipe.

Diffuser

The preferred method of compensating for uneven smoke distribution in a smokehouse was a periodic re-arrangement of the smokesticks. This task becomes much easier to accomplish with an installation of a diffuser which is a galvanized metal box, 1 foot (30 cm) square and 2 feet (60 cm) high, open at the bottom.

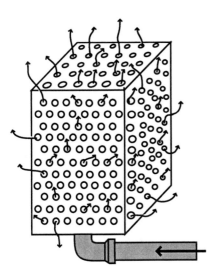

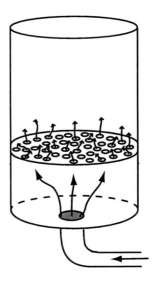

Fig. 11.3.5 Box diffuser in a large smokehouse.

Fig. 11.3.6 Baffle diffuser in a small smoker.

159

Three-quarter-inch (19 mm) holes are drilled or punched in the sides and top to permit the escape of smoke. The diffuser is placed over the mouth of the elbow and allows for an even distribution of smoke throughout the smokehouse. In most cases the smoke delivery pipe enters the smokehouse at the bottom but a side entrance is perfectly acceptable. It will even keep the pipe's mouth cleaner as there will be less grease or other debris falling down to it. It will be advisable to place a gas burner below the entrance of the pipe for two reasons:

- Less chance for the gas flames to go out.
- Gas burner will remain cleaner.

A good solution is to physically separate incoming smoke and the gas burner by installing a heat baffle, which is nothing more than a metal plate. It could be of conical or oval shape but the flat baffle is the easiest to find and install. A baffle can be placed on a few bricks and it will work fine.

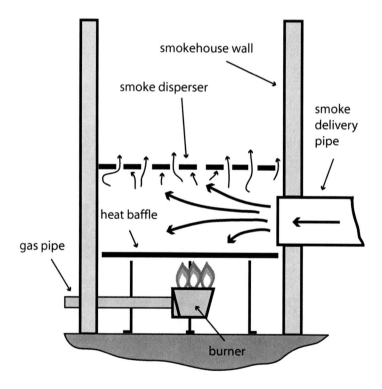

Fig. 11.3.7 Heat baffle.

Another advantage of the flat baffle is that you could place a metal pan with sawdust on it to generate smoke. You could even place wood chips directly on the heat baffle. The heat baffle will absorb the heat from the burner and it will then radiate heat up to the hanging products. This will allow for more even distribution of the heat. The smoke baffle (smoke disperser) is always a good idea as it allows for uniform distribution of the smoke. The same arrangement can be used for an electrical heat element. Although incoming smoke can not switch off the heating element, nevertheless the latter will stay cleaner.

It is not easy to visualize the way smoke behaves and flows inside the pipe or smoking chamber. The best way is to imagine *how water will behave if placed under the same conditions.* If water hits the wall straight on we can expect a heavy splash and turbulence. A heavy boulder in the middle of the stream will divide the stream. If the river takes on a gradual turn there will be a smooth flow of water, if there is a sharp 90 degrees turn, there might be a blind pocket of water in the corner. When planning to install a smoke delivery pipe, it may be beneficial to think in the above terms.

Wind - in mountains or windy areas it is a good idea to place a fire pit in a position where the smoke will follow the direction of the prevailing wind. For instance, if the wind blows from the south to the north, the fire pit should be placed south of the smoker. In this manner, we no longer fight against the wind but use it to lead smoke into the chamber.

Trench - digging a trench instead of installing a pipe creates a weaker and impermanent design. Nevertheless, for those in a hurry or on a tight budget, it is a viable solution. It can be constructed anywhere with almost no costs involved.

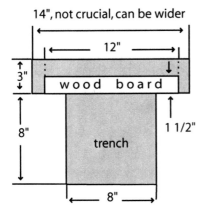

Fig. 11.3.8 Trench cross section.

A good trench is 8" wide by 11"deep (8" for the trench channel and 3" for the soil cover). The first dimension is crucial because the trench will be covered by a wooden plank 12" wide and 6' long, a size usually stocked by building supply stores. A gap of at least 12" is needed between the firepit and the beginning of the wood channel to eliminate the possibility of flames burning the wood boards. This gap is covered by a metal plate or a concrete slab measuring about 18"x18", available in any hardware store. In the wilderness, we have to find suitable rocks that will perform the same task. The last thing to do is to cover everything with at least 3" of soil.

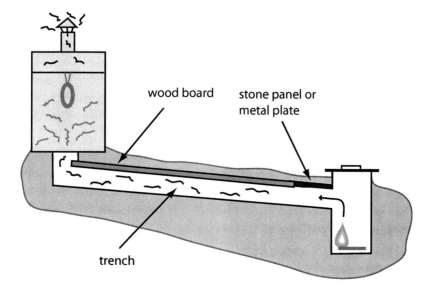

wood board

stone panel or metal plate

trench

Fig. 11.3.9 Safety gap (stone panel).

The trench should rise 1" per foot creating a 5 degree angle. Instead of a wood plank, four concrete slabs may be used, as long as they touch each other and prevent soil from falling between them. They come in different sizes, most often square and ranging from 12 inches to 18 inches and about 2" thick. A trench dug out in sandy soil will need some gravel and small rocks to reinforce it, or its walls may start to collapse.

Fire pit

The design is simple and consists of two holes in the ground and a trench. Connecting two holes with a pipe is not only faster to construct, it will also make a much better design.

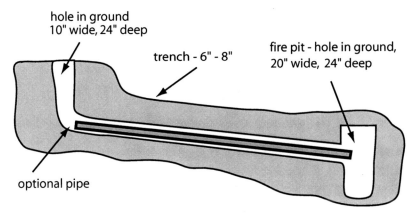

hole in ground
10" wide, 24" deep

trench - 6" - 8"

fire pit - hole in ground,
20" wide, 24" deep

optional pipe

Fig. 11.3.10 Trench and optional pipe.

Thermometers

Thermometers are one of the most important parts of your smoker. There is no way to determine the temperature inside the chamber simply by looking at the smoke, touching the drum, or inserting your hand into the smoker, no matter how experienced you are. When using a thermometer for the first time, most experienced individuals say they don't understand how they have been working so long without one. Well, one explanation is that for a long time they were not easily available in countries outside of the USA that were damaged by war. It turns out that these very countries are the ones with the longest tradition in smoking. Today, there is no excuse for not having one. The thermometer with the longest stem, 12" (30 cm), works best. When mounted on top of a smoker, it will read the temperature of the area where the meats are. It doesn't have to be permanently mounted. As long as there is a suitable hole, it can be inserted to determine meat temperatures, and then it can be removed when the smoking is finished.

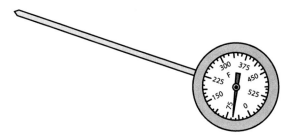

Fig. 11.3.11 Stem thermometer.

163

Photo 11.3.6 Bottle cork used to insulate thermometer from the metal.

Another thermometer is needed to read the temperature inside the meat while cooking. When the meats are smoked, they have the proper flavor and color, but they are still raw and need to be cooked inside a smoker or poached in water. In both cases a thermometer is needed to indicate when the meat reaches the safe internal temperature.

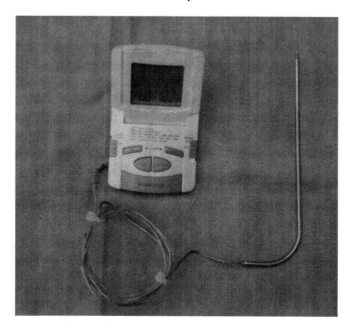

Photo 11.3.7 Meat thermometer.

This thermometer has a long temperature resistant cable. On one end there is a probe that is inserted into the cooked product and on the other there is the dial indicator, or electronic display that is kept outside. It is advisable to have a thermometer with a built-in sound alarm that would warn us when we have reached a pre-set temperature.

164

Electronic temperature control

There is little need for sophisticated thermometers when smoking meat. Any stem thermometer will indicate the temperature in a smokehouse and a digital meat thermometer with a remote probe will read the internal temperature of the meat. Such controls require manual supervision and are acceptable for short periods of smoking. Electric heaters may be wired with a thermostat making the smokehouse more user friendly. This requires some assembly and basic electronic skills.

Fortunately there is a wonderful and commonly available device called Line Voltage Thermostat which allows for very precise temperature control with 1° F accuracy. The device is inexpensive and can be ordered with preassembled extension cords. It is made by a number of companies (see Appendix B).

A heating element is plugged into the temperature control which is plugged into the electrical outlet or extension cord. The temperature sensor is placed inside of the smokehouse. The microprocessor monitors the temperature through the sensor and when the temperature is lower than the set point, the processor will energize the internal relay (switch). This allows the heater to draw current from the outlet. The drawing is not to scale and the typical unit is about: 6.5" x 2.7" x 2.5". These units can control coolers, heaters or any electrical device.

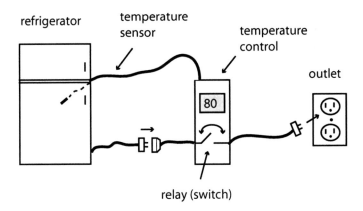

Fig. 11.3.12. Line voltage thermostat.

Draft

In simplest terms the draft is the sucking action of your smoker, it's pulling power that allows it to draw air into the fire pit for combustion and then pushes smoke into the smoking chamber. At the same time, it removes gases from the smoker through the exit opening, be it a stove pipe, chimney, or simply a hole in the top cover. In technical terms it is the pressure difference between the surrounding air of the firebox and the gases in the chimney. The higher the structure, the stronger the draft. *In a simple barrel smoker, starting the fire is enough to induce the necessary draft.* Masonry built smokers may include a chimney. However, this is more for looks than practical value because smokers work at rather low temperatures compared to other heating devices, which require more draft. Although smokers will produce smoke even with very little draft, the importance of draft cannot be understated. It is needed to suck out moisture and soot laden smoke that remains under the smoker's cover. Dry wood contains 20% moisture, and combined with the excess air that enters the smoke chamber, we would have to raise the temperature to almost 180° F (82° C) to prevent condensation, which would dry out the meat pieces. The right amount of draft solves the problem.

Smoking on uneven ground already creates some draft because one end of the pipe will be higher than the other. Factors such as chimney height, flue size, altitude, and the wind blowing over the chimney all contribute to the draft effect. Nevertheless, the single most contributing factor is the temperature difference between the outside air and the flue (chimney) temperature. This is why every smoker and wood stove operates better in cooler winter months than in the warmer days of summer.

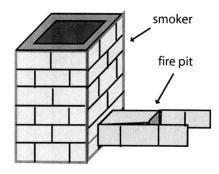

smoker

fire pit

Fig. 11.3.13 Simple smoker, no draft controls needed.

Some simple smokers are made from concrete blocks loosely arranged together and the smoke tunnel (about 3 feet long) is on the same level as the smoker. An old potato burlap sack is placed on top to control the smoke. The moment the air is warmed up, it goes straight up, and cold air takes its place creating a natural draft. This works fine for the simplest of smokers, but once accesories such as baffles, supports, smokesticks, hanging meat, and elbows in a pipe are added to the design, the smoke may need some extra sucking power (draft) to go up the chimney. Draft does not depend on the length of the pipe but on the difference in pressure (height) between the fire pit smoke outlet level and the smoke inlet level in a smoker. *A shorter steep pipe can create a stronger draft than a longer one with a smaller angle.*

What do we do if our smoker is not pulling out smoke? We could place our fire pit 2' under ground, but that would require running a connecting pipe or making a trench. In both cases we have to dig and if our construction rests on a concrete surface it creates a problem. Adding 2' of a metal pipe of 6" diameter to the top of our smoker is the solution. If a metal stove pipe is used as a smoke chimney, insulating it from the outside temperature will induce a stronger draft inside the system. The effect will be most noticeable in the cooler months of fall and winter when the draft is always the strongest.

Draft controls

Controlling smoke exhaust is of utmost importance when smoking meats. It is accomplished by installing a damper in a stovepipe, installing a smoke stack with a built-in damper, lifting up the smoker's cover, adding or removing burlap bags, covering open holes in the top cover, or any other means that we have at our disposal. There isn't a standard solution because there are so many different smokers. The two main reasons to control smoke exhaust are as follows:

- It has to be fully opened to warm up the smoker and to get rid of moisture.
- To control smoke outflow when smoking.

A smoker is not a wood stove whose purpose is to warm up the house or boil the water and its temperature expectations run much lower. That also means that there is no need to create an extremely strong draft. Once we start cooking meats inside the smoker and the temperatures are higher, draft becomes much more important. More draft is needed to burn wood cleanly and efficiently. The easiest device to control draft is a flat damper which is basically a flat piece of metal. The damper simply slides in and out of a slit in the stove pipe or brick chimney.

Smoked meats need a supply of fresh air that brings moisture with it. An adjustable opening is needed in the center of the smoker's cover to let the moisture out. Any cover will do, even cardboard can be raised an inch or two to accomplish this task.

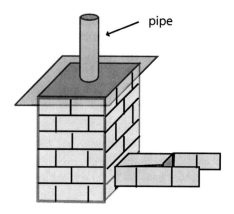

pipe

Fig. 11.3.14 Increasing draft by adding an extra section of the pipe.

A fire pit does not have to be totally sealed and enclosed when smoking. If smoke is coming out of the smoker, that means that the fire pit is doing its job. Once smoking is complete and we decide to continue cooking meats inside the smoker, enclosing and insulating the smoker and fire pit become more important. A little conical shield on top of a smoke exit pipe will give it a nice touch. At the same time it protects the pipe from rain and serves as a spark arrester. There is no preferred fixed diameter for a smoke exit pipe but a 6 inch (15 cm) pipe seems to be the unwritten standard.

All real smokers, whether home made or commercial quality, are vertically standing units where meats hang on smoke sticks. This is to isolate products from touching anything as that will obstruct smoke penetration and will leave pale marks on smoked products.

11.4 Drum Smoker

Without a doubt the most common design in the world is the 55 gallon (200 liter) drum smoker. Its well deserved popularity is due to the fact that it is:

- Easy to find and is practically free.
- Almost finished with the hardest work done by the factory.
- Very strong, made of metal.
- Versatile, can be used as a smoker, woodstove, or heating stove.
- Resistant to heat, lends itself to be used as a firepit.
- Easy to work with – no need for technical skills or specialized tools, the bottom can be cut out with a chisel and a hammer (top in many cases is removable).

Barrels come in different sizes but anything smaller than 55 gal (200 liters) should be reserved for use as a fire pit. After all the accessories are installed inside, a small barrel will offer little practical value. Even a regular size 55 gal (200 l) barrel requires a lot of attention when used as a smoker. At least 9" (23cm) of bottom space has to be designated as a fire pit area. Additionally, we need to add at least one baffle that eliminates another 4" (14 cm). Since there is 3" (8 cm) of unusable space on the top, we now have about 18" (46 cm) of vertical space for smoking. It is enough to hang one level of smoke sticks (2-3 in total).

However, the main problem is that because the smoker is confined to such a small internal space, it becomes very sensitive to any temperature changes. Every time we lift up the top cover, most of the heat escapes. When more wood is added, the temperature rises almost immediately. Baby sitting the smoking process becomes extremely labor intensive.

There are designs that incorporate increasing the size of the drum, but this involves adding an extra section from another drum which will require cutting and usually welding, making it a serious undertaking. The metal barrel conducts heat rapidly and also loses it quickly when the outside temperature is low. Increasing draft and adding more fuel (wood) will hopefully allow the barrel to maintain high enough temperatures (170°-190 °F) to cook the meat. Otherwise the barrel will have to be insulated on the outside.

This approach can be questioned for the following reasons:

- It becomes technically more involved.
- It does not solve the limitations of the barrel: little space, danger of jumps in temperature.

By leaving the barrel alone and building a 24" high masonry base, we can avoid all those problems and create a much better smoker. It looks better too. A bigger smoker can easily be made by replacing the drum with a wooden box or masonry smoker.

Fig. 11.4.1 Door in the barrel.

Large multi-drum smokers are popular when built on trailers which are moved from place to place. They are costly units and building them involves a lot of welding.

Drum preparation

In most cases the bottom and top of the barrel can be removed with a hammer and a chisel. Sometimes, the top cover is connected with a radiator type clamp. In this case we are lucky because we have the ready made removable top of our smoker. Hold on to the cut out bottom, because it can be used as a baffle plate. Painting the inside is useless, since the paint will be burned and the chemicals may enter the meat. However, it can be painted on the outside with heat resistant paint. Before its first use, the barrel should be heated for a few hours to remove any substances that may still be clinging to the inside. Keep in mind that your newly made drum smoker will in most cases remain outside the house. In 2-3 years it will be rusty and not pretty anymore. Nevertheless, it is still a fine first time smoker.

Photo 11.4.1 It is easy to cut out the bottom of the drum.

Drum base

The drum base has to be round with a wide enough cap to support a standing drum. Fire bricks must be used inside, with the mortar joints made of fireclay. These can be found at all building supply centers. The easiest way to start is to use a marker to outline the outside of the drum, right on the slab of concrete where the base will be constructed. Then follow the line with the mortar and bricks.

Photo 11.4.2 Drum base.

To allow easy access inside, the entrance to the base is about 12" wide. Loading wood or putting in an electrical hot plate is now effortless. The base shown on the photograph is only one firebrick high (9", 21 cm). It was designed to be the base for the barrel and serve as a grill at the same time. Going any higher will not provide enough heat to grill the meat. It should be noted that by increasing the height of the support base, we are actually improving the design of the barrel smoker by increasing the amount of usable space.

Photo 11.4.3 Drum base/grill with a screen/baffle.

Photo 11.4.4 Finished smoker.

The flame limiting baffle can be placed on top of the base. Another option is to place medium size river gravel on top of the grill screen.

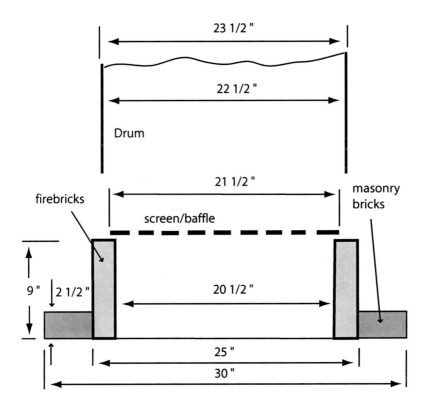

Fig. 11.4.2 Single baffle and a short base

Raising the base creates more space inside the drum. Increasing the base height to 24" (61 cm) provides ample space to install a second baffle, as well as an additional level of smoking sticks. This effectively doubles the amount of meat that can be smoked at any given time.

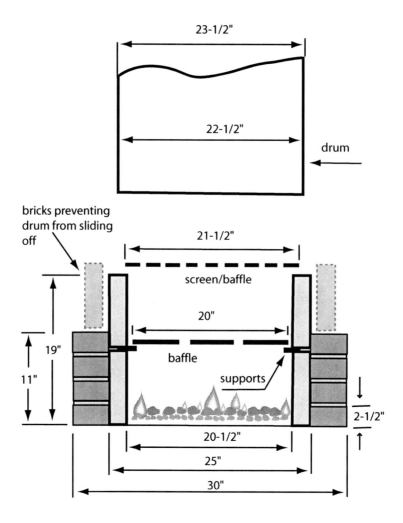

Fig. 11.4.3 Two baffles and a high base.

The lower baffle support is made of three 2" x 1/2" x 1/8" steel plates embedded every 120 degrees into refractory fireclay mortar. The upper baffle rests loosely on top of the fire bricks. The firebrick is 2 1/8" thick and this creates enough area to support the drum. Baffle supports should be inserted into damp mortar. If this becomes problematic, the easiest solution is to create an overlap by adding an additional level of bricks. An additional baffle can be installed in the lower part of the barrel. Now with two baffles, the barrel becomes an advanced smoker with lots of usable space.

The upper screen can be used as a baffle or to smoke fish fillets. Screens or baffles should be placed loosely on bricks or angle supports to facilitate cleaning. Loose placement offers the flexibility to change arrangements quickly and easily.

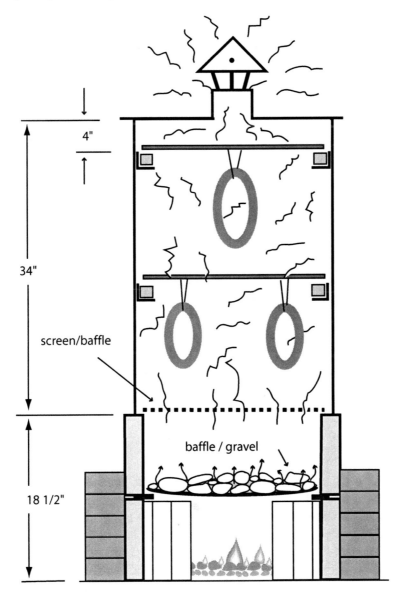

Fig. 11.4.4 High base and two levels of smoke sticks.

By laying two vertical rows of firebrick, we create a much bigger smoker with very little additional time or expense. It now becomes practical to install a second row of smoke sticks about 15" below the top one. This will double the usable smoking space. A little slope to help drain the inside of the base is a nice touch (1/8" per foot, 1 cm for 1 m), but don't forget to compensate for it when applying mortar to secure the bricks. Otherwise your drum will not be properly levelled (use a level). Water can drain out through the front opening, but you can make a couple of holes (1/2" diameter, 12 mm) in the mortar joints in the back. To make a hole, periodically insert a round stick in and out of the mortar while it is hardening. The drum can rest freely on the base and one person can easily put it on or take it down without any handles.

Smokesticks

Wood dovels can be found already precut in different lengths and diameters in building supply stores. Remember that sausages are often made into one long coil that will hang on on the smokestick. Wherever meat touches something (another meat, smoke stick or support) the color will be very pale since the smoke was not able to penetrate the meat.

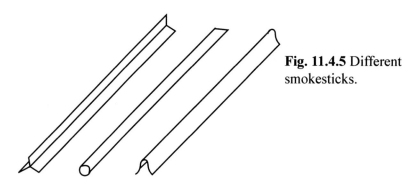

Fig. 11.4.5 Different smokesticks.

A smoke stick half an inch in diameter might bend under its own weight in the middle and the meats would slide down together. 5/8" is a better size. In many countries people just simply use a wooden broom stick, which is about 1" in diameter. In commercial establishments the smoke sticks are made from stainless steel and are usually a triangular shape so they don't roll over. These dovels are placed on a mobile cart and cannot be touched by hand when heated to high temperatures. Wooden dovels do not get as hot, which is why we use them in our home made smokers.

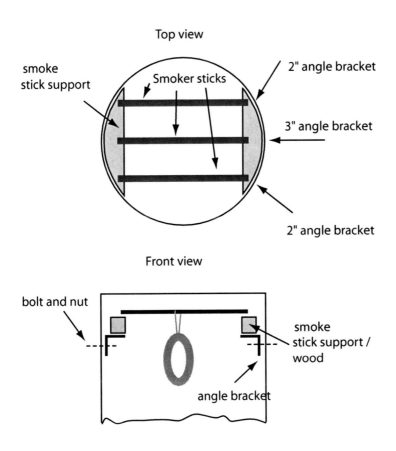

Fig. 11.4.6 Smokestick supports.

The support brackets should be v-notched to prevent the dovels from rolling over. The supporting bracket for the smokestick can be made of solid wood or metal. A common 2" x 4" piece is fine, but it should be mounted at such a height that its top should be about 2" below the top surface of the drum. Placing smokesticks on top of the bracket will give us about 4 inches (depending on smokestick's diameter) of unused space in the top area of the smoker.

We don't want our meats to hang there, because this area is very smoky, wet, and contains soot and other unburned particles. If the meats were hung there, they may acquire a bitter taste, lose some of their shine, and decrease in overall quality.

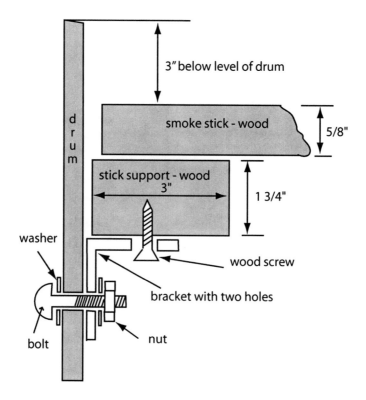

Fig. 11.4.7 Bracket attachment.

The easiest acceptable way to attach smokesticks is to leave them loosely on top of the drum. There is no work involved and the maximum usable space is created.

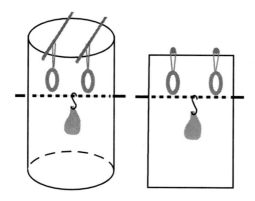

Smokesticks can also be pushed right through the body of the drum which will require drilling holes. This becomes inconvenient for loading sausages as the smokestick will have to be partially removed from the drum. Larger meat cuts may be hung on hooks.

Fig. 11.4.8 Simple ways of securing smokesticks.

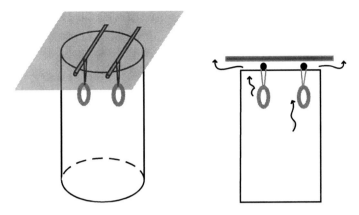

Fig. 11.4.9 Top cover resting on broom handles.

Top cover

The sophistication of the design will influence the type of cover. It can be:

- A metal plate with wooden handles for easier lifting.
- A wooden cover.
- A burlap bag.
- A piece of cardboard.

The top cover can be made of solid wooden planks that can have handles attached to them for easy lifting. A hole (round or square) of about 6" can be made in its center and a means to adjust its aperture should be provided. The hole can be omitted altogether by raising the cover over the barrel to let smoke escape. The way a top cover is designed and built has no bearing on the final quality of the product. It will only influence the cosmetic look of the smoker which is after all just a metal drum. In many simple barrel-smokers the meat hangs on broom handles that are placed loosely on top of the barrel. Any piece of plywood or flat cardboard box can serve as the top cover because the broom sticks provide enough clearance for the smoke to exit. More clearance can be created by inserting a section of a two by four piece of lumber on one or both sides. If the cover is made of metal, add wooden handles to it because it will get hot.

metal   wood handle

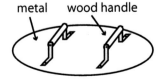

Fig. 11.4.10 Cover handles.

A burlap potato packing bag is a very practical design that allows just the right amount of smoke to sip through. If we need to confine more smoke inside we can simply place an additional bag on top of the first one.

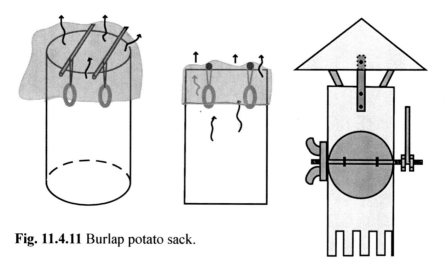

Fig. 11.4.11 Burlap potato sack.

Fig. 11.4.12 Controllable smoke stack can be mounted on top of the cover plate to enhance the look of the smoker and to control the smoke exhaust.

Barrel smoker with a separate fire pit

By placing a fire pit in a separate location the drum smoker is transformed into a smoker of higher caliber. This adds the following advantages:

- There is more usable space inside.
- There is no need for a baffle. A simple screen is sufficient to protect any meat that falls down.

Although it is possible to place the drum directly over the pipe supplying smoke, building a small drum base is highly recommended because it will protect the metal from water. There is no longer a need for firebricks because the fire pit is free standing and the temperatures inside the base will be much lower. Ordinary masonry bricks can now be used. The easiest way to implement this design is to find an uneven slope so that the barrel will be higher than the fire pit. Two drums can be used for that purpose. A small barrel is used for a fire pit and a bigger barrel becomes the smoker.

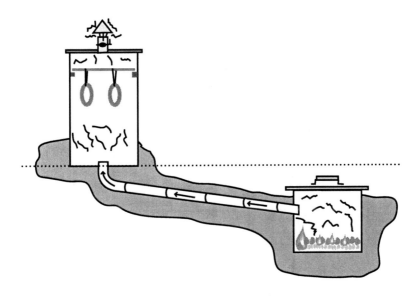

Fig. 11.4.13 Two barrels on uneven ground.

A support base eliminates the need for an opening to provide access into the smoker. The base can be built with bricks all around.

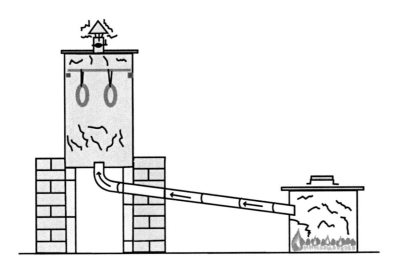

Fig. 11.4.14 Higher base, pipe above ground.

Smoke delivery pipe does not have to always enter the barrel from the bottom. Side entrance is perfectly acceptable.

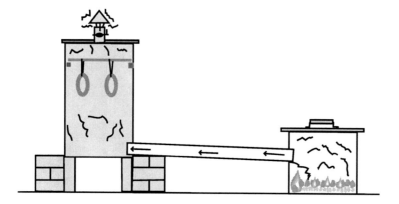

Fig. 11.4.15 Pipe on a side. No elbow connection is needed.

Photo 11.4.5 Pipe running above the ground, bottom entrance.

The higher the support base is built, the higher the smoker will become. This distance will create more space for smoking. A compromise is needed here since the smoker is loaded with meat on top. Creating too high a support base may make it impractical and difficult to use the smoker; it might even be necessary to use a step ladder to reach the top cover. The smoke delivery pipe should end with the elbow to prevent debris from falling into it.

It would be wise to install a shield over the pipe's outlet to prevent grease from dripping into the pipe. After smoking, a wooden plug should be inserted on both of the pipe's ends to prevent rodents from crawling inside it. The pipe should be made strong and well since it is often burried in the ground.

Screens

Screens are an optional addition to any smoker and are mainly used for smoking smaller pieces of fish that would otherwise break into pieces. Another product that requires screens is jerky, although most jerkys are only air dried. All that's required is the addition of three small angle brackets (every 120 degrees) to the wall of the smoker for a permanent screen attachment.

Fire pit

The fire pit could be just a hole in the ground or a sophisticated metal box with two doors and adjustable draft controls. Its main purpose remains the same: to burn wood. Some means to control the inlet of fresh air should exist to switch between smoking and cooking modes. When cooking, the temperature has to be raised by either providing more wood, allowing more fresh air in, or both.

11.5 Barrel And Box Smoker

An easy, practical solution is to place a box with a hole in the bottom on top of the barrel smoker. Think of it as a room addition to an existing house to increase interior space. It allows easier flame and temperature control, convenient loading, and effortless checking and removal of meats.

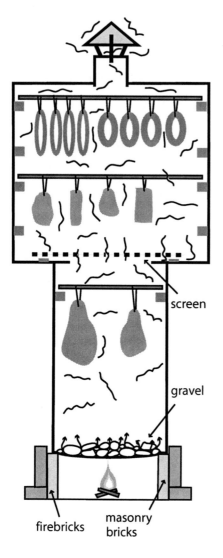

Larger meat pieces requiring a longer smoking time may be hung on smokesticks inside of the barrel and the sausages can be placed on a few rows of sticks inside of the box.

A baffle/screen is placed on the support base and an additional screen can be positioned on the bottom of the screen to smoke fish fillets or jerky. The box can be secured to the barrel by two angle brackets and the hinged door is secured on the front.

The top cover can be just a 6" hole in the top of the box that can be covered with any lid or piece of plywood to provide smoke exit control. The final result is a large and easy to operate smoker that can be built quickly, with minimal cost.

Fig. 11.5.1 Barrel and box, gravel baffle/screen, fire pit inside.

11.6 Box Smoker

There are no great technical skills or specialized tools needed to assemble a box smoker. Wood is quite forgiving, so any mistakes are easy to correct. For safety reasons a fire pit must be free standing. By using a barrel to build a smoker we have somewhat limited ourselves to the shape and physical dimensions of the barrel. However, we have much more design freedom when assembling a box smoker.

It makes little sense to include the wooden floor in the design since we will have to cut it for the smoke delivery channel. Besides, grease will be dripping down and it will have to be scrubbed off. The box can rest right on the ground, but it is still a good idea to place it on four bricks to prevent contact with wet ground. This helps prolong the life of the smoker.

If a smoker will be top loaded the top cover can rest loose or it can be secured to the back wall with hinges. An acceptable height will be anything from 24" to 40", the latter permiting the installation of two levels of smoking sticks.

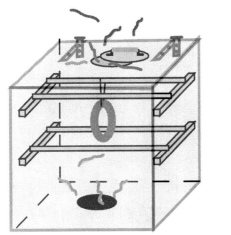
Fig. 11.6.1 Top loaded box smoker.

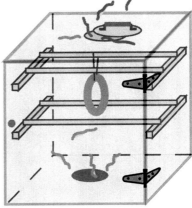
Fig. 11.6.2 Door loaded smoker.

The width and height should be dictated by the standard size of lumber available. Making the smoker 24" x 24" x 36" (height) will create a large but easy to move unit. Wooden handles can be installed on both sides of a box to facilitate lifting. After smoking, a smoke delivery hole should be well covered to prevent the accumulation of rain water. Otherwise, next time we will wonder why our smoker and sausages are wet.

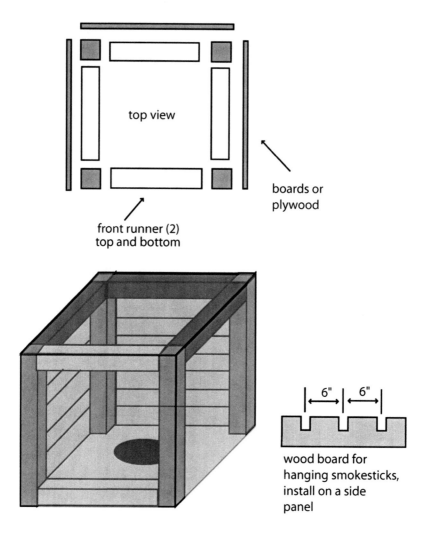

Fig. 11.6.3 Cross section view.

11.7 Outdoor Smokers

Wilderness smokers. Out in the wild you will use a boy scout's methods of smoking. If while on a camping trip you happen to catch a fish, all you need to do is clean it, salt it, and hang it on a stick over a small smoldering fire. If the small fire begins to burst into flames, throw more tiny wood chips on it. You have just built a great smoker and you don't even have to take it back home.

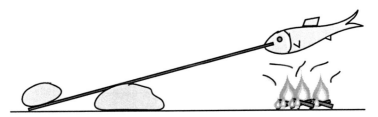

Fig. 11.7.1 Smoking over open fire.

Then, you could dig a hole in the ground and place meat on a wooden smoke stick and use branches with leaves as the cover.

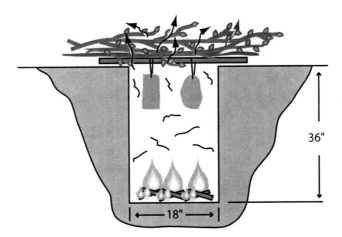

Fig. 11.7.2 Hole in a ground smoker.

The width of the hole is not important but you want it at least 24" deep to prevent the possibility of flames reaching the meat. Meat can be smoked in most primitive conditions far away from urban life. Place the smoked meat in a trunk of your car, drive home, and put the meat in the refrigerator and go to sleep. The following morning cook the meats in the oven or in hot water.

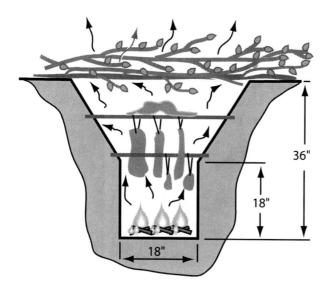

Fig. 11.7.3 This arrangement allows installation of smoke sticks at diferent depths, creating effective smoke screens.

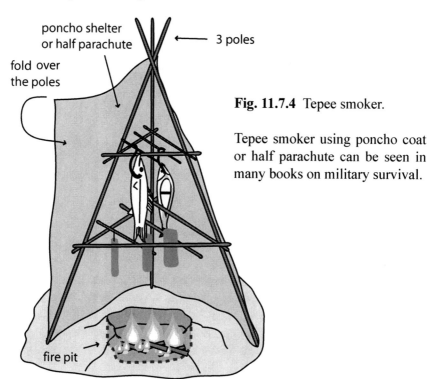

poncho shelter
or half parachute

fold over
the poles

3 poles

Fig. 11.7.4 Tepee smoker.

Tepee smoker using poncho coat or half parachute can be seen in many books on military survival.

fire pit

Most unusual but effective smoker made from the stump of an old oak tree. This original set up has been in operation for 20 years. Smoker located on Poliwoda Fishing Grounds, Opole, Poland. Smoked trout ends up on a dinner plate in a popular tourist restaurant which is located on the same grounds.

Photo 11.7.1 Brined fish being inserted on smokesticks.

Photo 11.7.2 A separate fire pit burning wood logs can be seen in the photo on the left.

A sheet of metal covers the smoke delivery channel and the bricks lying on top provide stability. It is connected with a smoker by an underground pipe. Black item lying on the ground to the right of the smoker is an old potatoe burlap bag that is used as the smoker's cover. Note that a potatoe burlap sack makes an excellent cover allowing just the right amount of smoke to sip through.

191

11.8 Metal Sheet Smoker

One of the easiest fully functional barrel smokers is made from a thin sheet of metal than can be carried anywhere. About 22" (56 cm) diameter and 48" (122 cm) high are acceptable dimensions. We want it to be on the high side as it will be embedded 1-2" into the ground and will not have any baffles that under normal conditions would separate the fire pit from hanging meats.

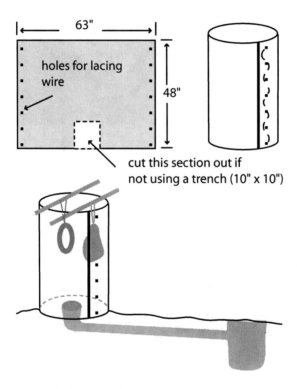

Fig. 11.8.1 Metal sheet smoker.

Just rudimentary math skills are needed and first we have to determine the length of the top side of the metal sheet to create a 22" diameter barrel. This length is nothing else but the length of the circle.

The length $L = 2 \times P \times r = P \times d$
Where P is the math constant = 3.14, r = radius, and d = diameter
That gives us $L = 3.14 \times 22 = 69.08 = 69$ inches
We are going to add an extra 1" (2.5 cm) to this length as the ends of the sheet have to overlap to prevent the leakage of smoke. The diameter of the

barrel is 22" (56 cm) and a standard 20" (51 cm) screen will fit inside without any trouble. Some wooden sticks have to be collected and they will become our smoke sticks on which we'll hang the meat. They have to be longer than the diameter of the barrel (22") and about 1" thick. A flat sheet of cardboard will rest on them and they establish the amount of clearance for the smoke to get out. A burlap sack can be used instead of a flat cover. Drill or punch a series of little holes, about 3/16" (5 mm) diameter, and every 2" (5 cm) at both ends of the sheet. A small diameter wire (without insulation) will be laced through them to hold the two sides together. You can use a few small nuts and bolts, too.

As this basically is a simplified version of the barrel smoker, a decision has to be made on the type of a fire pit that will be employed. That step is dependent on a terrain where a smoker will be placed. If it is hilly and stony, gather rocks and build a loosely compiled base support. If it is flat and grassy, dig a trench and you will have a much better smoker. A hole for a fire pit has to be digged, about 2' (61 cm) deep and 2' square. The 4' long, 8" wide by 8" deep trench should be deeper on the fire pit end. If possible try to find a grassy area for the location of the trench and before you start digging, score the grass with a flat shovel (about 4" deep, 10 cm) to make an outline of the trench. What you need is entire sheets of sod like the ones we buy for our garden. After the trench is dug, those big grassy plugs will be placed on top. The length of 4' is all we need and after the trench canal is made it should be densely covered with wooden sticks, exactly as a trap for wild game animals. The sheets of grass can now be repositioned over the trench and our smoker is almost completed. Now the barrel can be twisted in opposite directions a few times and firmly embedded into the ground right over the outlet side of the trench. If no trench is employed the following are needed:

- Wood chips holding metal pan.
- Kitchen colander or other baffle which will be positioned over the metal pan to prevent flames.
- Burning fire to re-ignite a new load of wood chips.

A very practical solution is to carry one or two grill screens which are commonly sold in all large department stores. The screen can be placed on rocks and used as a grill to satisfy the first hunger and then will become a crucial part of the smoker. The gravel or little stones can be found everywhere and placing them on the screen will create a fully operational and practical baffle. Three empty soda cans spaced 120 degrees will make workable spacers.

11.9 Cardboard Smokers

Refrigerator box smoker

There was a friend of mine in San Diego who has used the most original smoker I had ever seen and it was a refrigerator packing box. He would go to a large department store and get a heavy cardboard box that that holds a new refrigerator. This is very hard cardboard glued together. There wasn't any smoke stack or dampers, the top of the box was left intact and there were enough gaps and clearances for the smoke to exit. There is a hole for smoke exit control in the drawing below. He would cut the opening in the front with a box cutter on three sides only. This way he could open it, hang meat inside, and push it back to close it. Another opening was made at the botom to allow the placement of a metal pan with wood chips. A fire would be started in a large metal pan and after about 2" (5 cm) of hot coals were obtained, he would add sawdust on top to start smoking. The meats were hung on smoke sticks that were pushed through small holes on the sides of the box.

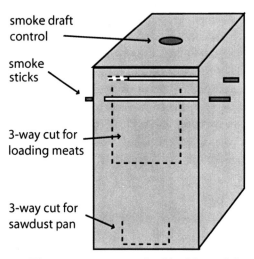

smoke draft control

smoke sticks

3-way cut for loading meats

3-way cut for sawdust pan

Fig. 11.9.1 Refrigerator empty box smoker.

The meats were smoked inside and the oven was used to cook them to ready to eat temperatures. The smoker was standing outside and water was no problem as it hardly ever rained in San Diego. To dispose of it he would just burn it after the last smoking session.

This real story is cited to demonstrate that almost anything can be used to build a smoker and all that is needed is some basic knowledge on the subject and some imagination.

Two box smoker

This is definitely the easiest smoker that can be built. It is popular in Asian countries. Disposable, yet fully functional, it can be built without any costs. This smoker may be the best introduction for the beginner to the world of smoking. Materials needed: 2 cardboard boxes of the same size, masking tape, smoke sticks, metal pan for sawdust, kitchen colander or a suitable baffle. A higher box will make a bigger smoker, although the size is not of real importance.

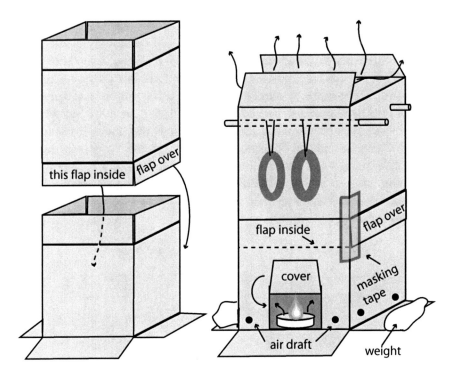

Fig. 11.9.2 Two equal size boxes.

Fig. 11.9.3 One box inserted into another.

Smoke exhaust can be adjusted by placing different weights on top covers. The cover flaps act as a spring and tend to open up. At the bottom a few holes may be punched out to supply air or the firebox cover may be left open. All corner joints should be reinforced with masking tape. A kitchen colander may be placed over the pan with sawdust. This is to prevent the possibility of sawdust bursting up in flames when grease drips down from the meat.

195

11.10 Concrete Block Smoker

An excellent smoker can be built in no time by using standard 8" x 8" x 16" concrete blocks. A firm support base is recommended and square patio stones of 12", 16", or 18" that are available at garden centers can be successfully used.

 Fig. 11.10.1 A concrete block.

Even bigger prefabricated concrete slabs 30" x 30" that are used to support outside air-conditioning heat pumps are commonly available in warehouses with building supplies. They may make an installation look prettier but are not necessary, a bare ground is fine. Just grade it well so it is leveled. The construction does not include using mortar, just arranging blocks in the manner that will be most practical. A separate fire pit built from blocks is attached to the smokehouse. This way the entire smoking chamber can be utilized for smoking meats and the process is easy to control. Nothing stops you from using mortar and making it a permanent structure, but a strong suggestion will be to try it out a few times. Make some observations that may help you with any future decisions regarding building a permanent smoker.

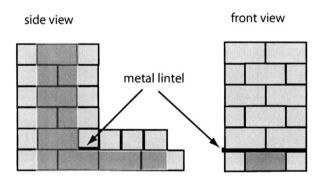

Fig. 11.10.2 Easy to build concrete block smoker.

This is a totally flexible design and imagine that you are building a smoker like a child who is erecting a house using little building blocks. This is how this smoker is built and the only difference is that the blocks are slightly bigger: 8" x 8" x 16". The required materials are available from a building supply store and the final cost will be incredibly low.

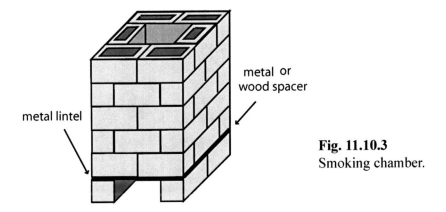

metal or wood spacer

metal lintel

Fig. 11.10.3
Smoking chamber.

Smokesticks support

The easiest and fastest way to support the smokesticks is to place them directly on top of the smoker. The sticks should be 1" in diameter as they act as spacers now, separating the top of the smoker from the cardboard or wooden cover that rests on it. This creates ample space for the smoke to exit from the smoker. This also limits us to two smoke sticks (one level). An old potatoe burlap sack has been used for that purpose for hundreds of years. Of course a flattened piece of cardboard or a piece of plywood can be used as well.

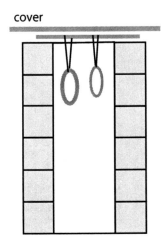
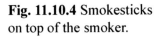

Fig. 11.10.4 Smokesticks on top of the smoker.

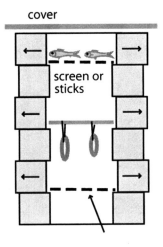

Fig. 11.10.5 Smokesticks on protruding blocks.

197

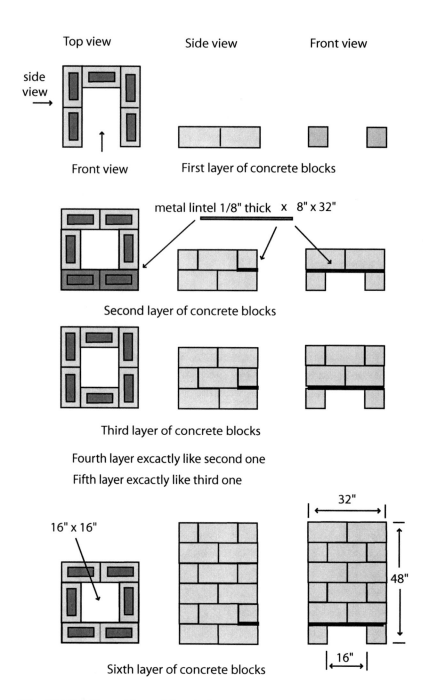

Top view   Side view   Front view

side
view
→

Front view   First layer of concrete blocks

metal lintel 1/8" thick   x   8" x 32"

Second layer of concrete blocks

Third layer of concrete blocks

Fourth layer excactly like second one

Fifth layer excactly like third one

16" x 16"

32"

48"

16"

Sixth layer of concrete blocks

Fig. 11.10.6 Top, side and front views.

Construction Details

A metal lintel about 1/8" thick is placed in front on top of the #1 layer. It's purpose is to support the subsequent concrete block levels. As this will slightly raise the front block (1/8"), it is advisable to put some spacers (wood is fine) under all blocks in # 2 layer to level the blocks. Spacers can be of the same size as the block, 8" x 16" or smaller (8" x 8") and placed wherever needed to make the floor level. Of course the spacers must be of the same thickness as the lintel. There is no need for spacers when using mortar. The block laying style repeats itself, uneven layers 1, 3, 5 have one pattern, even layers 2, 4, 6 have another one. There are 5 blocks in #1 level, all others require 6 blocks. In a six floor configuration a total of 35 blocks are used for the smoker and 7 blocks for the fire pit. Neither masonry bricks, mortar, half blocks or any tools are needed. As the fire pit is on the same plane as the smoker, in order to achieve enough draft, the smoker is built of six floors and is 48" high which makes it a comfortable height to work with. It will also work if the height is limited to 5 block levels (40") and if more draft is needed, an extra floor can be added in a matter of minutes. The blocks can be spaced so that every other row can have two blocks projecting inward from the wall on each side of the smoker. This arrangement creates support for the smokesticks, screens or racks.

Fire pit

There are only 7 blocks needed to construct the fire pit which is freely attached to the front wall. Any little smoke coming from the connection is negligible as long as there is smoke coming out of the chamber. A wet towel can be placed over the connection where the fire pit and smoker come together. A fire pit may be attached to the smoker with a mortar. As the concrete block is not designed to withhold high temperatures it is to be expected that once in a while one of the fire pit concrete blocks might crack. Obviously, the most practical solution is to replace it with a different one and go on happily smoking like before. Once smoking is completed, the cooking process begins and a long stem thermometer must be inserted between blocks or through the top cover. The temperature control and amount of heat generated is obtained by moving burning wood closer or away from the entrance to the smoker. A very practical solution is to place a propane camping burner or an electric hot plate inside of the fire pit. This is a fully functional and easy to operate smoker capable of producing smoked meats of the highest quality and it should not be judged by its looks. Its inside space is only 0.7 cubic foot (0.18 cubic meter) smaller than that of a typical metal drum. Resting smokesticks on two separate levels creates enough capacity to smoke about 22 lbs (10 kg) of meats.

Top view at smoker and firepit

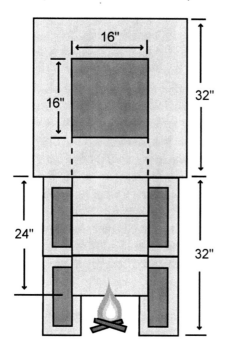

Fig. 11.10.7 Smoker with attached fire pit.

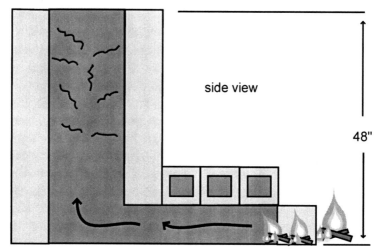

11.11 Appliance Smokers

Refrigerator smoker

Some books advocate making smokers out of refrigerators and many people try conversion. Many years ago refrigerators were made of metal and such a metal enclosure could be adapted as a smoker. More and more plastics are used in the construction of todays refrigerators and one may question the wisdom of such a design. Let's see some pros and cons of such a design:

Advantages: A smoking chamber is already made with screens included. Well insulated and roomy.

Disadvantages: Cannot burn wood in it. Needs electricity supply for a hot plate. Needs a lot of work: compressor, fan, radiator, rubber gaskets – all have to be removed. Holes have to be drilled for smoke sticks, bigger holes needed for smoke outlet. It is a one piece smoker, a baffle has to be installed. Many refrigerators have a separate freezer on top with its own door. The floor dividing the freezer from the refrigerator has to be removed to create one smoking chamber.

It will be more practical to use a refrigerator without a freezer. Holes have to be made to accomodate pipes, one in the bottom for a pipe connection from a separate fire pit, and one in the top to allow smoke to exit. After removing the door gasket, the door will not seal and we will have a leak there.

The easiest way to do a conversion will be to purchase a kit from the Sausage Maker, Buffalo, New York. The company sells entire kits and individual parts for electric and gas smokehouses.

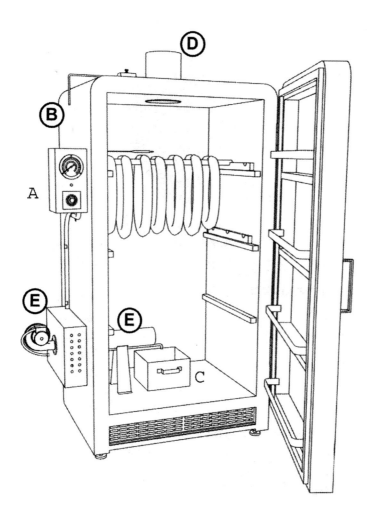

Photo 11.11.1 Electric smoker conversion.
Drawing courtesy the Sausage Maker, Buffalo, NY.

A - Smokehouse temperature control assembly.
B - Damper control.
C - Sawdust box.
D - 6" diameter damper.
E - Heating element and housing.

That does not mean it can not be done and to prove the point we enclose photos of wonderful work that was performed by Tomasz Abratkiewicz to convert an old Polish metal refrigerator into a smoker. The final result is a unit that will outperform all little and medium size factory built smokers.

Photo 11.11.2 Old refrigerator smoker.

Photos 11.11.3 &11.11.4 Fire pit and smoke delivery pipe.

Photo 11.11.5 Fire pit. There is a metal grate to receive wood and a locking handle to close the door tight.

Photo 11.11.6 Smoking in progress. Stem thermometer mounted on ceramic glass.

Photo 11.11.7 Smoke delivery pipe entering smoker.

Warming oven smoker

Wonderful smokers can be made from used restaurant equipment, especially from used warming ovens. In the following photos we can see beautiful work that was done on such a unit by Gary Zagrzebski of Wisconsin.

Photo 11.11.8 Used warming oven smoker.

Those well insulated units are made of stainless steel, there is a a factory made hole in the bottom for the cable, there is a screened vent hole on the top. They also include a built into the door thermometer and movable shelf supports.

Photo 11.11.9 Inside view.

 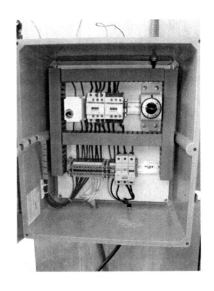

Photo 11.11.10 Control panels.

Photo 11.11.11 Control panel wiring.

Photo 11.11.12 Hot plate for producing smoke and heating elements for cooking.

The smoker has six 500 watt 220 volt elements for heating. They are controlled by a digital temperature controller. The controller has a range up to 220 degrees F. In the heating circuit there is also an infinite switch used to cycle the elements based on the outside temperature for heating.

There is a single 6 inch 650 watt element smoke burner. The element has two windings but only the center one is used. This element is controlled by a 0 to 60 minute timer. The timer is used to ignite the wood chips and then shut off. There are couplings at the bottom for draft. Pipe plugs are used to control the draft. The top has a stack with a damper. The inside of the oven has adjustable angles to support rods or racks.

Photo 11.11.13 Draft controls.

The smoker works great even in the winter temperatures of Wisconsin. Because it is electric and electronically controlled it is easy to use and does not have to be constantly monitored. Besides cold smoking it can also be used for hot smoking at 200 to 225 degrees F to do roasts, ribs, chops and brisket.

Above photos courtesy Gary Zagrzebski

11.12 Japanese Kamado Smoker

The Kamado or Japanese smoker has been used for centuries to cook rice, vegetables and meals. American soldiers, tourists, and Japanese immigrants brought the first units to the USA. You can't smoke 50 lbs of sausage or a whole ham but you can certainly impress your friends and neighbors. Traditional Kamado is a Japanese steam rice cooker known as Mushikamado. The Japanese word "mushi" means to steam. Those traditional rice cookers are still in use in Japan today.

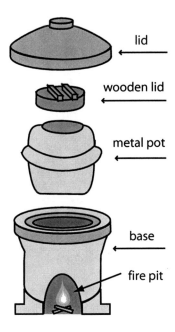

Fig. 11.12.1 Traditional Kamado cooker/smoker.

Rice was cooked with an open fire. When water containing rice was brought to a boil, the wooden lid started to pop up. That was indication that the boiling temperature was reached and the draft was closed to choke the fire. The cooker was then covered with a big lid and rice was allowed to steam for about 30 min. In all modern electrical rice cookers a thermostat stops boiling water and rice is steamed for 20 minutes. Think of the Kamado unit as a miniature traditional adobe bread oven. It has to be thick to store as much heat as possible during the burning process so it can slowly release this heat back to cook the meal.

Modern Kamado

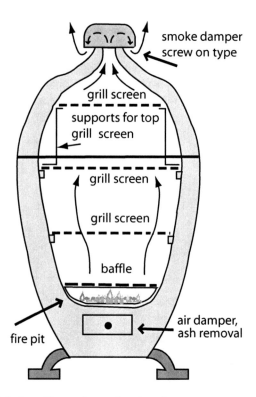

Fig. 11.12.2 Modern Kamado cooker/smoker.

The Kamado is a very efficient cooker and it can operate at 150–800° F (65-426° C) with very precise temperature control. It uses charcoal or specially made briquettes for fuel, or can be gas fired from a propane tank. They are usually made of clay and are painted red or green. Fancier units have a ceramic glazed tile finish on the outside and stainless steel hinges, handles and doors. Kamado looks like a big egg, with its smaller end flattened so it can stand upright. There is an adjustable smoke vent in the top part and a damper draft control near the bottom to control the air intake. Modern kamados are about 29"-63" high with grills of 13"-25" in diameter and about 90-600 lbs in weight. Both parts are connected with hinges and the top one is raised up. When the top cover opens, the Kamado works as a grill or barbecue. When it's down, the Kamado serves as an oven for roasting or smoking. To add more wood chips, one has to open the top lid and remove the grill screens which is rather inconvenient.

11.13 Masonry Smokehouse

Masonry smokers are a step up in smoker design, they look better and also cost more money. They need a permanent location and the design must be well thought of before laying down the foundation that is needed due to their size and weight. A good foundation should be about 4-6 inches thick and reinforced with wire mesh. Other details on mixing and pouring concrete and local codes and regulations can be obtained from the local library or the books written on the subject.

A masonry smoker can be built from concrete blocks, bricks, or combinations thereof. It is important to remember that the firebricks should be used wherever high temperatures will be present. For example, in a fire pit or in part of the smoking chamber that's in direct contact with a fire pit. That does not mean that the whole thickness of the smoke chamber wall must be made of firebricks, which cost more than a regular brick. The inside of the wall must be layered with firebricks, then additional layers can consist of the regular masonry bricks.

Description

It is best to think of this design as a brick replica of the barrel smoker design with a fire pit at the bottom. It follows the same design recommendations as the barrel smoker: fire pit, baffle, smokesticks, provision for screen insertion, and the flat damper to control the outflow of smoke. The only difference is the way of loading the smoke chamber with meat. In the barrel smoker it is done almost always from the top and in the masonry design the door will be installed in front.

The top of the smoker is the chimney. The other difference is the design of the fire pit which is capable of generating a lot of heat and high temperatures. As this is a more technically demanding project requiring more time and money, it makes sense to build a larger size smoker capable of smoking more meat at the same time. It is also easier to control inside temperatures of a larger unit. When used as an oven, this smoker should be able to roast a few turkeys or even a small pig.

You can easily eliminate 2' from its height and it will still be a very practical smoker. The usable space inside of the smoker is 24"x 24" x 80" high. The smoker is of the square shape, ie. length equals width. There are two doors, one about 26" x 59" for loading meats and providing access to baffles and the other 26" x 13" high that leads to the fire pit. There also is a drawer with a built in draft damper for ash removal. To support screens, every other brick course may have a few bricks protruding inward from the wall on each side of the chamber. That creates a lot of freedom for smoke sticks, screens and baffle arrangement. A single baffle, two baffles, or just a screen with medium size gravel can be inserted into the chamber. Baffles should be removable to facilitate cleaning.

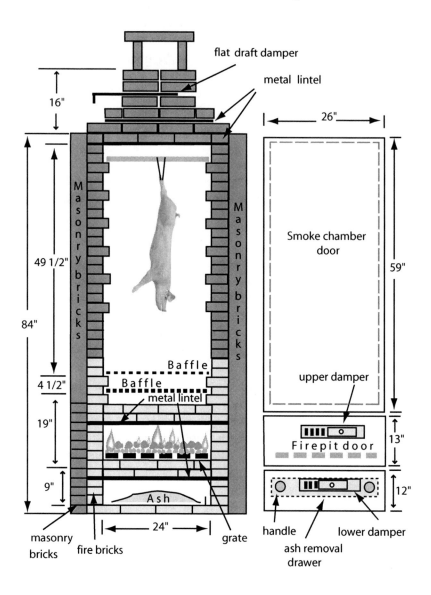

Fig. 11.13.1 Masonry smoker.

Fire pit

If your objective besides smoking sausages is to grill meats or roast a pig, your fire pit will become the most important part of your design. The fire pit door should have provisions for intake air draft control, one above the the grate for open fire smoking and one below the grate for additional air supply during cooking. Instead of having a separate fire pit door and the ash removal drawer, one could install just one bigger door that will provide access to the fire pit and the ash removal area. Just make sure you have one draft damper above the grate and another below it. Those dampers help to control temperatures during cooking. When smoking, the lower primary air damper located below the grate is shut and the wood gets air only from the main air inlet, located above the grate. With the top draft fully open (bottom damper closed) we are burning a regular open fire. By closing the damper and cutting off the air supply we are choking the fire forcing it to smoke. You may have two smaller separate doors installed, each with its own damper:

1. Bottom door (drawer) for the ash removal.

2. Upper door for wood supply. That makes construction more difficult but the design gives you even better control when smoking.

For those in need of very high temperatures a perforated pipe placed below the lower baffle will deliver pre-heated air for secondary combustion. Fire pit doors should be made of cast iron. If a glass peephole is desired it should be made of ceramic glass only. In addition to burning wood you may use gas burners and there is a lot of room to place them inside. Gas fired smokers have a lot of advantages: they are portable, inexpensive, and capable of providing large amounts of heat on demand. A metal pot with sawdust or wood chips can be placed on a gas burner to generate smoke. This degree of fine tuning can not be achieved when burning wood.

What is a firebrick?

Wherever high temperatures are present, the firebricks and refractory mortar should be used. In other areas use masonry bricks or concrete blocks. A firebrick is composed of clay and has been fired in a kiln. It is different from a concrete brick, which is composed of portland cement and inert aggregate (sand and gravel) and is hardened by a chemical reaction instead of by heat. A firebrick is lighter in color (usually light yellow) than a common clay brick which is red. This red color is due to impurities such as iron, and those impurities lower the melting point of the clay. In a fire clay brick those impurities are removed to give it a higher melting point and that is why it can tolerate higher temperatures. It is also slightly larger (9" x 4" x 2 ¼") than a masonry brick. When building a fire pit, remember that a firebrick expands when heated. When laying firebricks the refractory fireclay mortar must be used as the regular mortar will not stand such high temperatures. The fireclay mortar joints are much thinner 1/8" – 1/4". Some elaborate designs cover bricks with ceramic tiles and other finishes, which may crack if proper expansion joints are not provided (mineral wool).

Chimney and draft

In most smokehouses, barbecue units and stoves, a huge amount of heat is lost passing into the air through the chimney. This loss can be diminished by the construction of a damper that will restrict some heat from escaping. A chimney should end with a masonry or stainless steel cap which will prevent rain from going inside. In windy weather a cap can protect the chimney from downward wind turbulance which would decrease the draft of the system.

To control smoke draft a flat damper is chosen which is nothing else than a rectangular 8" x 26" flat metal sheet of 1/8" thickness that is pushed in or out of the chimney. The damper should be installed when the mortar is still wet and by moving it in and out during the mortar curing process we create a space for the damper. The smoker is a square unit and a damper can be installed on any side.

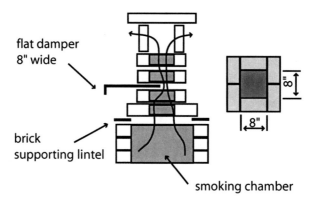

Fig. 11.13.2 Chimney damper control.

Spark arrester

When there is a possibility of a fire hazard, the chimney should be equipped with the spark arrester and a damper control. The spark arrester is a box of woven wire screen, attached to the top of the chimney. It can be held in place by clamps, bolts or hinges. The last being the best solution as it provides an easy access to the flue of the chimney. Any kind of a dense wire mesh will make a spark arrester. It can be a flat sheet bolted down to the chimney, or a box screen attached to flat or angle brackets, clamps or hinges. As long as it is physically stable it will do the job.

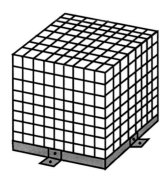

Fig. 11.13.3 Spark arrester.

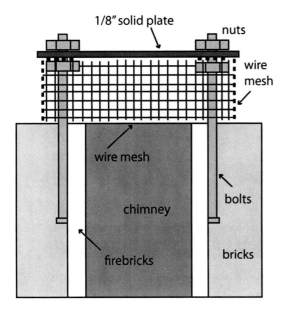

Fig. 11.13.4 Spark arrester.

11.14 Masonry Smoker/Grill

The dimensions are for informational purpose only, please feel free to improvise your own design.

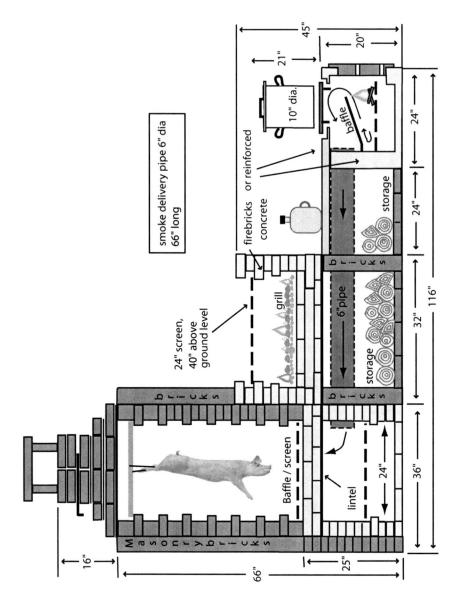

Fig. 11.14.1 Smoker/grill.

Description

This design takes the masonry smoker one step further by adding a grill and a hot plate stove to it. It may be of interest to people who smoke meats outdoors for extended periods of time. The area below smoking chamber can be used as a storage area or as an additional fire pit providing extra heat if needed. An electrical heating element or a propane burner can be placed there or regular wood can be burned. A safety baffle can be placed on protruding bricks. The smoking chamber and the storage area below (secondary fire pit), both have their own access doors.

Grill

On the right side of the smoker there is a grill with its own fire pit and storage space underneath. The front of the grill is left open and the back end is the brick wall. A grilling rack is located at a comfortable level of 40" but can be placed at different heights. Protruding bricks provide support for the grilling screen at different heights. The top can be covered with a metal plate. The smoke delivery pipe runs under the grill and the area can be utilized for wood storage. A wooden door is optional. There is a working area on the right with a smoke delivery pipe underneath and more room for storage. Its height is only 20" but can be easily increased by laying an additional level of bricks.

Fire pit

The fire pit is the main smoke and heat generating unit and an optional metal hot plate can be added on top to allow water boiling. The plate could be round but the bricklaying will be much easier if a square shape is chosen. The plate depicted in the drawing is quite large and accomodates a 10" diameter pot. You can always place a smaller vessel on a large plate but not vice versa. The hot plate concept will definitely be appreciated by people smoking at low temperatures. The fire pit is of stool grate type with one draft above the grate and another one below. The controls are located on the fire pit door.

There is a 24" x 12" bent baffle inside the fire pit to redirect the heat back towards the upper front of the fire pit where an optional cooking plate is located. There is an option for installing a secondary combustion air draft above the two main draft controls. Though not included in the main plan in order not to cloud drawings with too many details, a secondary combustion can be easily obtained by drilling a 1" hole through the fire pit door. Then a 6" section of a steel pipe 1 – 2" in diameter, with pre – drilled 1/8" diameter holes, may be inserted into the door and secured on both sides with nuts or welds. You can get threaded steel pipes from plumbing supplies stores. This pre-heated air will generate much higher temperatures right under the metal hot plate and the pot. This concept is described in detail in the chapter on fire pit design.

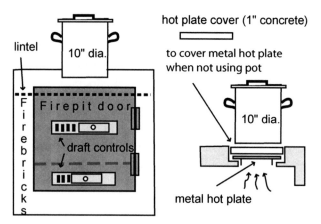

Fig. 11.14.2 Fire pit.

Keep in mind that air draft controls are only effective if your door shuts tight.

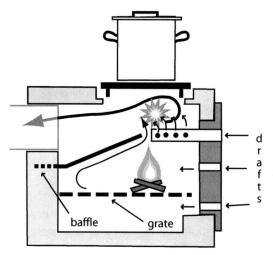

Fig. 11.14.3 Secondary combustion perforated pipe.

When smoking the draft control below the grate remains shut and the control above the grate is open. That supplies enough air to slowly burn wood and create smoke. To cook meats we need more heat and this is accomplished by opening the draft below the grate. That supplies more fresh air and the only way it can go is straight up through the gate with smoldering wood. With more available air the wood starts to burn cleaner, faster and at a higher temperature. An optional secondary combustion perforated pipe will push the temperatures even higher.

Smoke delivery pipe. A 66" (162 cm) long, 6" (15 cm) diameter smoke delivery pipe runs through the storage area under the grill. It is possible to make the unit shorter by 24" by eliminating the smaller storage area next to the fire pit. That will also decrease the length of the smoke delivery pipe by 24". The smoker is 82" (208 cm) high and that creates a sufficient draft.

Construction tips

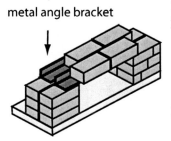

metal angle bracket

1. Build up the wall at each side opening.
2. Place a 3 -4" steel angle bracket over opening, supporting it at each end. In certain cases like building up the chimney, you won't be able to use the angle bracket, use metal lintel (flat steel) instead.
3. Apply mortar under and behind the bricks, bracket will be hidden by the bricks.

Fig. 11.14.4 Supporting lintel - angle brackets.

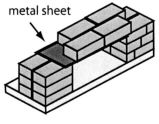

metal sheet

A 3/16" - 1/4" flat sheet of metal will do fine too. Make sure it is not thicker than a mortar joint, otherwise the next level of bricks will not be even.

Fig. 11.14.5 Supporting lintel - metal flat steel.

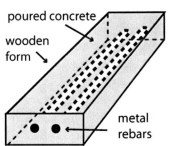

poured concrete

wooden form

metal rebars

Make a wooden u-shaped form, insert and support with spacers, two 3/8" rebars and pour concrete. Make sure that the finished lintel is not higher than a brick. In place of rebars you may use wire mesh.

Fig. 11.14.6 Rebar lintel.

11.15 Storm Water Pipe Smoker

The majority of masonry smokers are rectangular in shape thus the smoker below looks different and more original. The firebox design is based on a round fire pit which is popular in Argentina. A storm water pipe is used to build the smokehouse. Such pipes are laying around wherever new housing projects are built in developing areas. They come in 10' length and are made of reinforced concrete about 3" thick. Inside diameters vary from 12" to 40" in 2" increments.

Photo 11.15.1 Concrete storm water pipes.

Due to its length and size an average pipe weighs about 800 lbs and its transport is one of the most difficult parts of a project. The pipe will have to be cut down to size and the openings for a smoke delivery channel and clean out access have to be made. That can be accomplished with a portable motorized saw with a 12" diamond blade. A saw can be rented out or a paving contractor can perform the service.

When cutting a pipe down to size a section of it can be saved to be used as an inside part of the fire pit, although an opening will have to be made for the smoke delivery channel. This way we can eliminate laying down the fire bricks. It is recommended to place masonry bricks on the outside of the round fire pit and the smoker to give it a more elegant look.

This smoker has many advantages:

- Smoke flows very evenly inside as the smoker is round in shape (no blind pockets).
- Smoker has a very good natural insulation due to its very thick walls.
- Neither a meat loading door nor fire box door are needed.
- It is very simple to build, there are no precise measurements or difficult hardware or hinges to install. What is basically needed is some intelligent planning.

Due to its massive weight a solid 6" reinforced concrete foundation has to be poured down. Using concrete pipes for making smokehouses is quite common, see photo 11.3.4 on page 157.

Photo 11.15.2 Argentinian barbecue known as "asado". A round fire pit is a very practical, visually pleasing and inexpensive solution for confining hot fire in a designated area.

Photo courtesy of the Calitina Wine Resort,
San Rafael, Mendoza, Argentina.

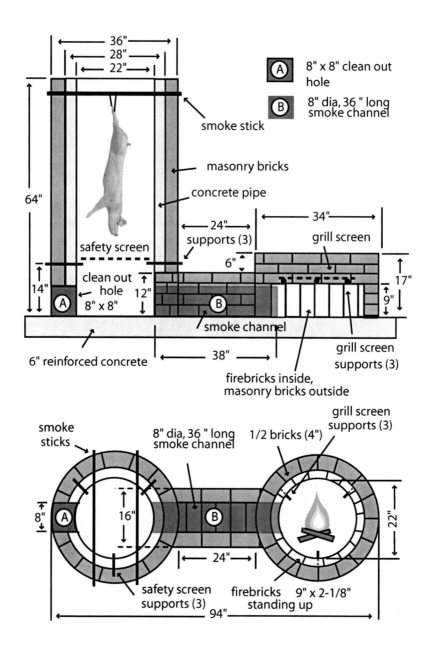

Fig. 11.15.1 Smoker and grill.

In place of smoke channel "B" the round pipe at least 6" in diameter may be installed.

Description

The beauty of this design is that both a smoker and a grill use the same fire pit. The amount of smoke or heat going into the smoker is adjusted by moving burning wood towards or away from the entrance to the smoker. This is accomplished by burning an open fire right on the concrete foundation floor. A metal grate with short legs can be placed in the fire pit and the wood will be burning faster and at a higher temperature having an extra supply of fresh air from below. The fire pit can be covered with a metal cover that will send all available heat to the smoker.

Neither the smoker nor the fire pit employ any doors which greatly simplifies construction. Instead a round metal cover is placed on top of the smoker. By moving this cover a smoke draft control is established.

Smoke sticks can be easily mounted by drilling with a masonry drill right through the pipe walls. This is inconvenient when loading many small items such as sausages and impossible to hang a long rope sausage. A more professional solution is to install smokestick supports that allows for loading smokesticks outside. Supports for a safety screen can be drilled right through the concrete pipe wall. It is a wise precaution to install a safety screen to prevent the possibility of meats falling down on the floor during smoking.

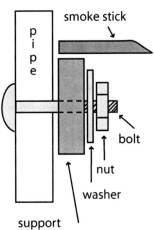

Fig. 11.15.2 Smokestick support.

A good idea is to make the brick corbel about 2" longer than the pipe. This creates a very strong support for hanging heavy pieces of meat. Metal rebars may be used as smokesticks and the cover will sit on top of the bricks above them. A crossbar with three arms separated by 120 degrees can be constructed and will permit to hang more meats in the lower part of the smokehouse.

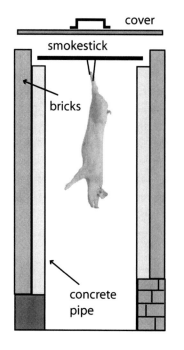

Fig. 11.15.3 Smoke stick support.

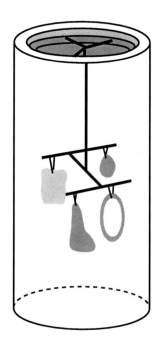

Fig. 11.15.4 A cross bar support.

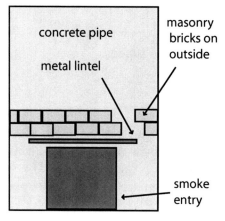

Fig. 11.15.5 Brick support over smoke channel.

Grill/fire pit

A grill is nothing more than a metal screen suspended on supports inside of the fire pit. Such round screens are available in standard sizes at all department stores.

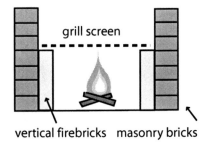

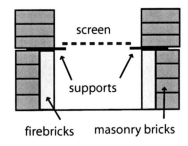

Fig. 11.15.6 Firebricks used as a grill screen support. The easiest approach.

Fig. 11.15.7 Three metal supports imbedded between bricks and spaced equally every 120 degrees.

The supports can be 4" long pieces of rod or flat metal and should be inserted into damp mortar between the bricks. They can go on top of vertically standing firebricks which determines the height of the screen that is 9". The screen is surrounded by an additional 8" of bricks and that will confine heat in the grill area.

When cutting the pipe down to size, it is a good idea to cut another section for the inside wall of the fire pit, providing that fire pit and smokehouse are of the same diameter. Remember to also cut an opening for the smoke channel. This way the smoker and the fire pit will be of the same diameter. This is not a rule and the fire pit can be made wider than the smokehouse.

The smoker is top loaded and at first it may seem too high and awkward but the top of the smoke delivery channel "B" serves as the 11" high step ladder and loading the smokehouse becomes quite easy.

Using the smoke delivery channel as a step ladder is the reason why the smoke sticks should be installed perpendicular to the smoke delivery channel. This provides a strong grip and facilitates their insertion or removal. There is a 8" x 8" clean out access "A" to facilitate cleaning the smoker or recovery of the fallen items. An electric heating element can be inserted through this hole when wood is in a short supply. It is a very unusual looking smoker which works very well.

The following photos provided courtesy Mr. Peter J. Van Brussel from Ohio:

Photo 11.15.3 Laying bricks around concrete pipe.

Photo 11.15.4 Building fire pit.

There is no need to buy sawdust or wood chips. Logs of wood are used and smoking can continue for days or weeks with little supervision. If it stops at night, it can be very easily re-ignited the following morning.

Photo 11.15.5 Smoke delivery pipe.

Photo 11.15.6. Laying firebricks inside fire pit.

Photo 11.15.7 and **Photo 11.15.8** Finished smokehouse. On the lower photo note a clean out door at the bottom of the smokehouse.

Photo 11.15.9 Some serious smoking takes place here. Pulling a pig out.

Photo 11.15.10 A job well done. Sitting from left to right: Jeff Banks, Jim Comerford and the proud owner Peter Van Brussel.

231

11.16 Masonry Smokehouse # 5352

The following smokehouse was designed in 1933 by the North Dakota Agricultural College and the U.S. Dept. of Agriculture. This is a big walk - in smokehouse requiring a foundation reaching below the frost line. This is the depth where water can still be found frozen depending on a particular geographical location.

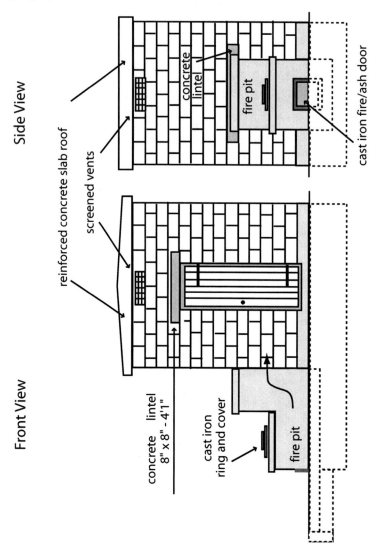

Fig. 11.16.1 General view of the smokehouse.

These plans have a great value from an educational point of view and can be easily adapted to an existing shed or other already erected structure. The smokehouse can also be built up right from the beginning.

Description of the smokehouse

The smokehouse is entirely built from commonly available concrete blocks (8" x 8" x 16"). The 5" thick roof slab is made from concrete that is reinforced with # 9 fencing wire. Meats hang on 2" x 6" hangers that are placed 6" apart in slots of the 2" x 8" wall plates (2). One wall plate is located on the front wall just above the door and the other is on the back wall. The wall plates are secured every 12" with ½" bolts and washers on both sides of the concrete blocks. That will require drilling holes through the blocks and the bolts will have to be about 14" long to accommodate the 8" block, 2" wall plate and washers. See detail A and B.

There is a concrete lintel (8" x 8" - 4'1") above the door to provide support for the upper 3 levels of concrete blocks. Lintel is reinforced with two 3/8" - 3'10" steel rebars. The door frame is attached to the blocks with six (3 on each side) ½" countersunk bolt anchors. The 2'6" x 6'6" built-up door is covered with a tin sheet on the inside. See detail B. The smoke exit and ventilation are provided by four screened vents attached on the outside – detail E.

Fire pit

What separates this smokehouse from others is its original fire pit design. In almost all traditional smokehouses smoke delivery is provided by an underground pipe connecting the fire pit with a smoking chamber. In this design a fire pit is an integral part of the smokehouse and the smoke is delivered through the opening in the wall that is situated above the ground level. The fire pit and its vertical safety baffle are made of reinforced concrete to prevent flames from reaching the inside of the smoking chamber.

There is a cast iron ring and cover on top of the fire pit and water may be heated for butchering or cooking. The cover can be removed altogether and the cooking vessel can be placed directly over the fire. A cast iron door is provided for ash removal. Due to the height of the smokehouse (10') there is a sufficient draft for smoking.

Floor Plan

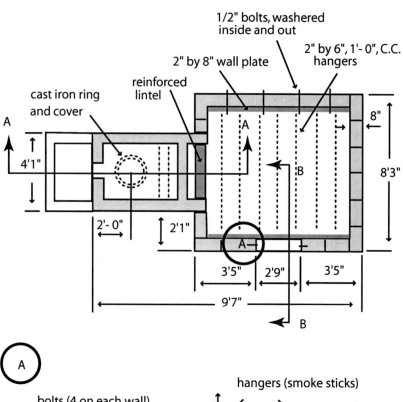

1/2" bolts, washered inside and out

2" by 6", 1'- 0", C.C. hangers

2" by 8" wall plate

reinforced lintel

cast iron ring and cover

A

A

A

A

4'1"

8"

8'3"

2'- 0"

2'1"

B

3'5"

2'9"

3'5"

9'7"

B

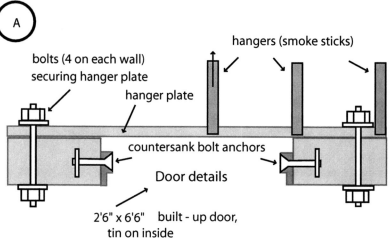

A

hangers (smoke sticks)

bolts (4 on each wall) securing hanger plate

hanger plate

countersank bolt anchors

Door details

2'6" x 6'6"   built - up door, tin on inside

Fig. 11.16.2 Floor plan.

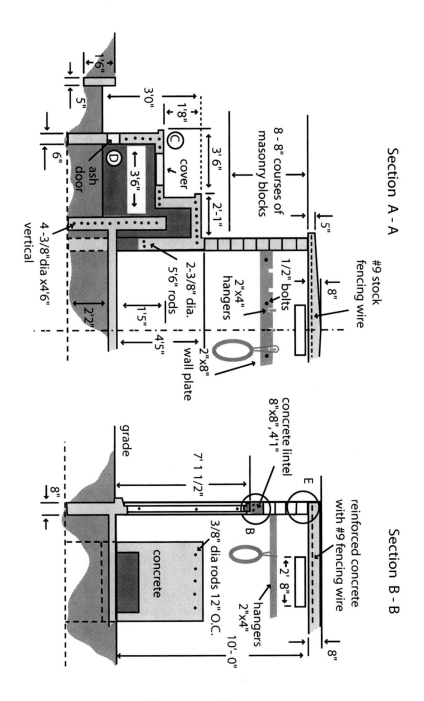

Fig. 11.16.3 Cross-sections A-A and B-B.

235

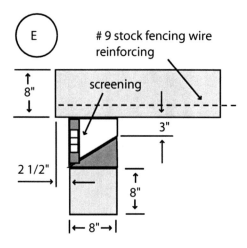

Fig. 11.16.4 Detail E – smoke exit and ventilation.

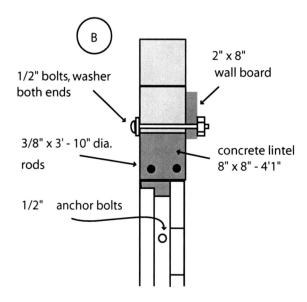

Fig. 11.16.5 Detail B – door and wall plate support.

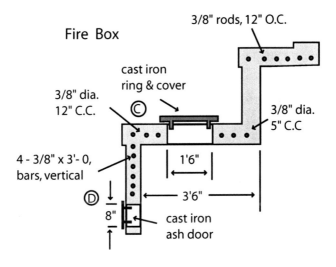

Fig. 11.16.6 Details C and D – fire pit.

United States Department of Agriculture Smokehouse Plans

The smokehouse plans (5352, 5351, 5695 Frame, 5695 Masonry) compiled in this section pertain to the traditional gravity type of smokehouse technology. Although they will not be used by a commercial facility anymore, they make a wonderful reading. And they can still be of practical use by someone living on the farm and smoking a lot of meat.

The Smokehouse Plans: 5352, 5351, 5695 (Frame) and 5695 (Masonry) courtesy North Dakota State University.

11.17 Frame Smokehouse # 5351

The above smokehouse was designed in 1933 by the North Dakota
Agricultural College and the U.S. Dept. of Agriculture.

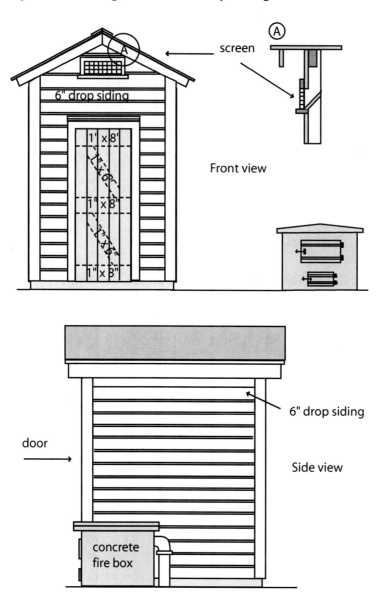

Fig. 11.17.1 General view.

This is a big walk-in smokehouse requiring a foundation reaching below the frost line. This is the depth where water can still be found frozen depending on a particular geographical location.

Description of the smokehouse

This is a frame smokehouse built from standard size wood beams and panels. It is covered on the outside with 6" drop siding. The 6" x 14" vent at both ends (front and back) is screened on the outside. The minimum distance between the firepit and the smokehouse is 4'. This is a big smokehouse and there is a room for a removable utility bench and a barrel with salt. There are 2" x 4" beams with round movable hangers placed every 24". The roof is covered with tight sheathing and the frame is secured to the foundation with 5/8" x 12" anchor bolts.

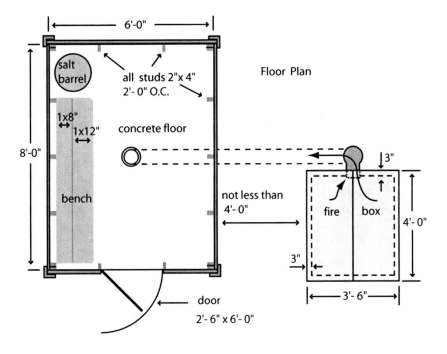

Fig. 11.17.2 Floor plan.

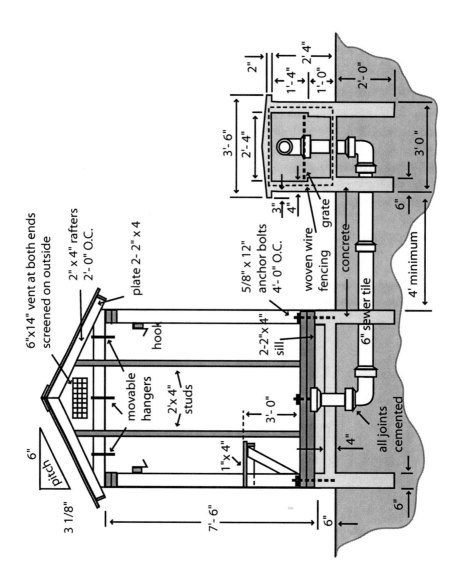

Fig. 11.17.3 Cross section.

240

Fire Pit

This plan incorporates a rather unusual design of a fire pit as the smoke pipe is going down into the ground and then up again into the smokehouse. Although the smoke delivery pipe is going down into the ground and then up again through the smokehouse floor, there is enough draft as the smokehouse is over 8' high.

The firebox is made of concrete that should be reinforced with woven wire fencing and additional rods around metal doors. The top should also be reinforced with 3', 1/4" rods or their equivalent in addition to woven wire fencing. The doors can be made of sheet metal. Doors from an old heating stove can be used. Grates can be made of pipes, rods or old stove or furnace grates. A hole may be made in the top slab to heat water for feed or butchering.

Photo 11.17.1 Frame smokehouse built by Joachim Czekala of Poland. This smokehouse works all year round, even at freezing temperatures.

11.18 Frame Smokehouse # 5695

The following smokehouse was designed in 1965 by the North Dakota State University and the U.S. Dept. of Agriculture. This is a big walk-in smokehouse requiring a foundation reaching below the frost line. This is the depth where water can still be found frozen depending on a particular geographical location.

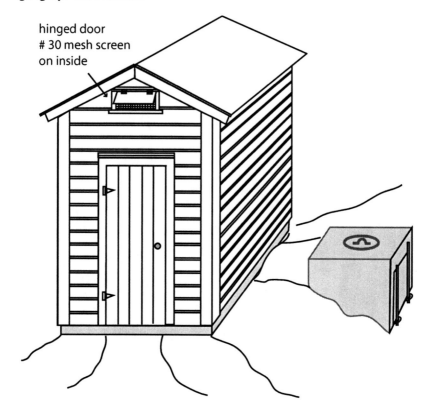

Fig. 11.18.1 General view.

Description

This is a classical design of a smokehouse that has been used in Europe and later in the USA for centuries. About 10' high, ventilation on both sides, # 30 mesh screen on the inside and a hinged door on the outside. Roof covered with tight sheathing and the frame secured to the foundation with ½" anchor bolts. A removable utility bench inside and the barrel with salt in the corner.

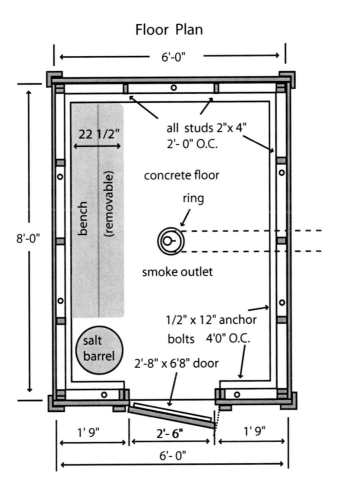

Floor Plan

6'-0"

22 1/2"

bench (removable)

8'-0"

all studs 2"x 4"
2'- 0" O.C.

concrete floor

ring

smoke outlet

1/2" x 12" anchor
bolts 4'0" O.C.

salt barrel

2'-8" x 6'8" door

1' 9"   2'- 6"   1' 9"

6'- 0"

Fig. 11.18.2 Floor plan.

Fire Pit

The firebox in best of tradition is placed below the smokehouse floor and the smoke delivery pipe is pitched up towards the smokehouse. The minimum distance between the firebox wall and the smokehouse's wall is 4' and the pipe has a perfect length of 7 feet. There is a wood plug with a ring covering the smoke pipe when not in use. The firebox is made of reinforced concrete (rods and wire mesh). There is a 24" tapered concrete plug on top of the firebox that when removed will allow the placement of a large vessel for heating water or cooking.

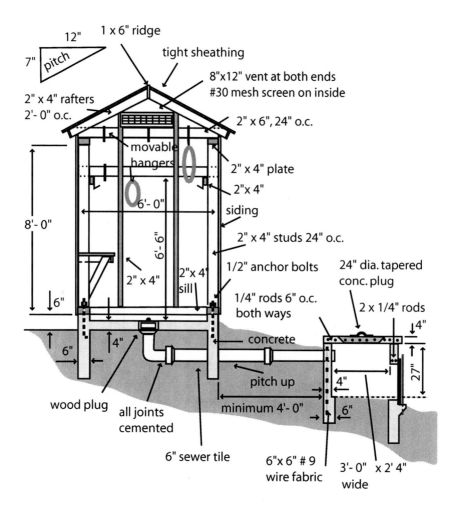

Fig. 11.18.3 Cross section.

A simple but functional sliding metal door is secured by pipe uprights. The door will be hot and it should have hook holes or handles. Earth mound over the pipe completes construction.

11.19 Masonry Smokehouse # 5695

The following smokehouse was designed in 1965 by the North Dakota State University and the U.S. Dept. of Agriculture. This is a big walk-in smokehouse requiring a foundation reaching below the frost line. This is the depth where water can still be found frozen depending on a particular geographical location.

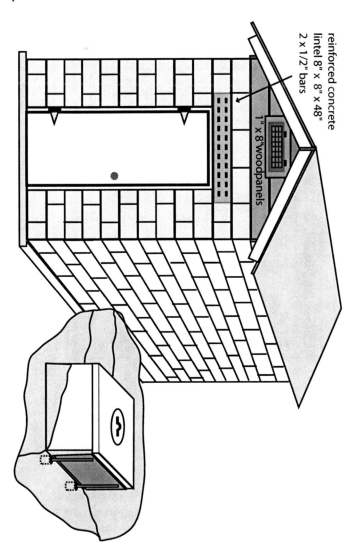

Fig. 11.19.1 General view.

Description

This plan is very similar to the # 5695 Frame Smokehouse, the difference being in the materials used for construction. This is a classical design of a smokehouse that has been used in Europe and later in the USA for centuries. About 10' high, ventilation on both sides, # 30 mesh screen on the inside and a hinged door on the outside. A removable utility bench inside and the barrel with salt in the corner.

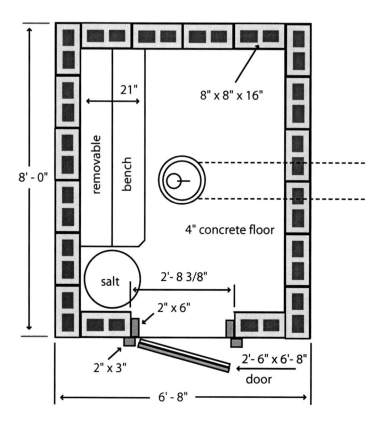

Fig. 11.19.2 Floor plan.

The smokehouse is built using standard size concrete blocks 8" x 8" x 16" which make the project inexpensive and easy to complete. It is almost like building a small house foundation, concrete walls and a wooden roof that can be covered with shingles. The floor is made of 4" concrete, the door is covered on the inside with sheet metal. The advantage of this design is an excellent insulation and a very strong design.

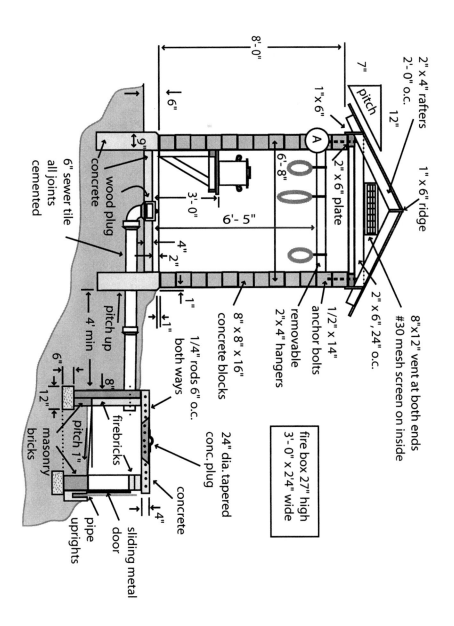

Fig. 11.19.3 Cross section.

247

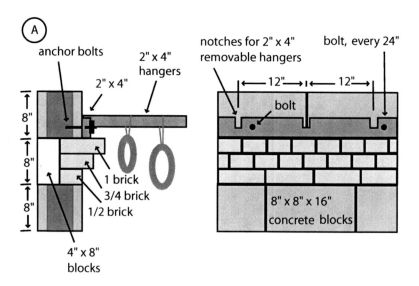

Fig. 10.11.4 Supports for hangers.

This type of smokehouse is an overkill for a home sausage maker but becomes a very attractive proposition for someone who wants to make products for sale. Commercially made smokehouses of this capacity will be very costly and the main difference will be in used materials-stainless steel, computer control, automatic showering and all types of advanced settings.

All those functions can be easily accomplished by using a few thermometers and obeying the basic rules of smoking meats. The proper curing of meats before smoking is more important than all the bells and whistles that come with an expensive industrial unit. Another advantage is that there is almost no maintenance as the smokehouse is so simple. If including this type of smokehouse in a regular meat processing operation it would be a good idea to submit the plans to the local fire department to see what changes may be needed.

They may require a concrete slab roof instead of the framed one (see Masonry Smokehouse #5352 page 232), different thickness of the floor or drain. This type of design has proven itself for hundreds of years and cannot be beaten. Many professional butchers use their own brick layered smokehouses with a great deal of success.

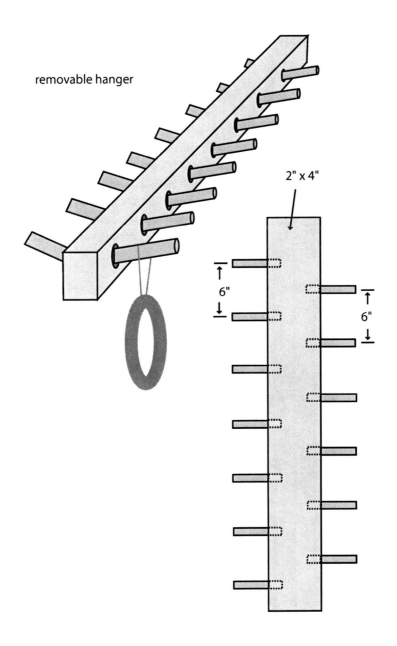

Fig. 11.19.5 Hangers.

11.20 Factory Made Smokers

The photo on the left depicts a very well designed smoker with the following features: 120 V, 800 W, heating element with an adjustable control, sawdust pan, smoke chimney with adjustable damper control, smoke diffuser, removable screens and smoke sticks for hanging meats and sausages. This unit is capable of maintaining internal temperatures of 160-170° F while the outdoor temperatures are as low as 5° F. Thermometer mounted on front door.

Photo 11.20.1 Insulated 20 lb smoker. *Photo courtesy the Sausage Maker, Buffalo, N.Y.*

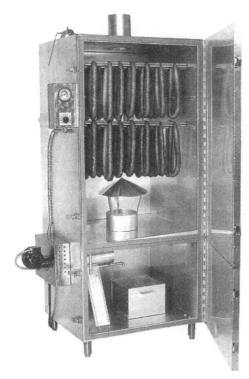

This is a bigger electrical unit, 220 V, 500 W, heating element with thermostat control, electrical blower and built in smoke generator. Larger commercial units have a high wattage (1000-5000 W) heating element or gas burner mounted inside of the smoker.

Photo 11.20.2-100 lb smoker. *Photo courtesy the Sausage Maker, Buffalo, N.Y.*

Different methods are used to generate smoke. A widely used technique is to pyrolise hardwood chips or sawdust. Wood pieces are fed into a gas or electrically heated metal surface at 662-752° F (350-400° C).

With other methods, a block of wood is pushed against a rotating metal wheel and temperatures become high enough for the wood to start smoking. Electrical blowers push the smoke into ducts leading into the smokehouse. There is a small smoker made by Bradley Technologies with a separate smoke generator that employs an original way of producing smoke. Prefabricated blocks of wood (flavor bisquettes) are fed vertically into the smoke generator unit and one by one burn there generating smoke. The smoke generator has a short pipe that fits into the smoking chamber. A nice unit but there is a catch... you are dependent on the company or its distributors to deliver bisquettes which come in different flavors (hickory, apple, alder and others).

Photo 11.20.3 & 11.20.4
-600 lb smoker.

Photos courtesy Koch Equipment, Kansas City, MO.

When properly set, steam, water spraying, and other microprocessor controlled functions take care of the entire smoking and cooking operations. The smoke generator is a separate unit standing outside of the smoker and is connected to it with a pipe. Such units can generate cold smoke as well and permit easy control of temperature and humidity. Immediately after smoking the products are cold showered. The water is released through the smokehouse drain.

11.21 Combustion Theory and Fire Pit Design

For more than a million years the fire was the most precious treasure man possessed. When lightning started a fire, a designated member of the tribe known as "The Fire Keeper" was carrying it with him wherever the tribe decided to move. A fire was not just for cooking, it was a center of social activity since man can remember. This ancient relationship has been forever embedded in our consciousness and even today nothing compares with the beauty of a camp fire with people sitting around playing guitars and singing songs. There is something mystical in those dancing flames and a man's instinct draws him to fire like a magnet.

For people living in urban areas the only fire they know is the fire on the news and firemen running with water hoses. If they are lucky they may see a story about the first chimneys that were built 2,000 years ago in Han – China. Agriculture is only 10,000 years old so fire is without any doubt the oldest thing a man has always had.

A complete wood combustion occurs in three stages:

- Drying-moisture is cooked out of wood to allow it to burn. Even well seasoned wood still contains about 20% moisture that has to go away. Wood drying process continues at temperatures up to 338° F (170° C).

- Pyrolysis-wood molecules are changed by heat, producing smoke, gases and tar particles. As the temperature rises wood breaks down chemically into charcoal and different gases. Dry wood ignites at 400-575° F (200-300° C) and the charcoal and some of the gases start to burn. *At this stage the smoke is given off.* It is accepted that the best quality smoke is produced between 650-750° F (343-398° C) This temperature is not high enough to burn other volatile gases that escape up the chimney. Those escaping gases combine with moisture inside of the chimney creating "creosote" that is dangerous and if not cleaned out on a regular basis it might start a chimney fire.

- The charcoal stage - stage of fire after hydrogen and other gases burned out. CO_2 and CO are still produced but no more water or steam are present. At 1000° F (540° C) charcoal burns away becoming ash. Most gases burn out but some will ignite only when the temperature reaches 1100° F (600° C). To reach such high temperature a lot of oxygen is needed and usually a process called the "secondary combustion" is employed. At such high temperatures wood burns very clean leaving no unburned particles behind. One cubic meter of dry wood corresponds to about 1 drum of oil (55 gallons).

Wood combustion is an involved chemical process consisting of many reactions taking place at the same time. The basic wood composition is:

		Air dried wood	Oven dried wood
Carbon	(C)	41.0%	50.0%
Hydrogen	(H_2)	4.5%	6.0%
Oxygen	(O_2)	37.0%	42.0%
Water	(H_2O)	16.0%)	---
Ash		1.5%	2.0%

The percentage of ash varies from 0.5-2%. There is also a small percent of sulfur (0.02%) and nitrogen (0.5%) produced in gases and smoke during combustion. Freshly cut wood contains about 50% of moisture. Firewood stored in a ventilated area has a moisture content of about 20%. If kept in a warm space indoors the moisture content can drop lower to even 10%. To further lower moisture content the wood has to be oven dried.

The reaction during efficient burning   the reaction during smoking

$$C + O_2 = CO_2$$
$$2H_2 + O_2 = 2H_2O$$

$$2C + O_2 = 2CO$$

CO_2 is carbon dioxide used in soda water.

H_2O is water or steam.

CO is carbon monoxide, dangerous and potentially lethal. It affects us physically at concentrations as low as 1:100.

By adding more oxygen (air) CO will start burning:

$$2CO + O_2 = 2CO_2$$

When smoking meats we are purposely choking the air supply to create smoke which normally is considered an undesirable inefficient combustion. Other important factors are the firebox shape, construction materials, and the moisture content of the wood. A properly designed masonry heater can reach temperatures as high as 1650-1800°F (900-1000° C).

Fire pits

A fire pit or firebox is the area of the smoker where we burn wood to produce smoke or to generate heat to cook meat. It can be an integral part of the smoker or free standing separate unit connected to a smoker by a pipe or digged out trench in the ground. It may be made of metal, reinforced concrete, or firebricks. The combustion efficiency inside the fire box depends on the ways fresh air is supplied into the burning wood.

All smokers employ a very simple system of draft control as the temperature requirements for creating smoke are rather low. That can be often accomplished without any draft system but in order to cook products inside the smokehouse, some means of temperature control must be created. This involves using air dampers and different methods of placing wood inside.

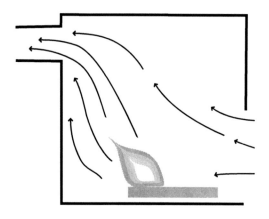

Fig. 11.21.1 Simple firebox.

Note: warm air or smoke will always go up.

A baffle can be placed vertically and it will direct heat in a different direction now. The less clearance between the top of the baffle, the more heat will be supplied to the top of the fire box.

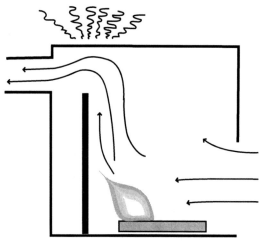

Fig. 11.21.2 Fire box with a vertical baffle.

The three classical ways of placing wood in a firebox follow below:

- Directly on the ground, known as the hearth botom-grate.
- Above the ground on a grate, known as a stool-grate.
- Above the ground on a grate, known as a raised stool-grate.

Hearth Botom Grate

The drawing below shows the most common way of positioning wood when smoking. When wood is placed directly on the ground the air enters from above. This is the way fireplaces work and though all air seems to bypass the wood, enough of it reacts with fire to maintain combustion. It is obvious from the drawing that a strong draft has very little influence on a combustion process as the air will only stream faster over the fire.

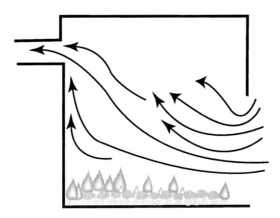

Fig. 11.21.3 Hearth bottom grate. A typical open fire.

The rate of combustion and temperature is controlled by the amount of wood placed in a fire pit and as the air is consumed, a new fresh air comes into its place. *The rate of combustion is independent of the draft and the fire burns as if no chimney existed.* To be able to control burning, the air opening has to be greatly decreased and a damper will start exercising control. Wood burns from front to back. When placing wood on the ground in a firebox with fresh air flowing in freely, the higher temperature will be in the back of a firebox or the barrel. Wood burns from front to back and the higher temperature will be in the back of a firebox.

Stool Grate

The drawing below is an example of a closed firebox used in a heating stove. The air that enters under the wood has a greater density than the hot air above. This creates a difference of pressure (draft) and the only possible way for the air to move is to go up through the wood.

The burning coals will deprive the streaming air of its oxygen and that sets the temperature. Placing wood on a grate permits the introduction of primary air below the burning wood and better combustion. The coal bed physically separates fresh air below from the warm air above, a natural draft is created and *all* air has to flow through the burning coals. *This design permits total control of incoming air.*

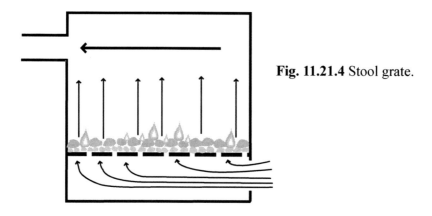

Fig. 11.21.4 Stool grate.

Raised Stool Grate

The drawing below depicts a smaller amount of air flowing through the burning wood and the larger portion blows over the wood increasing the rate of burning. In this case the rate of combustion can be easily controlled by adjusting the air supply under the fire.

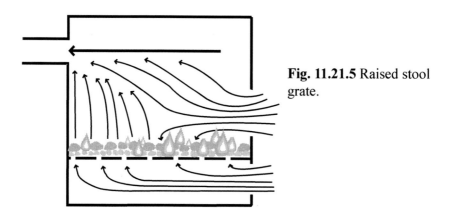

Fig. 11.21.5 Raised stool grate.

The grate significantly increases the efficiency of combustion. The firebox design is further enhanced by sloping the floor of the firebox from the sidewalls down to the grate. By adjusting the doors/dampers in the firebox, the amount of draft and intensity of combustion is controlled. This design becomes especially useful when moist wood is used.

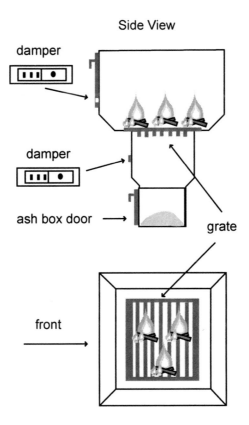

Fig. 11.21.6 Sloping the floor towards the grate.

* bluish flames indicate complete combustion

The rate of combustion is easiest to control in the stool-grate design and most difficult in the hearth bottom-grate type. Smoking can be easily done with an open fire (hearth-bottom grate) and adding more sawdust to a kindling fire allows for some control at least in respect to smoke.

The raised stool grate type can be an effective tool for switching over from smoking to the cooking process. When smoking, the bottom damper has to be shut tight and the top damper open. The firebox becomes the hearth bottom-grate type and by adjusting the top damper we can choke down the air supply and the wood will start smoking. Needless to say we still need to add sawdust or wood chips into the hot coals.

To control combustion and temperatures when cooking, a bottom damper can be adjusted to provide more air which will increase the burning rate and will create more heat and higher temperatures. By the same token the amount of smoke created will be decreasing. A correctly designed raised stool-grate fire pit will allow to switch from smoking to cooking by opening the fresh air damper located below the grate level.

The way most smokers operate is to have an unrestricted flow of incoming air into the pipe. The temperature is set by the rate of burning wood and the excess fresh air is rushing into the pipe together with the smoke. This is a welcome scenario as this fresh air brings moisture with it into the smoker preventing the drying out of sausage casings. In order for the dampers to perfom their designated function, *the firebox and its door must fit tight.* If proper rules for efficient combustion are observed, the wood becomes a very clean fuel.

Secondary combustion

Secondary combustion means adding pre-heated fresh air above the burning wood. This results in higher temperatures and cleaner and more efficient combustion. There will be less soot and other unburned particles and less smoke as well. This is not needed during the smoking process but may be of use when cooking meats. A baffle is placed in the rear of the fire pit to prevent smoke from rushing directly into the flue and to re-direct it into the area where a secondary air (B) is entering the chamber.

In old times the blacksmith was manually pumping more air into the fire to create high temperatures that made metals softer and pliable. That was a very effective technique as he delivered air under higher pressure into the fire.

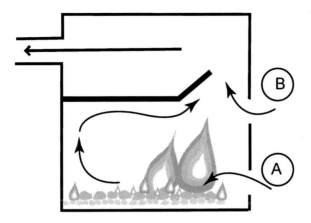

Fig. 11.21.7 Secondary combustion.

Incoming air is preheated in a confined but hot area before being divided into two separate streams: the **(A)** primary (lower) and the **(B)** secondary (higher). The smoke cannot go straight up the flue anymore and has to return through the only available opening where it picks up fresh air **(B)**. This air becomes very hot and burns cleaner due to much higher temperatures. The air for secondary combustion is delivered in a higher part of the firebox, just before smoke enters the pipe. Secondary combustion can be employed in any of the fire pit arrangements as long as there is a baffle and secondary air **(C)** coming close to the flue as shown in the following drawing.

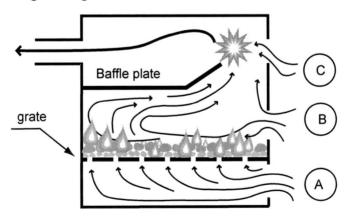

Fig. 11.21.8 Raised stool grate stove with a baffle and secondary air.

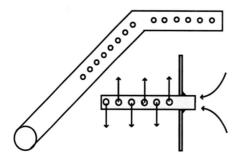

In the above drawing the pipe travels through the flame area and the air inside gets heated and escapes through a series of holes drilled in the end section of the pipe.

Fig. 11.21.9 Perforated pipe.

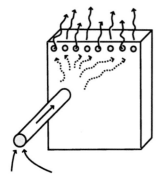

The drawing on the left depicts a very clever solution where the baffle preheats air. Depending whether a grate is employed, a pipe can be connected to the baffle on the bottom of a fire box or can run over the grate.

Fig. 11.21.10 Perforated baffle.

The simplest secondary air delivery system is just a covered hole located near the upper part of the baffle. Due to high temperatures firebox baffle plates should be made of a thicker material. The hole can be drilled in the required area and the pipe can be directly inserted into the hole. It can be welded or threaded and secured with nuts.

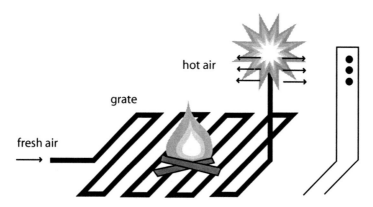

Fig. 11.21.11 Grate made of metal pipe 1/2"-1" diameter. Small holes 1/8" diameter supplying secondary hot air.

A fire pit that is used for smoking and cooking only is subject to different requirements than a fire pit which must supply high heat for grilling. The size of the firebox is determined somewhat by the amount of surface which is desired for cooking. A large firebox may have the following dimensions: height 8 to 10", width 12 to 18", and length 20 to 30". There should be a slight slope from the back to the front, in order to drain out any water which accumulates inside. Because the unit will be standing outside it will be exposed to sudden changes of temperature. Different materials such as stone, brick, firebrick or metal, will expand at different rates when a high heat is generated and the firebox may weaken. The best practice is to line the firebox interior with firebricks in order to protect the outside stonework or masonry from direct exposure to high temperatures.

There are different classes of firebrick, classified according to heat resistance. The firebrick generally used for building fireboxes has a melting point around 2,905° F (1596° C) and its maximum expansion is one-sixteenth inch per foot at a temperature of around 2,200° F (1204° C). Concrete can withstand temperatures of 1000° F (537° C) but it should be noted that the temperatures in the stove or fireplace fall into 800-1500° F (426-815° C) range. It is of no importance whether firebricks are laid on its natural bed, side or standing up. What is important is that a fireclay mortar is applied when joining bricks. The mortar joints are much thinner (less than 1/8") when laying firebricks. The reason for such thin joints is that fireclay used in mortar joints between the bricks is not as resistant to heat as is the firebrick itself. The 1/4" or thicker joints will have a tendency to shrink and cause damage to the joint. A common brick mortar will not withstand high heat because it contains lime which fluxes under heat and because it contains sand which does not posess such heat resisting qualities which are required in these joints.

A properly mixed fireclay mortar is available from lumber or brick supply stores. If only powdered fireclay is available, it should be mixed with about 20-25% portland cement and the joints should be less than 1/8" thick. Once when the firebricks are laid, they should be submitted to intense heat for about 5 hours. This would create a solid and permanent bond. There should not be any space between firebricks and the regular bricks or stonework. The joints must be completely grouted and sealed at the top to prevent any water from entering. In some high heat producing units, an air space between firebricks and the regular bricks is provided. This gap is usually filled with mineral wool or other suitable thermal insulators. It is recommended to build the floor of the firebox with firebricks as well.

There is a special material rated at 3000° F (1600° C), used for making forges. You can cast the entire refractory liner for a forge or just the floor using this material. This specialized cement known as *castable refractory*, consists of calcium aluminate cement, also known as fondue cement or lumnite, and sand with crushed firebrick. A firebox can be constructed from a heavy gauge sheet iron with a grate and doors attached. If such a unit will be covered with bricks or stonework, it must be noted that steel expands much more than firebrick.The top of the fire pit may consist of a solid plate which can be used as a stove base for cooking pots. This will keep them away from smudging on the outside. Such a plate should be at least 3/8" thick, otherwise it may warp and sag in. If a thinner plate is used it should be reinforced with angle brackets. The easiest solution is to have a removable plate. If a permanent plate is installed, it must be kept in mind that some clearance shall be provided for expansion of the points where the plate is attached to the masonry. A fire pit can be an open fire type, a tight firebox with the door and a damper or an open type covered with a metal plate. The plate can be removable or can be attached to the masonry or stonework with hinges. This plate gets very hot and is sometimes used for camp cooking. As metal expands faster than masonry, in order to secure a permanent and lasting installation, a provision for expansion should be included in the design.

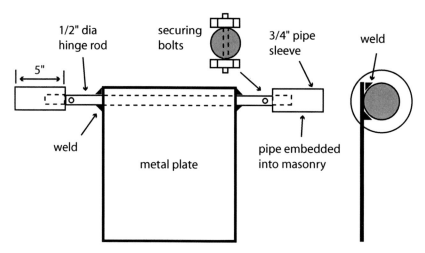

Fig. 11.21.12 Rotating plate. Metal plate and hinge rod will expand due to heat. The design comes from the 1936 book "Camp Stoves And Fireplaces" published by the Forest Service, United Stated Department of Agriculture.

There is a space inside the pipe sleeve for this expansion but the pipe sleeve itself will not expand. As a result there will not be damage to masonry even after many hours of operation.

11.22 Baffles

Controlling flames is a serious problem for small smokers since the distance between the fire pit and the hanging meat is so short. That is why smaller smokers must have a safety feature called a "baffle" that physically separates the fire pit from the smoking chamber. A baffle is a perforated or solid metal plate, rectangular or round, of about 1/8" (3 mm) thickness or more, strong enough to support the weight of river gravel or another baffle. There are three kinds of baffles:

- directional baffles.
- safety baffles.
- heat baffles.

A directional baffle is a solid metal plate whose purpose is to direct heat and flames into a specified direction. The directional baffles could be installed vertically, horizontally or a combination of the two. Directional baffles are used most often in wood stoves.

A safety baffle, commonly used in one unit smokers**,** is a perforated metal plate that separates the firepit from the meat compartment and its main purpose is preventing flames from reaching the smoke chamber. Better designs advocate the use of two or three baffle plates separated by 3 - 4 inches, though that complicates the smokers construction and uses valuable space.

A heat baffle is a metal plate whose job is to absorb heat and then to re-radiate it into the smoking chamber above. In a large smokehouse the heat from a centrally positioned gas burner will go straight up and may not reach all areas of the smokehouse. A metal plate placed above the heat supply will slow down the flow of the hot air and will provide a more even distribution.

Baffles are a very important design feature of any small smoker with a firepit located in its bottom part as they safeguard products from flames and wild jumps of temperature. They provide a piece of mind when smoking making the entire process more organized and controlable and they also help to disperse smoke slowly and evenly to all parts of the smoking chamber. If a smoker is connected by a pipe with a separately standing fire pit, the baffles are not necessary.

The flames in a long narrow firepit of a masonry heater can reach 5' in length. The reason we see them shorter when burning an open fire is that they are cooled by the air above. Meat hangs in different sections of the chamber but the smoke pouring out of the pipe, or the one raising up from the fire pit is using the path with the least resistance and that means it is rushing straight up. A baffle puts some brakes on the smoke forcing it to slow down and disperse evenly in all sections of the smoker. During cooking the baffles contribute to more even heat distribution and the smoker is more efficient. The diameter of the baffle should be about 1" (2.5 cm) smaller than the diameter inside of a barrel to facilitate removal for cleaning. The holes between ½ - 1" (12-25 mm) diameter should be drilled at random so when the two baffles are used, there will be some offset between holes for better smoke distribution.

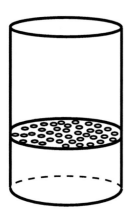

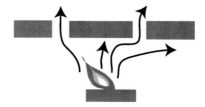

Fig. 11.22.1 Single baffle smoker.

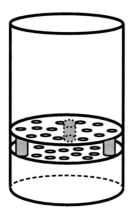

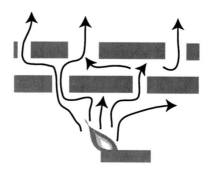

Fig. 11.22.2 Two baffle plates with spacers.

The smoker will work even better when a second baffle is installed. The bottom baffle will rest freely on three right angle metal supports secured to the barrel with bolts and nuts and positioned every 120 degrees. The top baffle will rest freely on three spacers, about 4" high and placed every 120 degrees.

There is a simple but very practical baffle with overlapping plates. It allows the smoke to flow freely but acts as a heat baffle at the same time. You may use two solid 1/8" overlapping plates and the size should correspond to about 60% of the depth of the smoking chamber. The top one should be 4" higher than the bottom one and will overlap it by 4".

Baffle plates are made of metal and will expand when heated so don't install them tight. They may be placed on any suitable supports, even bricks. More plates can be added to make the system even more efficient. Curved plates will facilitate heat and smoke flow.

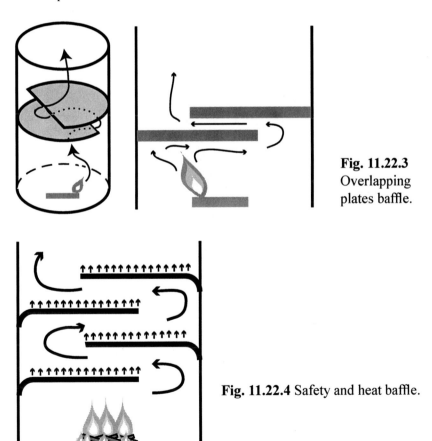

Fig. 11.22.3 Overlapping plates baffle.

Fig. 11.22.4 Safety and heat baffle.

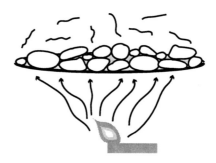

Fig. 11.22.5 Gravel baffle. One of the easiest, most effective baffles can be made by placing medium size river gravel on a suitable screen.

Photo 11.22.1 Colander makes a great smoke disperser/baffle and can be found in every kitchen.

Colanders are made of stainless steel and come in many shapes and sizes. What makes them especially suitable is that they fit nicely over sawdust holding pans. As a result, a little and easily movable smoke generator is created.

Photo 11.22.2 Very functional although not a typical baffle. This stainless steel enclosure with hundreds of holes creates a formidable safety screen to stop any flames from below.

11.23 Smokehouse Heating Systems

There are three types of fuel used in smokers

- Wood – commonly used in home made smokers situated outside.
- Electricity – factory made smokers. Wood chips or sawdust are still needed for smoke generation.
- Gas – natural or propane. Preferred fuel in large industrial smokers. Wood chips or sawdust are still needed for smoke generation.

Wood is traditionally used fuel in outside smokers because:

- It is easy to obtain.
- It is free.
- It is dependable.
- It is fun - when burning wood a simple home made smoker it looks prettier than any factory made model.

On a drawback side it requires more attention when smoking especially when using a small smoker. Wood presents very few safety problems. There is a remote chance of a fire but no chance of explosion which may occur in gas fired systems. Charcoal briquettes may be an acceptable fuel for a barbecue but don't belong in a real smoking category as they often leave an unpleasant undertaste in smoked products. If as the last resort you have to use them, make sure they burn outside of a smoker first until thoroughly covered with white ash before entering the smoking chamber.

The wood fired traditional smoker is a beautiful design capable of producing the highest quality products, but a smoker can become more user friendly by using additional types of fuel, such as electricity or gas. Smoke will still be generated by burning wood chips in a preferably free standing smoke generator (fire pit), but the smoking chamber, which now becomes a cooking chamber, will benefit greatly with the addition of a controlable heating element or a gas burner. This will give us the following advantages:

- Heat on demand – just with the turn of a dial.
- Very accurate temperature control – a thermostat can be added to a heating element.
- Total portability of a propane gas tank and burner.
- A source of additional heat - a smoker can fully operate in its wood burning mode and the electric or gas option could be applied in very cold weather.

Electricity, depending on location, can be inexpensive or very costly and can be a cost factor when smoking a product for a long time. The advantages are that it is easy to use and allows for a precise temperature control especially when the smoker has a thermostat. An extension cable can provide electricity to the outside located smokehouse but a permanent electrical connection will be more practical. A conduit pipe can be run underground to the point where a junction box could be installed. Small 500 W or 1000 W heating elements will use 115 volts but anything bigger than 2000 W will need 220 volts. With electricity there are are no safety or pollution concerns. In the worst case we may blow a fuse which is not a great deal.

From a technical point of view, installing electrical burners is much easier than putting together a gas system as we dont't have to deal with safety issues like a flame blow out. There is no need for thermocouples and safety valves and the installation costs are much lower. Much less of a technical know-how is needed to put a system together. If a smokehouse is the size of a refrigerator or larger, you will need a stronger electrical burner (5000 W). Another burner can be easily added, too. Other devices (thermostat, control lamps, outside lamps, blower, smoke generator etc.) need 115 volts and you will probably end up needing 115 V and 230 V.

Photo 11.23.1 240 V, 2100 W, 8" diameter, heating element from *The Sausage Maker, Buffalo, N.Y.*

Although it is possible to shop around to find all the necessary components for assembling a complete system, it will be faster and cheaper to order the complete kit from the Internet.

The complete kit comes with detailed assembly instructions and costs less than buying individual components. Many factory made smokehouses can be ordered to run on either electricity or gas.

Gas is the cheapest energy and that is why it is used in commercial smokers and other kitchen equipment. Gas burners are easy to control and are able to supply huge amounts of heat. On a downside they present a few safety problems. There are basically two types of gas:

Natural gas – no color or smell, consisting mainly of methane (80-95%) and other gases such as carbon dioxide, carbon monoxide, nitrogen, helium and argon. Its characteristic and unpleasant odor is achieved by purposely adding chemicals that create that smell. The natural gas pressure is very low and it varies from 6 to 10" of WC (water column). This is less than 1 PSI.

To use natural gas a gas pipe, commonly ½" diameter, has to be brought into the smoker and terminated with a valve. On the other side of the valve there will be a fitting and supply line to the burner. Large metropolitan areas are normally piped for natural gas but in some states, for example Florida, natural gas is not available in all areas. The disadvantage of a natural gas connection is that it requires metal pipe lines which once in place, can not be moved with a smokehouse to a new location. The amount of gas that can be delivered to the smokehouse depends on the pressure in the local system, length of pipe run, pipe size, the number of turns and the meter capacity. The disadvantge of a gas installation is its very permanent installation, metal pipe lines and more technical expertise needed for making connections. Its main plus is that you never run out of gas.

Propane – made by distilling a natural gas. Propane is heavier than a natural gas or air and it is stored in tanks as a liquid under pressure. At 0° F the tank pressure is 24 PSI, at 30° F the pressure is at 51 PSI, at 70° F the pressure is 100 PSI, at 90° F it is 150 PSI and at 130° it is 260 PSI. When a propane tank reaches 120° F, the pressure inside is trippled and the tank may release some of the excess pressure through the safety relief valve. There are many camping units with one or two burners and different size propane bottles available at all major department stores. A typical grill's 20-pound cylinder holds five gallons of propane. Almost all outdoor cooking equipment runs on propane gas and we are going to cover propane burners in more detail. The propane tanks and related hardware are available everywhere and the installation of a customized system neither requires heavy technical skills nor professional tools.

Since BTUs are measurements of energy consumption, they can be converted directly to kilowatt-hours (3412 BTUs = 1 kWh) or joules (1 BTU = 1,055.06 joules). A wooden kitchen match produces approximately 1 BTU, and air conditioners for household use typically produce between 5,000 and 15,000 BTU. An average home consumes between 25 and 100 million BTU per year. A BTU is the amount of heat required to increase the temperature of a pint of water (which weighs exactly 16 ounces) by one degree Fahrenheit.

Basic gas system components

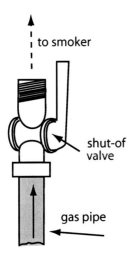

to smoker

shut-of valve

gas pipe

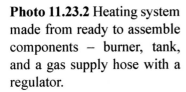

Fig. 11.23.1 A typical natural gas connection.

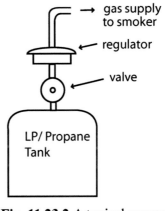

gas supply to smoker

regulator

valve

LP/ Propane Tank

Fig. 11.23.2 A typical propane connection.

Photo 11.23.2 Heating system made from ready to assemble components – burner, tank, and a gas supply hose with a regulator.

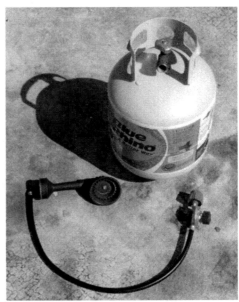

Photo 11.23.3 A typical department store sold system: burner, regulator hose and stand.

A burner is connected to a tank by a flexible hose that runs through a hole in the bottom of the smoker. If very high temperatures are expected, a hose may be inserted into a section of a car radiator hose tubing that can withstand higher temperatures.

Photo 11.23.4 Dual heating system: wood and propane. A separate firebox is used for smoke generation and for cooking. A propane burner is employed for additional heat when needed.

Even though a propane tank is kept outside it is still a dangerous system and unless the safety features are incorporated, such a system should be avoided. The flame can go out inside of the smokehouse but the gas will continue to flow. A peep hole could be drilled through the wall of the smoker to allow viewing of the flame. The hole will also provide fresh air to the venturi. Unfortunately, such measures depend entirely on the awareness of the operator and they are not the right substitute for the safety valve.

11.24 Gas Burners

Both natural gas and propane burners work on the same principle called the "venturi effect". The principle says that as gas or fluid passes through a pipe that narrows or widens, the velocity and pressure of the gas or fluid vary. As the pipe narrows, the gas flows more rapidly.

What sounds like a surprise but holds true, is that when the fluid or gas flows faster through the narrow sections, the pressure actually decreases rather than increases. The venturi tube is a large diameter tube, gradually feeding into a smaller tube and then gradually becoming a larger tube.

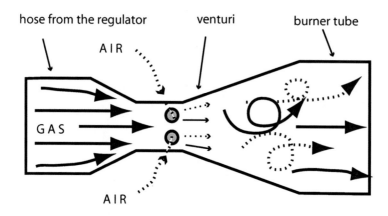

Fig. 11.24.1 Venturi principle.

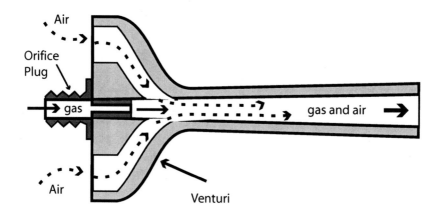

Fig. 11.24.2 Venturi burner.

The regulator hose nut screws on the orifice plug and supplies gas. Gas leaves the orifice plug through a tiny hole and flows at a higher speed but at reduced pressure. That creates a vacuum inside the venturi head and sucks in the air from outside. The air now mixes with gas inside of the tube and flows towards the burner head. This is how most natural and propane burners work today. One of the main advantages of venturi burners is that they work without electricity.

There are very strong power burners where venturi is not needed. In those, gas and the air supply are two independent systems where air is supplied by the electrical blower. These powerful burners are capable of melting glass or metals and have no practical use in a smokehouse.

The most important part of the burner is the orifice plug with the hole in it. This is the point where the gas escapes from the hose or pipe and enters the mixing bell of the burner. Orifice plugs are replaceable and screwed into the orifice spud. Nearly all atmospheric (venturi) burners have a gas orifice that is accurately fixed in the burner throat providing air intake.

Photo 11.24.1 Screen venturi and attached orifice plug.

Photo courtesy Tejas Smokers, Houston, TX.

There are orifice charts that specify what diameter the orifice hole should be drilled for a particular burner. Those holes are normally very small, about 1/16" (1.5 mm) or less. They may be bigger when burning natural gas. An example of how a 1 mm orifice hole used at different gas pressures effects the amount of generated heat is presented below:

Low Pressure Chart						High Pressure Chart- Liquid Propane		
BTU / hr						BTU / hr		
Drill Size	Deci-mal	Met-ric	N-Gas	N-Gas	L-P	5 PSI	10 PSI	15 PSI
60	0.040	1 mm	4" WC (Water Column)	7" WC	11" WC			
			4350 BTU/hr	5750	11175	39689	56130	68745

It can be seen in the table that for the same hole the heat output of the burner will increase with the rise of pressure. At 15 PSI, a propane burner will supply 16 times more heat than a natural gas burner at 4" WC. Complete tables with different orifice holes and pressures up to 25 PSI can be obtained for free on the Internet. The pressure of natural gas in a pipe is very low and its venturi is able to suck in only about 40% of the needed air into the burner. The burning flame consumes the rest of the needed air from the air that surrounds it. This is the reason why all natural gas appliances have such generous air openings near the burners. This also means that the gas burner may not work too well when placed inside of the smoking chamber when heavy smoke keeps pouring into it. Because of the natural gas low pressure there is no need for a regulator.

Pressure Conversion Chart	
Inches of water (WC-Water Column)	Pounds per square inch (PSI)
4	0.1445
7	0.2529
11	0.3974

Propane gas is flowing out of a regulator at a much higher pressure and is being able to suck in all needed air into the burner, providing that the venturi chamber is located outside of the smokehouse. Propane gas leaving the tank goes to the regulator first, which may be either fully adjustable (0-20 or 0-30 psi) or a preset type (10 or 20 psi). The adjustable regulators usually have a large knob for adjustments. All regulators do basically one function: they reduce pressure and keep it constant (regulated). There are propane gas regulators that are preset to 6 ounces of pressure and they are considered low pressure regulators. Although they are preset they may have a small range of adjustment. Needless to say they will supply less heat than a high pressure burner.

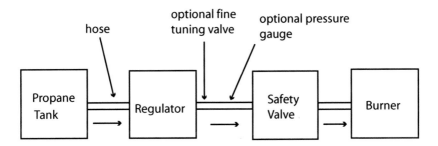

Fig. 11.24.3 A typical propane system

Smokehouse Burners

If the smokehouse is small, you are better off installing an electrical heating element. It will be faster, easier and cheaper. Choosing a gas burner for a large smokehouse presents a little problem. Let's say that on the inside your smokehouse is 36" wide, 2' deep and 6' high, a total of 36 cubic feet. Most gas burners are very short, 4 - 6" and if placed inside will provide heat by the side wall only.

The venturi part and the connecting hose should be outside of the unit and you are left with a burner head situated a few inches from the wall. There will be uneven heat distribution in the smokehouse chamber as the heat will go straight up where the burner is placed. You could of course use a blower but that complicates the design that we try to keep very simple. If the entire burner must be placed inside, replace the hose with an iron pipe. Keep in mind that now when venturi is inside it needs air supply. The air may come in the smoke delivery pipe or some opening must be provided. Using such an adjustable length burner it is possible to place a burner in the center of any size smokehouse (see Photo 11.24.4 on page 281).

Burner Safety Issues

According to United States regulations burners used in outdoor cooking equipment don't require safety valves. It is believed that when the flame goes out, the gas can safely escape to the atmosphere and the cook will eventually discover the fact. Smokehouses like many other gas heated appliances (ovens, water heaters) present safety hazards. If the flame of the burner or the pilot light becomes extinguished for any reason, the gas will keep on going into the smokehouse creating both a risk of fire and a health hazard. The risk will deepen even further if the smoke generator will be supplying smoke at the same time as this may deliver a spark to ignite the gas.

To eliminate this danger a device called a thermocouple is used to sense when the pilot light is burning. A thermocouple consists of two dissimilar metals that are joined together at the sensing end. A different voltage is generated, typically between 1 to about 70 microvolts per degree Celsius which increases with temperature. When this voltage reaches a pre-set level, the thermocouple shuts down the gas supply.

The tip of a thermocouple is placed in the flame and as long as the thermocouple remains hot it holds the pilot gas valve open. If the pilot flame goes out, the temperature of the thermocouple will drop and the gas supply valve will close, shutting off the gas to the pilot light. The same thermocouple controls the main gas valve in the same manner. The thermocouple voltage, typically around 20 mV, operates the gas supply valve responsible for feeding the pilot.

To start the burner again we have to open the flow of gas. When the thermocouple is cold its voltage is too low for the solenoid to pull the valve down. The *manual reset button has to be pushed down* to open the gas supply and the pilot can be re-lit. The reset button has to be held down for 20 more seconds to warm up the thermocouple. Now when the thermocouple is hot again, it produces enough voltage for the solenoid to hold down the valve and the gas starts to flow again.

Hoses, Gauges and Regulators

The gas from the tank flows to the regulator and then through the safety valve (if used) into the burner. In most cases the hose comes with a regulator already attached to it. There are two types of regulators:

1. Pre-set pressure type - the pressure is fixed in the factory and the small dial allows for some finer tuning.
2. Variable pressure regulator - the regulator has a much bigger knob and allows for adjusting pressure in a much wider range, for example from 0 - 35 PSI or from 0 - 20 PSI.

Using an adjustable pressure regulator we can not determine what is the exact gas pressure flowing into the burner. A pressure gauge is needed to display the actual pressure reading.

Photo 11.24.2 An adjustable regulator, 30 PSI.

Photos courtesy Tejas Smokers, Houston, TX.

Photo 11.24.3 An adjustable regulator, 20 PSI with a pressure gauge.

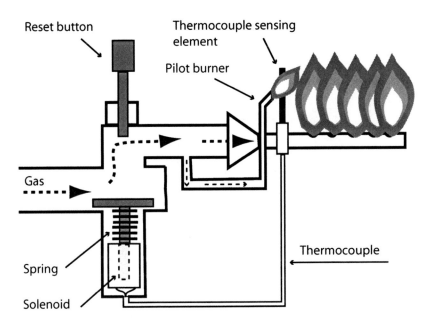

Fig. 11.24.4 Safety valve. Thermocouple hot. Solenoid energized. Gas flowing ino main burner and into the pilot light burner.

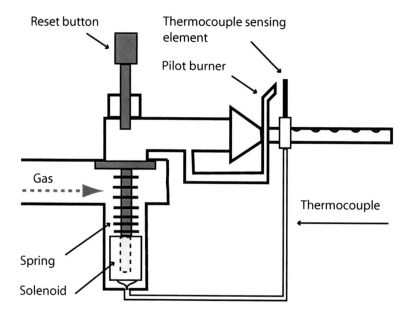

Fig. 11.24.5 Thermocouple cold. Solenoid de-energized. Spring pushes the valve up preventing gas from flowing into the main or pilot light burner.

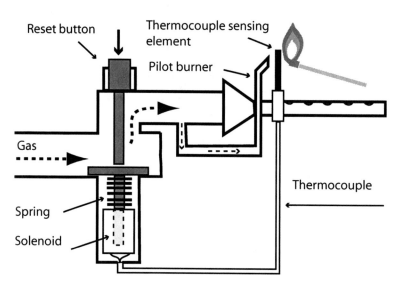

Fig. 11.24.6 Reset button manually pushed down, valve pushed down, gas flows into the burner.

Making Your Own Burner

Why would anyone want to build his own burner? Or a smokehouse? In some countries procuring a burner may be very difficult or simply too expensive.

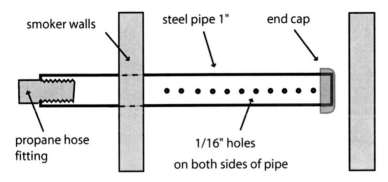

Fig. 11.24.7 Homemade burner - basic idea.

In a large smokehouse it will be extremely difficult to maintain cooking temperature using wood only. Without electricity or natural gas nearby, our choice is narrowed to a liquid propane system. Quite often a very large gas burner is needed. There is a very clever burner design from Tejas Smokers, Texas. They have physically separated the burner head from the venturi by a common, adjustable length steel pipe.

Photo 11.24.4 Adjustable length venturi burner.

Photo 11.24.5 Burner head. **Photo 11.24.6** Venturi and orifice plug.

Above photos courtesy Tejas Smokers, Houston, TX.

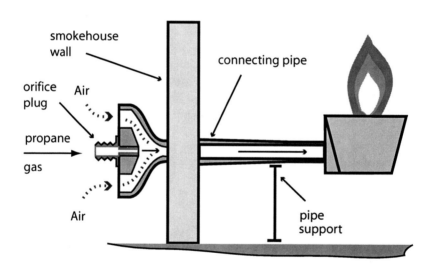

Fig. 11.24.8 Burner head connected by adjustable length pipe.

A section of pipe threaded on both ends connects the venturi with a burner. A centrally placed burner will not distribute heat equally in all parts of the large smokehouse unless a metal plate/baffle will be installed above the burner.

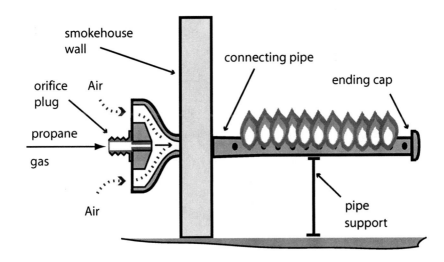

Fig. 11.24.9 Connecting pipe becomes a burner.

This is a home made burner solution. A section of the steel pipe is threaded into the venturi. Pre-threaded pipes are commonly available. The other end is capped. A series of 1/16" holes are drilled on both sides throughout the length of the pipe and the pipe becomes the burner itself.

Larger holes may create problems as the pressurized propane may extinguish the flame. This will not happen with natural gas as the pressure is much lower and the holes can be drilled slightly larger. If the regulator is not able to meet the demand, there might be a case where a back section of the pipe burner will lose a flame as there is not enough pressure to sustain the flame. The simplest solution is to drill slightly larger holes in the area of the pipe that is having difficulty. Another solution will be to get a stronger regulator.

Fig. 11.24.10 Insufficient gas pressure. The rear end of the burner not burning.

Fig. 11.24.11 Larger holes drilled out in the back of the burner.

The holes should be drilled at a 45° angle. This is much simpler than it looks - just drill two rows of holes at a 90° angle (drawing below), then turn the pipe 45°.

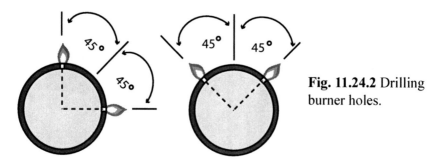

Fig. 11.24.2 Drilling burner holes.

All smokehouse gas burners are subject to burner safety issues explained earlier on this page. Natural gas or propane must go first to the safety valve and only from there it can flow into the burner. All connections must be checked for gas leaks. Although it is feasible to design and install our own gas heating system, the fastest approach will be to order a gas kit with assembly instructions.

Warning:

The information provided in this chapter on making your own burners and installing your own gas heating systems is for educational purpose only. The gas systems of any kind are very dangerous and the actual work involved of making or assembling any components or the whole systems should be performed by a qualified and licensed plumber or contractor only.

Chapter 12

Smokehouse And The Local Law Regulations

Smoke consists of many gaseous components such as unburned solid particles, carbon monoxide, resinous particles, hydrocarbons, formaldehyde, acids, water, alcohols and many others. The final composition of smoke will vary depending on wood composition, humidity, smoke generation temperature, even the product type. The temperature control is probably the most effective factor in controlling the process. To control smoke emissions from large industrial smokehouses and to meet ever increasing pollution standards, new more effective methods have been devised:

1. Afterburner is a secondary combustion heating device which creates high enough temperatures to burn most smoke components that would normally escape into the atmosphere. The device is placed on top of the smokehouse, between floors or on the roof of the building. Afterburner is an effective device but energy hungry which makes it costly to operate.

2. Wet scrubber is a wet devices that try to capture smoke particles, mix them with water and drain them away. Mist scrubbers inject water mist into the chamber where they collide with smoke exhausting from the smoking chamber. Packed bed scrubbers are lined with a special wet material that absorbs smoke. Smoke liquefies and is drained away. Vortex scrubbers use a whirling flow pattern which breaks water into fog like droplets. Smoke mixes with droplets and then liquefies.

3. Electrostatic precipitator is a filter that works on the same principle used in car catalytic converters. The exhausting smoke is first heated, then it passes through a catalyst, causing a chemical reaction that eliminates harmful emissions leaving CO_2 and water. Precipitators are effective for controlling solid smoke particle emissions. Electrostatic precipitators are commonly used in restaurant hood filtering systems.

Combined methods, such as a wet scrubber for gaseous emission control may be used with an electrostatic precipitator for particle removal. Needless to say all technologies are applied to smoke that is exiting the smoking chamber and not before.

All above methods are quite expensive to implement and it is not expected that a hobbyist will find much use for them. Nevertheless for those interested in starting a commercial enterprise this information might be of value. A smokehouse can be built or installed for a commercial purpose or for private use and depending on its location it will face different regulations. There is not much in the Code of Federal Regulations that covers the subject and the only federal institution that may come into play is the Environmental Protection Agency (EPA) as they deal with the problems of pollution. The Food Safety And Inspection Service does not care about the smoker, its location, size or the amount of smoke it discharges. They worry about factors which influence meat safety such as the plant's sanitary conditions or processing temperatures.

What should be noted is that a store which smokes fish for retail sale will be subject to less stringent requirements than an establishment that smokes meats wholesale. There are stores where smoking meats takes place in a horizontal smoker outside and then they are brought inside of the store. The store itself conforms to the safety requirements such as plumbing, wash sinks, garbage disposal etc., of the local county. An insignificant amount of smoke is discharged and if there are no complaints from local businesses, the little store should be fine. Most smart operators start smoking at 5 AM and by 9 AM the bulk of production is done.

A commercial plant smoking thousands of pounds of meat an hour will definitely need to install a filtering system. The EPA document Compilation of Air Pollutant Emission Factors AP-42, Section 9.5.2, covers emission standards in Meat Smokehouses.

Every state or county will have a final word on its air pollution restrictions and local authorities should be consulted before construction is started. For example the following comes from California regulations:

Section 5 - List of Title V, Insignificant Activities

I. General Criteria for Insignificant Activities

An insignificant activity is any activity, process, or emission unit which is not subject to a source-specific requirement of a State Implementation Plan, preconstruction permit, or federal standard and which: 1) meets the "Criteria for Specific Source Categories" below; or 2) emits no more than 0.5 tons per year of a federal hazardous air pollutant (HAP) and no more than two tons per year of a regulated pollutant that is not HAP.

E. Food Processing Equipment

1. Any oven in a food processing operation where less than 1,000 pounds of product are produced per day of operation.

Justification:

13.7 lb VOC/2,000 lb product * 1,000 lb product = 6.9 lb VOC/day

(Reference AP-42)

2. Any smokehouse in which the maximum horizontal inside cross section area does not exceed 20 square feet.

Justification:

0.3 lb PM10/ton of meat * 1 ton/day = 0.3 lb PM10/day

0.6 lb CO/ton of meat * 1 ton/day = 0.6 lb CO/day

(Reference AP-42).

3. Any confection cooker, and associated venting or control equipment, cooking edible products intended for human consumption.

Justification:

Insignificant air pollutant emissions from this source.

Note:

- VOC = Volatile organic compound.
- PM = Particulate matter.
- CO = Carbon monoxide.

Federal standards include:

40 CFR Parts 60 (New Source Performance Standards), 61 (National Emission Standards for Hazardous Air Pollutants), 63 (National Emission Standards for Hazardous Air Pollutants for Source Categories). HAPs are toxic substances listed pursuant to Section 112 (b) of the Federal Clean Air Act.

A home made smoker can be a simple inexpensive unit, sometimes even portable and we may not even involve any officials. On the other hand if one intends to build an expensive combination island (grill, smoker, water sink, lights) that will require electrical wiring and gas and plumbing connections, it will be a good idea to find out from the local city hall about regulations. *In every state each county has a County Nuisance Ordinance.* If someone finds that your campfire or open burning is a nuisance to him or her, you will be asked to put the fire out. That will apply to meat smoking as well. If you live in a metropolitan area and smoke meats for hours at the time, someone might call the officials. The local Fire Department does not have much information about smokers or meat smoking, all they are concerned with is the common sense safety: keep fire away from any structures, don't smoke under low hanging trees, have a garden hose (water source) close by, don't use any flammable or combustible liquids, have adult supervision when the kids are present, make sure the fire is completely out after the event is over, etc.

If you plan to build a sophisticated smokehouse, by all means show the fire department the plans and they will gladly review them and make some recommendations. Without a doubt the first step is to talk to the Local Zoning Office to see whether such a structure is allowed and in most cases it is. The second step is to check with your county city hall if a building permit is required. They will have everything there is to know about building a smokehouse in their area.

For example, in Maryland the Air Quality General Permit to Construct "Charbroilers and Pit Barbecues" applies to every person who owns, constructs (installs), or operates a non-residential charbroiler or pit barbecue with a total cooking area greater than 5 square feet (0.46 square meters). The permit is not required for residential units.

In St. Louis City the smokehouses are permitted within residential zoning districts as long as they conform to city ordinances. Any building or structure intended to be used as a smokehouse within a residential zoning district which exceeds fifty (50) square feet in size shall require a permit from the building commissioner prior to construction and shall conform to all applicable regulatory codes for such structure (Ord. 65944 #2, 2003).

In the state of Milwaukee the General Building Code has Section 239-4 which says that: In addition to the regulations 239-1, Detached Private Garages, smokehouses shall:

- have walls of not less than 2 hours fire-resistive construction with a noncombustible floor and roof, and a metal door overlapping the door opening at least one inch at the top and on both sides, and shall have a noncombustible vent or smoke flue.
- may be located within the principal building if constructed of 3 hour fire-resistant construction throughout.

No matter where you are located *you may expect requirements such as:*

- Non-combustible or masonry wall structures.
- Metal door.
- Concrete slab (at least 3 1/2" thick).
- Minimum distance of 15' from property lines and from any other structure.
- No sale of smoked meat that was prepared in a smokehouse.

As you can see there isn't any set of government instructions or regulations on building smokehouses and you have to do your own homework by visiting your local court house or city hall.

Chapter 13

Smokehouse Construction Photos

The smokehouse depicted on these photos has been designed and built by Joachim Czekała in Poland.

Photo 13.1 Smoke delivery system - back of the smokehouse. Firebox doors, smoke channel and the foundation are being constructed.

Photo 13.2 & Photo 13.3 Building frame.

Photo 13.4 Smokehouse on foundation, rear view.

Photo 13.5 Gravel baffle for an even smoke distribution.

Photo 13.6 Door opened - smoking in progress.

Photo 13.7 Smokesticks tray.

292

Photo 13.8 Smokehouse thermometer.

Photo 13.9 Firebox. Top door - loading firewood, bottom door - ash removal.

Photo 13.10 & Photo 13.11 Front view.

Appendix A

Tables and Formulas

How To Calculate Cure # 1 in Comminuted Products (Sausages)

In case you are really curious and would like to know how to calculate ppm (parts per million) of nitrite when using Cure #1 here is the formula and an example:

How much Cure #1 is needed to cure 200 lbs of meat?

ppm = cure mix x % sodium nitrite in cure x 1,000,000 / weight of meat

Note that the weight of cure mix and the weight of meat must be in the same units (pounds, ounces, grams, kilograms)

Maximum allowed limit of sodium nitrite is **156 ppm**
Cure #1 contains 6.25% sodium nitrite = 0.0625
Solving equation for cure #1:

cure mix = ppm x meat weight/% sodium nitrite in cure x 1,000,000
n = unknown amount of cure mix

156 = n x 0.0625 x 1,000,000 / 200
n = 156 x 200 / 0.0625 x 1,000,000
n = 0.4992 lb of Cure #1, which equals 7.98 oz (226 g)

To cure 200 lbs of meat and stay within the prescribed 156 ppm nitrite limit we should use no more than 0.4992 lb of Cure #1. This formula applies to the dry method of curing when the nitrite is directly applied to meat. The example will be meat that was ground and then will be mixed with spices and Cure #1 to make a sausage.

The same example using the metric system:
1 lb = 0.453 kg, 200 lbs = 90.6 kg
n = 156 x 90.6 / 0.0625 x 1,000,000
n = 0.226 kg (226 g) of Cure #1

If 0.0625 is removed from the above formula, not Cure #1 but sodium nitrite will become a part of the equation:

ppm = sodium nitrite x 1,000,000 / weight of meat

sodium nitrite = ppm x meat weight/1,000,000

N = unknown amount of sodium nitrite

156 = N x 1,000,000 / 200

N = 156 x 200 / x 1,000,000

N = 0.031 lb of sodium nitrite, which equals 5 oz (14 g)

To find the amount of Cure #1 required, we have to divide the amount of sodium nitrite (14 g) by the percentage of sodium nitrite in the Cure #1 (6.25%)

14 / 0.0625 = 224 g of Cure #1

How to Calculate Cure #1 in Brined Products

Calculating cure in mixed products is more difficult when the traditional wet curing method is used. It is easy to calculate how many parts per million of sodium nitrite is in the brine, but it is harder to estimate how much sodium nitrite has made it into the meat. A meat piece can be immersed in brine for a day, a week or a month and a different amount of sodium nitrite will penetrate the meat.

Brines with different salt concentrations will exhibit different speeds of salt and nitrite penetration. One will have to weigh the meat to estimate the amount of brine the meat has picked up.

All modern curing methods rely on injecting brine directly into the meat which eliminates this guessing game. We know exactly how much brine we inject and precise calculations can be performed. These figures are based on pump percentages and revolve around 10% average pump pick up. What it means is that a 10 lb meat piece will be injected with the amount of brine corresponding to 10% of its weight. In this case 1 lb of brine will be injected into 10 lbs of meat.

Maximum allowed limit of sodium nitrite in brined products is **200 ppm**
Cure #1 contains 6.25% sodium nitrite = 0.0625

Example:
Hams are to be pumped at 12% using Cure #1. How much cure can be added to 100 gallons of brine? Brine weight is 9.5 lb per gallon.

ppm = cure mix x % of sodium nitrite in cure x pump% x 1,000,000 / brine weight

cure mix = ppm x brine weight / % pump x 0.0625 x 1,000,000
n = unknown amount of cure mix
n = 200 x 950 / 0.12 x 0.0625 x 1,000,000
n = 25.33 lb of Cure #1

One gallon of water weighs 8.33 lb but saturated brine (100 degree) contains 26.4% salt in it. One gallon of saturated brine contains 2.64 lb of salt and weighs 10.03 lb. Depending on the strength of your brine you can estimate its weight or use brine tables to arrive at more accurate values.

Example:
A meat piece is to be pumped at 10% using Cure #1. How much cure can be added to 1 gallon of brine? Brine weight is 9.5 lb per gallon which corresponds to the brine strength of around 40°.
n = 200 x 9.5 / 0.10 x 0.0625 x 1,000,000
n = 0.30 lb (4.8 oz, 136 g) of cure #1.

If 0.0625 is removed from the above formula, not Cure #1 but sodium nitrite will become a part of the equation:
ppm = sodium nitrite x pump % x 1,000,000 / brine weight
sodium nitrite = ppm x brine weight / % pump x 1,000,000
N = 200 x 9.5 / 0.10 x 1,000,000
N = 0.019 lb of sodium nitrite

To find the amount of Cure #1 required, we have to divide the amount of sodium nitrite (0.019 lb) by the percentage of sodium nitrite in the Cure #1 (6.25%).
0.019/0.0625 = 0.30 lb of Cure # 1

Only established meat plants have access to sodium nitrite and they may formulate their own cures. A hobbyist will use Cure #1 which is pre-mixed and safer. It is our belief that it is beneficial to know how to calculate the amount of Cure #1 that is needed to cure meat for two reasons:

1. More confidence is obtained by understanding the process.
2. Unproven recipes can be easily checked for the correct amount of cure.

Brine Tables and How to Use Them

If you come across a recipe and you would like to determine what is the strength of the brine, just follow the two steps:

1. Find the percent of salt by weight in the solution: weight of salt/(weight of salt plus weight of water), then multiply the result by 100%.
2. Look up the tables and find the corresponding salometer degree.

For example let's find the strength of the brine that is mentioned in many recipes and calls for adding 1 pound of salt to 1 gallon of water (8.33 pounds).

% salt by weight = 1lb of salt/1 lb of salt + 8.33 lbs (1 gallon) of water = 0.1071
0.1071 x 100 % = 10.71 % of salt

Looking in the table at Column 2 (percent salt by weight) we can see that 10.71% corresponds to **40 ½ degrees**.

Another popular brine is made by adding 3/4 cup of salt (219 g) to 1 gallon (3.8 liters) of water

219 g / 219 + 3800 g = 0.05
0.05 x 100 = 5% of salt

Looking in the table at Column 2 (percent salt by weight) we can see that 5% corresponds to **19 degrees**.

Adding salt to water and checking the reading with a salometer is a rather time consuming method and you can make brine much faster by using tables, the way professionals do. For example we want 22 degrees brine to cure chicken. If you follow the 22 degree row to the right you will see in Column 3 that 0.513 lb of salt has to be added to 1 gallon of water to make 22 degree brine. To make 80 degree brine we need to mix 2.229 lbs of salt with 1 gallon of water. Then check it with your salinometer and you can add a cup of water or a tablespoon of salt to get a perfect reading.

If you end up with not enough brine, make some more. If you think you may need just 1/2 gallon more of 80 degree brine, take 1/2 gallon of water and add 1/2 of salt that the table asks for. In this case looking at 80 degree brine (Column 1), going to the right you can see that in Column 3 the amount of the needed salt is 2.229 lbs. Yes, but this amount is added to 1 gallon of water to create 80 degree brine. Because we use only 1/2 gallon now, this amount of salt needs to be halved: 2.229 lbs/2 = 1.11 lbs. In other words if we add 1.11 lbs of salt to 1/2 gallon of water we will also create 80 degree brine.

Let's say you need about 10 gallons of 60 degrees SAL brine (15.8% salt) to cure ham. Locate 60 degrees SAL in Column 1 and then go across to Column 3 where it is stated that 1.567 pounds salt/gallon of water is needed. Multiplying 1.567 (pounds salt/gallon of water x 10 gallons of water gives us 15.67 lbs of salt. This is how much salt needs to be added to 10 gallons of water to make 60 degrees SAL brine.

Sodium Chloride (Salt) Brine Tables For Brine at 60° F (15° C) in US Gallons

Salometer Degrees	% of Salt by Weight	Pounds of Salt per Gallon of Water
0	0.000	0.000
1	0.264	0.022
2	0.526	0.044
3	0.792	0.066
4	1.056	0.089
5	1.320	0.111
6	1.584	0.134
7	1.848	0.157
8	2.112	0.180
9	2.376	0.203
10	2.640	0.226
11	2.903	0.249
12	3.167	0.272
13	3.431	0.296
14	3.695	0.320
15	3.959	0.343
16	4.223	0.367
17	4.487	0.391
18	4.751	0.415
19	5.015	0.440
20	5.279	0.464
21	5.543	0.489
22	5.807	0.513
23	6.071	0.538
24	6.335	0.563
25	6.599	0.588
26	6.863	0.614
27	7.127	0.639
28	7.391	0.665
29	7.655	0.690
30	7.919	0.716

31	8.162	0.742
32	8.446	0.768
33	8.710	0.795
34	8.974	0.821
35	9.238	0.848
36	9.502	0.874
37	9.766	0.901
38	10.030	0.928
39	10.294	0.956
40	10.588	0.983
41	10.822	1.011
42	11.086	1.038
43	11.350	1.066
44	11.614	1.094
45	11.878	1.123
46	12.142	1.151
47	12.406	1.179
48	12.670	1.208
49	12.934	1.237
50	13.198	1.266
51	13.461	1.295
52	13.725	1.325
53	13.989	1.355
54	14.253	1.384
55	14.517	1.414
56	14.781	1.444
57	15.045	1.475
58	15.309	1.505
59	15.573	1.536
60	15.837	**1.567**
61	16.101	1.598
62	16.365	1.630
63	16.629	1.661
64	16.893	1.693

65	17.157	1.725
66	17.421	1.757
67	17.685	1.789
68	17.949	1.822
69	18.213	1.854
70	18.477	1.887
71	18.740	1.921
72	19.004	1.954
73	19.268	1.988
74	19.532	2.021
75	19.796	2.056
76	20.060	2.090
77	20.324	2.124
78	20.588	2.159
79	20.852	2.194
80	21.116	**2.229**
81	21.380	2.265
82	21.644	2.300
83	21.908	2.336
84	22.172	2.372
85	22.436	2.409
86	22.700	2.446
87	22.964	2.482
88	23.228	2.520
89	23.492	2.557
90	23.756	2.595
91	24.019	2.633
92	24.283	2.671
93	24.547	2.709
94	24.811	2.748
95	25.075	2.787
96	25.339	2.826
97	25.603	2.866
98	25.867	2.908

| 99 | 26.131 | 2.948 |
| 100 | 26.395 | 2.986 |

- Seawater contains approximately 3.695% of salt which corresponds to 14 degrees salometer.
- At 100 degrees brine is fully saturated and contains 26.395% of salt.
- 1 US gallon of water weighs 8.33 lbs.
- 1 US gallon = 3.8 liters = 3.8 kilograms.
- Bear in mind that when you add Cure #1 to your solution (it contains 93.75 % salt) you will be changing the strength of the brine, especially at higher degrees. Simply subtract this amount from the salt given by the tables.

Salinometer readings are calibrated to give a correct indication when the brine is at 60° F temperature. Each brine tester will have its own instructions for temperature compensation but the basic rule of thumb says that for every 10° F the brine is above 60° F, one degree should be added to the reading before using table. If the brine is below 60° F subtract 1 degree for each 10° F from the observed salinometer reading before using table.

For example, if a salinometer indicates 70 degrees brine and the brine's temperature is 40° F, the corrected salinometer reading would be 68 degrees (for each 10 F below 60 F, one salinometer degree is subtracted). If the brine temperature is 80° F and the salinometer indicates 40 degrees, the corrected reading would be 82 degrees SAL (for each 10° F above 60° F, one salinometer degree is added). These are very small differences which are of bigger importance for a meat plant curing huge amounts of meat at one time. Needless to say a thermometer is needed too.

Baumé Scale

You may come across a scale in Baumé degrees that is based on the specific gravity of the brine measured with a hydrometer. It is a popular scale in metric countries and you can often find reference given in Baumé degrees. One can measure the gravity of the brine with a specially designed float (like a brine tester) and one can refer to the table and look up the % NaCl (salt) by weight. One Baumé degree corresponds to 10 g of salt in 1 liter of water. The table below compares brine strength degrees with Baumé scale.

Baumé Scale

Specific Gravity	% Salt by Weight	Baumé Degrees	Salometer Degrees
1.007	1	1.0	4
1.014	2	2.0	8
1.022	3	3.1	12
1.029	4	4.1	15
1.037	5	5.2	19
1.044	6	6.1	25
1.051	7	7.0	27
1.058	8	7.9	30
1.066	9	8.9	34
1.073	10	9.8	37
1.081	11	10.9	41
1.089	12	11.9	46
1.096	13	12.7	50
1.104	14	13.7	54
1.112	15	14.6	57
1.119	16	15.4	61
1.127	17	16.3	65
1.135	18	17.2	69
1.143	19	18.1	72
1.151	20	19.0	76
1.159	21	19.9	80
1.168	22	20.9	84
1.176	23	21.7	88
1.184	24	22.5	92
1.192	25	23.4	95
1.201	26	24.3	99

There is another set of brine tables for UK Gallons (UK imperial gallon = 4.54 liters) and it can be looked up on Internet.

Humidity

Humidity or better said the "relative humidity" defines how much water (vapor) is present in the air at a particular temperature. The air almost always contains some water vapor and although we don't see it, it is there and it has a certain mass (weight). *The higher the temperature the more water can be held by air and vice versa.* As the amount of moisture in the air is fixed for at least some time (the clouds can bring moisture and rain), raising the temperature lowers the relative humidity. There is a point for each temperature reading when air can hold the maximum possible amount of water and we call it a saturation or a dew point. At this point the relative humidity is 100%. If the dew point is below freezing, it is called the frost point and the water vapor will form the frost or the snow. Air with a temperature of 30° C (can hold more than three times as much moisture as air at 10° C (50° F). In the same room at 100% relative humidity, if we suddenly lower the temperature, the air can now hold less moisture and the droplets of water will start condensing on smooth surfaces such as mirrors, knives, or even meat itself.

The humidity control in a meat plant is based on dew point control. *Dew point is the temperature at which condensation forms.* When air comes in contact with a surface (often metal or glass surfaces) that is at or below its Dew Point temperature, condensation will form on that surface. In a meat plant the item that is at risk is meat taken out from the cooler as its temperature will be about 2° C (35° F). In the processing room the temperatures are about 10-12° C, though they may reach even up to 16° C (60° F) if the meat will not remain there longer than one hour. By adjusting the room temperature and its humidity levels we can control the temperature of the dew point. In a well designed meat plant the temperature will stay more or less the same. If the facility is climate controlled, the amount of relative humidity should also remain at the same level. In the kind of "improvised" facility without automatic control, the relative humidity can be controlled by any of the following factors:

- Meat temperature - the worst solution as the meat's temperature will have to be increased which will lead to bacteria growth and shorter shelf life of the product.
- Room temperature - will have to be lowered which is acceptable.
- Room humidity - the best idea as it allows moisture removal (dehumidifier) or moisture introduction (humidifier) by separate devices. Those simple units will control the relative humidity without the need for room temperature adjustments or worrying

about meat temperature. In the table below only a part of the table that contains temperatures that might be encountered in a meat processing facility is quoted. Tables that include all temperature and humidity readings can be obtained on the Internet. It is very unlikely that an average home sausage maker will ever bother with humidity control but those interested in making fermented sausages will need to know humidity control very well.

Dew Point Table in ° F

Air Temp. in ° F	% Relative Humidity								
	100	90	80	70	60	50	35	30	25
65	65	62	59	55	50	45	36	32	
60	60	57	53	50	45	41	32		
55	55	52	49	45	40	36			
53	53	50	46	43	39	35			
52	52	48	44	43	37	33			
50	50	46	44	39	35	32			
45	45	43	39	35	32				
40	40	37	34						
35	35	32							
32	32								

Example: if the temperature in the sausage factory is 60° F (16° C) and the relative humidity is 50%, the intersection of the two shows that the Dew Point is reached at the temperature of 41° F (5° C), or below. This means that the moisture that is present in the air at 60° F (16° C) will condense on any surface that is at or below the Dew Point temperature of 41° F (5° C). This also means that if the meat having a temperature of 35° F (2° C) was brought from the cooler into this room (60° F, 16° C) the moisture would condense on its surface. The meat's temperature of 35° F (2° C) is below the Dew Point limit of 41° F (5° C). Until recently, measurements of humidity required knowledge of terms such as wet and dry bulb temperatures and a good command of relative humidity tables. Today, there are very accurate digital humidity meters, devices such as a humidistats which measures humidity and will switch a humidifier on and off as needed. For typical meat smoking applications such humidity control is not needed unless one starts producing fermented products.

How to Measure Humidity - The Dry Bulb and The Wet Bulb

To measure outside humidity all is needed is a simple humidity tester which is very inexpensive. To measure continuously humidity inside of the smokehouse or the drying room is harder and the manufacturers of commercial humidity sensors that could be inserted into a smokehouse can be located on the Internet. For a home made system the most economical way to go will be the dry bulb and the wet bulb system that has been around for long time.

The simplest hygrometer known as "a sling psychrometer" can be made from two thermometers attached (tape, string or wire) to a wooden board and the mercury or liquid filled ends sticking over the edge of the board about 1" (2.5 cm). This thermometer is called the dry-bulb thermometer. The second thermometer has a wet cloth (gauze, muslin bag) around the thermometer bulb, and secured with the rubber band or other ways, This thermometer is called the wet-bulb thermometer. The fan is needed to blow the air on the thermometers until both temperatures will stabilize and the readings are taken. Water will evaporate from a little bag cooling the wet-bulb thermometer. Both thermometer readings are taken and the difference between them allows us to calculate the humidity using tables.

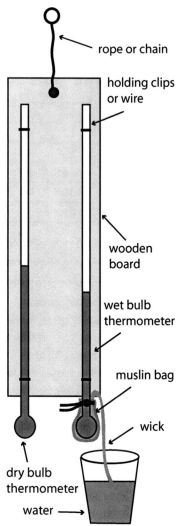

rope or chain

holding clips or wire

wooden board

wet bulb thermometer

muslin bag

wick

dry bulb thermometer

water ⟶

Fig. A.1 The dry bulb humidity tester

A better model can be made by drilling a hole in the top of the board and attaching a handle with a rope or a short piece of chain so that the whole assembly can be whirled around (no fan needed now). During the whirling, the water evaporates from the wick, cooling the wet-bulb thermometer.

For the most accurate reading, swing your psychrometer for several minutes, until the thermometer wrapped in cloth gives a constant temperature reading. If the ambient air is dry, more moisture is removed from the bag or wick, cooling the wet-bulb thermometer more and the temperature difference between two thermometers will be greater. The wet-bulb thermometer always gives lower readings than the dry-bulb because of the cooling effect of moisture evaporating from the muslin bag. If the air is very humid the difference will be smaller. If the relative humidity is 100 %, there is no difference between the two temperatures.

Relative Humidity Table

The following is just a small section of the complete humidity tables.

Dry Bulb ° F	Difference between dry bulb and wet bulb temperatures									
	1°	2°	8°	9°	10°	11°	12°	13°	14°	15°
64	95	90	60	56	51	47	43	38	34	30
66	95	90	61	57	53	48	44	40	36	32
68	95	90	62	58	54	50	46	42	38	34
70	95	90	64	59	55	51	48	44	40	36
72	95	91	65	61	57	53	49	45	42	38
74	95	91	65	61	58	54	50	47	43	39
76	96	91	66	62	59	55	51	48	44	41
78	96	91	67	63	60	56	53	49	46	43
80	96	91	68	64	61	57	54	50	47	44

Example: Dry bulb thermometer shows reading of 70° F and the wet bulb thermometer shows 60° F. Find the relative humidity. The difference between readings is: 70-60= 0° F. Following 70° F dry bulb temperature to the right and 10° F difference between dry bulb and wet bulb temperature down we can see that they intersect at 55% relative humidity. There are also tables in °C and they can be found on the Internet.

The most complete set of tables can be obtained on Internet from the National Weather Service (http://www.wrh.noaa.gov/sto/rhtbl.php): *"Relative Humidity and Dew Point Tables for Different Elevations using Dry-bulb and Wet-bulb temperatures".*

Appendix B

Useful Information

Sausage Making Equipment and Supplies	
The Sausage Maker Inc. 1500 Clinton St., Building 123 Buffalo, NY 14206 888-490-8525; 716-824-5814 www.sausagemaker.com	**Allied Kenco Sales** 26 Lyerly #1, Houston, TX 77022 713-691-2935; 800-356-5189 www.alliedkenco.com
The Sausage Source 3 Henniker Road, Hillsboro, NH 03244 603-464-6275 www.sausagesource.com	**Butcher & Packer Supply Co.,** 1468 Gratiot Avenue, Detroit, MI 48207 888-521-3188; 313-567-1250 www.butcher-packer.com
Koch Equipment LLC 1414 West 29th Street, Kansas City, MO 64108 816-753-2150; 816-753-4976 www.kochequipment.com	**The Ingredient Store** Division of Ames Company, Inc. PO Box 46 New Ringgold, PA 17960 www.theingredientstore.com
Sausage-Stuffer 1501 A Wimbledon Drive, Alexandria, Lousiana 71301 888-588-7267 www.sausage-stuffer.com	**LEM Products, Inc.** 107 May Drive Harrison, Ohio 45030 1-877-536-7763 www.lemproducts.com
Northern Tool+Equipment 2800 Southcross Drive West Burnsville, Minnesota 55306 952-894-9510 www2.northerntool.com	**The Ranco ETC Store** 330 Sunderland Road, Delphos, OH 45833 419-371-1742 www.rancoetc.com
American Weigh Scales, Inc. 2 Carriage Ln., Suite 2 Charleston, SC 29407 843-225-7282 www.amaricanweigh.com	**Mid-Western Research & Supply** 430 N. Mosley Street, Wichita, KS 67202 316-262-0651 www.midwesternresearch.com

Masonry Construction, Fireplace Design, Supplies
Maine Wood Heat Co., Inc., www.mainewoodheat.com   **Masonry Institute**, http://masonryinstitute.org   **The Masonry Heater Association of North America**   http://mha-net.org   **B4UBuild**, www.b4ubuild.com/links/masonry.shtml   **Earth Stone**, http://earthstoneovens.com/

Smoker Pits, Charcoal Grills, Gas Burners, Gas Regulators
Tejas Smokers   P.O. Box 4158   Houston, Texas 77210-4158   (713) 932-6438; fax: (713) 222-6096   www.tejassmokers.com

Wood stoves - Grills - Barbecues - Chimneys
Wood Heat, www.woodheat.org   **Hearth Net,** http://hearth.com   **Hearth Education Foundation,** http://heartheducation.org/   **Hearth, Patio and Barbecue Association,** http://hpba.org/   **National Fireplace Institute,** http://nficertified.org/   **Chimney Safety Institute of America,** www.csia.org/

Air Pollution Control
U.S. Environmental Protection Agency www.epa.gov/

Food Information
United Stated Depertment of Agriculture - Food Safety and Inspection Service, www.fsis.usda.gov   **U.S. Food and Drug Administration - Center for Food Safety and Applied Nutrition,** www.fsis.usda.gov   **American Association of Meat Processors,** www.aamp.com

Recipes
Wedliny Domowe, www.wedlinydomowe.com   **Sonoma Mountain Sausage**, http://home.pacbell.net/lpoli/

Recipe Index

Index

Also by Stanley and Adam Marianski

ISBN: 978-0-9824267-1-5

6 x 9 Paperback

274 pages

Published date: July 2009

2nd Edition

Publisher: Bookmagic LLC
www.book-magic.com

The majority of books written on making fermented sausages do not tackle the subject of fermented sausages at all. The topic is limited to a statement that this is an advanced field of sausage making which is not recommended for an amateur sausage maker. Well, the main reason for writing this book was that the authors did not share this opinion. On the contrary, they believed that any hobbyist could make wonderful salami at home, if he only knew how.

In The Art of Making Fermented Sausages readers are provided with detailed information about how to:

- Control meat acidity and removal of moisture.
- Choose proper temperatures for fermenting, smoking and drying.
- Understand and control fermentation process.
- Choose proper starter cultures and make traditional or fast-fermented products.
- Choose proper equipment, and much more...

With more information obtainable every day and commercial starter cultures available to the public, there is little reason to abstain from making quality salamis at home, regardless of the climate and outside conditions.

Also by Stanley and Adam Marianski, Miroslaw Gebarowski

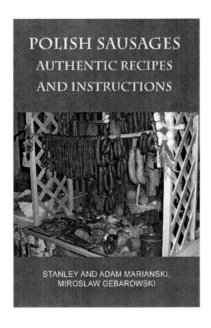

ISBN: 978-0-9824267-2-2

6 x 9 Paperback

286 pages

Published date: July 2009

2nd Edition

Publisher: Bookmagic LLC
www.book-magic.com

Most books on sausage making are filled with unknown quality recipes, this book is different, it contains carefully compiled government recipes that were used by Polish meat plants between 1950-1990. They were written by the best professionals in meat science the country had.

The recipes presented in *Polish Sausages* come from those government manuals and they were never published before. These are recipes and production processes of the products that were made by Polish meat plants and sold to the public. Most of those sausages are still made and sold in Poland. In Polish Sausages, readers are provided with detailed information about:

- The history of Polish sausages.
- How meat is classified.
- Methods of curing, grinding, and cooking.
- All about cold smoking and how to create a finished smoker.
- The truth about food safety & chemical additives.